Business Process Blueprinting

Michael Hewing

Business Process Blueprinting

A Method for Customer-Oriented Business Process Modeling

Michael Hewing
Berlin, Germany

Dissertation Freie Universität Berlin, 2013

D 188

Printing subsidy by the Ernst Reuter Foundation, Freie Universität Berlin

ISBN 978-3-658-03728-4   ISBN 978-3-658-03729-1 (eBook)
DOI 10.1007/978-3-658-03729-1

The Deutsche Nationalbibliothek lists this publication in the Deutsche Nationalbibliografie; detailed bibliographic data are available in the Internet at http://dnb.d-nb.de.

Library of Congress Control Number: 2013950135

Springer Gabler
© Springer Fachmedien Wiesbaden 2014

Printed on acid-free paper

Springer Gabler is a brand of Springer DE.
Springer DE is part of Springer Science+Business Media.
www.springer-gabler.de

Dedicated to my parents

Foreword

The approach to understand companies as complex systems of business processes has become a central theme of Information Systems and a major instrument to reflect and solve business challenges. Process models are the fundaments of Business Process Management and crucial to understand, analyze and design processes. Therefore it is quite surprising and astonishing, that the processes of the customer are just sparely considered in science and practice. Although customer orientation is seen as one of the most essential aspects for a long-lasting success in business, Business Process Management tends to focus on the production processes of the supply side – sometimes with the inclusion of external factors from the customer ("customer integration"). Yet, in order to increase the worth of one's offers, it is important to understand where and how value originates for the customer. In order to do so, one needs to establish a process-based customer intelligence which reflects current and future needs, especially with regard to the processes on customers' side.

In this book the author approves by a comprehensive literature review the lack of customer process models, calls for further research in this area and points with the development of a method to an approach that may solve this problem.

By reflecting the transformation on value creation in marketing from a product-over-service to an experience-oriented focus, the author underpins in detail the importance of a process-based customer orientation, which is barely implemented in Business Process Management. The literature review shows that only a few publications mention customer processes – quite apart from customer process models. In this respect, Michael Hewing succeeded very well with his in-depth study to present the current state of research and identify a highly relevant and quite visible research gap.

Further, the author presents with the Business Process Blueprinting a method to visualize customer processes in a consistent and structured way. As a first step, the marketing approach "Service Blueprinting", which assigns process elements depending on the managerial context to specific activity levels, has been combined with established modeling languages. Next, the logic has been expanded towards customer processes. Empirical data has been collected by a field study in cooperation with the medical technology company BIOTRONIK SE & Co. KG, which is one of the biggest producers of implantable electronic cardiovascular devices worldwide.

This book addresses a problem of academic and practical relevance and includes, with the Business Process Blueprinting, a first solution. Most important, Michael Hewing links with his approach two disciplines that usually operate independently from each other. The Business Process Blueprinting bridges the existing gap between the two fields and incorporates the respective other point of view into their familiar perspective. This way, a dialogue with experts outside the respective subject area can be initiated that seems long overdue, yet very promising.

For the sake of the professions, I hope that Michael Hewing's plea for a process-based customer orientation will meet high response in academic and practical communities and initiate further research.

Prof. Dr. Martin Gersch

Table of Content

List of Figures

List of Tables

List of Abbreviations

ACIS	=	Australasian Conference on Information Systems
ACM	=	Adaptive Case Management
AISeL	=	Association for Information Systems Electronic Library
AMCIS	=	American Conference on Information Systems
ARIS	=	Architecture of Integrated Information Systems
B2B	=	Business-to-Business
B2C	=	Business-to-Consumer
BP^2	=	Business Process Blueprinting
BPM	=	Business Process Management
BPMN	=	Business Process Modeling and Notation
BPMJ	=	Business Process Management Journal
BPO	=	Business Process Outsourcing
BPR	=	Business Process Reengineering
BSR	=	Behavioral Science Research
C2C	=	Consumer-to-Consumer
CRM	=	Customer Relationship Management
DSR	=	Design Science Research
DSRM	=	Design Science Research Methodology
ECIS	=	European Conference on Information Systems
eEPC	=	Enhanced Event-driven Process Chain
GDL	=	Goods-dominant logic
GPRS	=	General Packet Radio Service
GSM	=	Groupe Spécial Mobile
HM	=	Home Monitoring
ICD	=	Implantable cardioverter-defibrillator
ICIS	=	International Conference on Information Systems
ICT	=	Information and communications technology
IDEF0	=	Icam DEFinition for Function Modeling
IECD	=	Implantable electronic cardiovascular device
IHIP	=	Intangible, heterogeneous, inseparable and perishable
IS	=	Information Systems
IT	=	Information Technology
LED	=	Light-emitting diode
PACIS	=	Pacific Asia Conference on Information Systems
PM	=	Pacemaker
SDL	=	Service-dominant logic
WTP	=	Willingness to pay

1 Introduction

For the past two decades customer orientation and the creation of customer value has grown in interest and is intensively discussed especially in marketing literature (Jayachandran, Hewett and Kaufman 2004, p. 219). Yet, customer orientation, which is described as "...the organization wide generation of market intelligence pertaining to current and future customer needs..." (Kohli and Jaworski 1990, p. 6), is insufficiently picked up in Business Process Management (BPM) (Maddern et al. 2007, pp. 1001–1003). Focusing on the production and its technical quality, comparative advantages are mostly aspired via BPM through gains in efficiency. Although customer orientation seems relevant to sustain and level revenues, current methods provide a rather inside-out view on processes. But as value (for money) originates from solutions that address and satisfy the customers' needs, companies also have to understand and meet customers' requirements in order to enhance customer satisfaction and create customer value. Thus, it is beneficial to broaden the focus of business processes to the customers' side.

Consequently, modern Business Process Management methods not only need to concentrate on the internal process performance, but also have to include the customer's perspective for s/he takes the role of an active participant in the value creation process. The design of service processes should take the customer's expectation and perception into account. Although the customer's view on service processes has been mentioned in literature since the early nineties (Davenport 1993), there is still a lack of embedding a comprehensive customer perspective and his or her perception of value into methods of BPM. For instance, the discussion on service-dominant logic proposes that the application of specialized knowledge and skills by all involved actors is the fundamental basis of economic exchange. This means that the customer is always a co-creator of value. Thus, firms cannot create value by themselves. Because the customer participates in the value creation, providers can only prefabricate value to a specific degree. The customer always participates actively in the process of value creation. The provider can therefore only make a value propositions to the customer. Value always results from co-creation in a reciprocal and mutually beneficial relationship between the firm and the customer. Concepts in terms of abstract objects that emerge from this discussion are not considered in BPM. This especially relates to usage processes, which are performed autonomously by the customer after the completion of a service transaction. As usage processes significantly impact the customer's overall experience, it is important to factor in these processes when (re-)designing processes.

However, because recent research in BPM barely considers customer processes, usage processes are neglected too. In total, BPM lacks of a comprehensive approach to capture, document and design customer processes. As process models are especially crucial to understand and design processes, the arising question is:

RQ: How can customer processes be modeled in Business Process Management?

In order to answer the research question this thesis reflects, after a description of the scientific context in chapter 2, currently evolving process-based concepts on the customer in the relative fields of marketing and BPM and sum ups the current knowledge on customer processes. An extensive literature review in chapter 3 uncovers conceptual and methodical deficits of a customer-oriented process management in BPM. A management of customer processes is currently barely considered. Because the author wants to raise awareness of the importance of customer processes in management (research), this thesis concentrates on the development of an artifact that bridges this academic void.

Chapter 4 describes the artifact that has been introduced by Gersch, Goeke and Lux (2006) and enhanced towards usage processes throughout research at the Competence Center E-Commerce of the Freie Universität Berlin. It merges two well-known approaches of both disciplines to a method that is capable of modeling customer processes. The deriving process model can be seen as a basic requirement to manage customer processes. Thus, the artifact that has been developed in this research supports a process-based customer orientation. The development of the proposed method is based on the Design Science Research Methodology (Peffers et al. 2007), which contains a procedure model with a series of activities that need to be conducted throughout the development process. The thesis describes each of these activities in detail.

Chapter 5 strengthens the rigor of the artifact by describing its evaluation that bases on a case study in the field of health care. The evaluation can be seen as a first proof of the artifact's concept. It demonstrates the relevance of customer processes and points to new possibilities with regard to how to differentiate one's service offer by supporting usage processes. By doing so, one may strengthen efficiency and effectiveness in the creation of value.

Before the last chapter summarizes the findings of this thesis, the method's limitations are critically reflected and an outlook of future research possibilities is given in chapter 6. Accordingly, the developed artifact can be seen as the basic element of a toolbox to which other methods and concepts can be aligned. Hence, additional research for an enhancement of method is necessary.

2 Research Concept

Before the manuscript focuses on the research depicted in the introduction, some opening words are called on the scientific foundation that structures this thesis. In the first two sub-chapters the underlying research paradigm and methodology will be elucidated in order to classify this work. The third sub-chapter outlines the work's structure and goes into more detail about the procedure of this thesis.

2.1 Research Approaches in Information Systems

Kuhn describes paradigms as "...achievements that some particular scientific community acknowledges for a time as supplying the foundation for its further practice" (Kuhn 2012, p. 10; first published in 1962). It can be seen as a scientific consensus and conceptual framework within a community of researchers that determines with its mental map and view on the world a specific way of thinking that provides through education patterns, practices and prime examples for the solution of problems. As the association is a base element of this definition, the social component represents an important part of paradigms. This is why the term "school of thought" is often used in science to refer to paradigms (i.a. van Aken 2004, p. 220).

This thesis is assigned to the domain of Information Systems (IS), in which the differences between the paradigms are of particular importance and significance. Due to its dichotomy IS is a good example of a multi-paradigmatic community (Vaishnavi and William 2007, p. 8). The IS discipline can be described as the study of "...interrelated components that collect (or retrieve), process, store, and distribute information to support decisions making and control in an organization" (Laudon and Laudon 2012, p. 47). Accordingly, IS deals with behavioral as well as technical research.

In the domain of IS two science paradigms have been solidified over the years which coexist to a large degree independently of each other (Frank 2006). These paradigms are namely Behavioral Science Research and Design Science Research. Although the two paradigms are not contrary but rather complementary, they are often considered in competitive terms. Both paradigms aim to evolve value in the discipline of Information Systems, but with different approaches.

Behavioral Science Research (BSR) has its origins in natural science (Frank 2006, pp. 2–3), which accumulates empirical knowledge through the measurement and surveying of natural phenomenon. The model of natural science and its paradigm has been adapted to many fields such as social science and psychology. The intention in these contexts is to understand a problem by developing and approving theories that can explain or even predict the phenomena observed. In IS the object of interest is the interaction between human and computer. Accordingly the discipline strives to understand "…organizational and human phenomena surrounding the analysis, design, implementation, management, and use of information systems" (Hevner et al. 2004, p. 76) by justifying cause-effect and target-means relations. As BSR is very much oriented on the paradigm of natural science it is a very much accepted and internationally widespread approach, particularly in the Northern American hemisphere (Baskerville 2012, p. 581). Nonetheless, due to its close relations to other disciplines, the approach struggles with its scientific identity. Moreover, the relevance of the results it arrives at is frequently disputed as these often have little practical impact.

In contrast to the behavioral approach, whose objective is to deduce statements of truth in the form of hypotheses and theories, Design Science Research (DSR), which originates from the engineering discipline and is rather established in Europe (especially in German speaking countries), deals with the development of useful artifacts to solve a problem. So instead of trying to understand a specific problem and provide truth, DSR focuses on the identification and development of useful solutions to a problem in the form of artifacts. Information Technology related artifacts for such solutions range from "…constructs (vocabulary and symbols), models (abstractions and representations), methods (algorithms and practices) to instantiations (implemented and prototype systems)" (Hevner et al. 2004, p. 77). Even though the relevance of this research approach and its practical impact are held in high regard, its scientific contribution and value are often disclaimed. While the process of artifact creation still builds on core theories the research relies on, innovative artifacts often touch the boundaries of existing theories (Markus, Majchrzak and Gasser 2002). Furthermore, no consensus exists for the evaluation of artifacts (Cleven, Gubler and Hüner 2009, pp. 1–2). DSR lacks evaluation principles and a body of methodical and empirical standards. As a result it can be rather difficult to publish articles based on DSR in international channels which most likely follow the BSR approach (Baskerville 2012).

The two paradigms are often treated as contrary and mutually exclusive. Discussion of the two paradigms and the relationship between them is commonly known as "rigor versus relevance" (i.a. Österle, Winter and Brenner 2010). Rigor refers to the scientific conclusiveness and stringency of research. It considers a systematic methodical approach, which is compliant with academic research standards and rules that facilitate evaluation of the quality and validity of research. The BSR paradigm in particular strives to generate rigorous research outcomes. The term relevance, in contrast, points to the impact of research results in practice. As DSR seeks to originate applicable solutions for a specific problem, it is often associated with relevance.

Although each paradigm tends to emphasize one and neglect the other, both – rigor and relevance – are essential in IS research. Hevner et al. (2004) try to settle the difference by arguing that the approaches are complementary to each other. They state that both are very much of importance and that the challenges or disadvantages one paradigm faces can be covered by the other. Accordingly, artifacts have the potential to sort out not yet dissolved problems, while theories analyze the implementation and use of those artifacts as well as their impact on the organization and may, in doing so, discover further challenges that need to be solved. Thus, results that base on one paradigm initiate research that refers to the other.

As the present work proposes to bridge an academic void by means of a methodical conceptualization of a customer-oriented process management, it is rather allocated to DSR. In order to give the reader a deeper insight into the approach and basic elements of DSR, the next chapter will comment on the methodology of DSR.

2.2 Research Methodology

As DSR originates from engineering and the design of the artificial, it also includes parts of their body of principles and techniques. In reference to the methods of engineering, in the early 1990s researchers began discussing DSR frameworks and procedure models for a systematic development of artifacts in DSR. Those frameworks can be seen as mental models for the demonstration and evaluation of DSR in IS. Peffers et al. (2007) reviewed proposed frameworks in their article on Design Science Research Methodology (DSRM) and united them by appropriately combining their elements.

The presented DSRM process model is widely accepted in IS related DSR publications due to its consensus building approach (Hevner and Chatterjee 2010, p. 28). Figure 1 illustrates the course of action, which consists of six activities that need to be taken consecutively. Based on Peffers et al. (2007) each activity is described in further detail in the following:

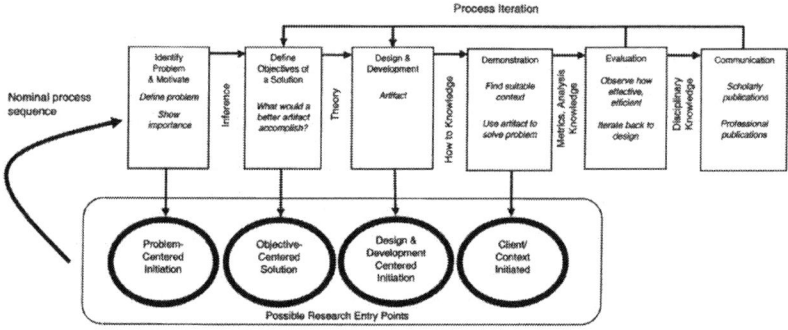

Figure 1. DSRM process model (Peffers et al. 2007, p. 54), full-page illustration in Appendix 1.

(1) The first activity focuses on identifying the problem and motivation of research. In order to set research to the right direction, it is fundamental to explicitly define the problem that needs to be solved. It is important to show the relevance of the problem and the significance of a solution that solves it. Thus, identification of a need justifies the entire research.

(2) Once the problem and the relevance of a solution has been depicted, the requirements a solutions needs to meet have to be extracted from the problem definition (i.a. Eekels and Roozenburg 1991, pp. 199–200). When the required specifications of a solution are elucidated clearly, the audience can follow the line of argumentation more easily and approve whether the developed artifact pursues the identified

problem. Objectives can be of a quantitative (e.g. measurements) and/or qualitative (e.g. description of the support to problem solving) nature.

(3) All of the proposed research frameworks see the key element of DSR in the design and development of artifacts. Once the specifications are outlined, the creative phase of developing an artifact that addresses the desired functionalities can be initiated. As artifacts' functionalities are often developed step-by-step, they may need revision and adjustment. This step is therefore an iterative one. In order to provide insight into the steps taken, the functionality specifications and the process of development are often documented in further detail.

(4) With regard to the framework, a demonstration of the artifact's application is appropriate (Nunamaker, Chen and Purdin 1990, p. 100). This allows for the basic idea of how the artifact provides a solution to the problem to become more tangible and comprehensible. This step can be seen as an informal evaluation, ensuring that the idea to solve the problem works properly. It can be demonstrated, for instance, by exemplifications or even concrete examples.

(5) Once the artifact is developed and its suitability has been demonstrated, the artifact has to be evaluated (Hevner et al. 2004, pp. 88–90). The main purpose of this activity is to measure to what extent the artifact solves the problem that has been defined at the beginning of the research. Stated more concretely, the evaluation verifies whether its functionalities suit the requirements of activity 2. This can be obtained by logical proof or empirical evidence, such as performance indicators (quantitative) or client feedbacks (qualitative). The results of the evaluation show whether the objectives are fulfilled or further adjustment is necessary. For example, one may revise the artifact in order to raise performance indicators. However, due to a lack of principles almost no guidelines are currently available for the choice of evaluation method, which complicates the justification of one's selection.

(6) After research is completed, the created process needs to be documented and made available for insight so that the gathered knowledge is spread and can be discussed in respective academic and/or practicing communities (Hevner et al. 2004, p. 90). The DSRM can be seen as a structuring element for publications. Books, working papers or theses are formats that can cover all research activities at once. Parts of the research project such as the literature review, the design or evaluation can also be published a priori in the form of articles.

Though the DSRM follows a nominal process, iterations are considered and advised. It also can be stated that research does not necessarily need to start with the first activity. Entry points for research are given throughout activity 1 to 4. Instead of the common problem-centered start of research, also objective, design/development or context-oriented initiations are conceivable. Also leaps between the activities might be conducive and informative. In summary, the DSRM with its sequence of six activities reflects a typical procedure in DSR. Though procedure details depend on the nature of the specific research (e.g. problem context, design situation), it provides a well-founded guideline (Hevner and Chatterjee 2010, p. 28).

2.3 Outline of Research

As recommended by Hevner and Chatterjee (2010, p. 31) the nominal DSRM explained above has been used to structure the further proceeding of this thesis and the relative research. Chapter 1, 2 and 7 of this thesis are not further considered in the outline as they are rather of a framing and summarizing character. Figure 2 illustrates which chapter and sub-chapters cover which of the six DSRM activities. As the last activity "communication", which focuses on documentation and publication of the research proceedings, is complied with this thesis, it contains an outlook on further research possibilities instead.

Chapter 3 highlights the problem and its relevance by referring to recent research on customer orientation and customer processes in the domain of marketing and BPM. In chapter 3.1 evolving marketing concepts and current findings as well as the significance of customer processes for business performance are described. Chapter 3.2 pans the view to BPM and analyses in a comprehensive literature review the extent to which the customer and his or her processes have been picked up in BPM. Besides an explanation on the review procedure, the literature review contains a quantitative and qualitative analysis. In chapter 3.3 the critically analyzed findings of the literature review are transformed into a problem definition, on which the subsequently described objectives and requirements of solution are based.

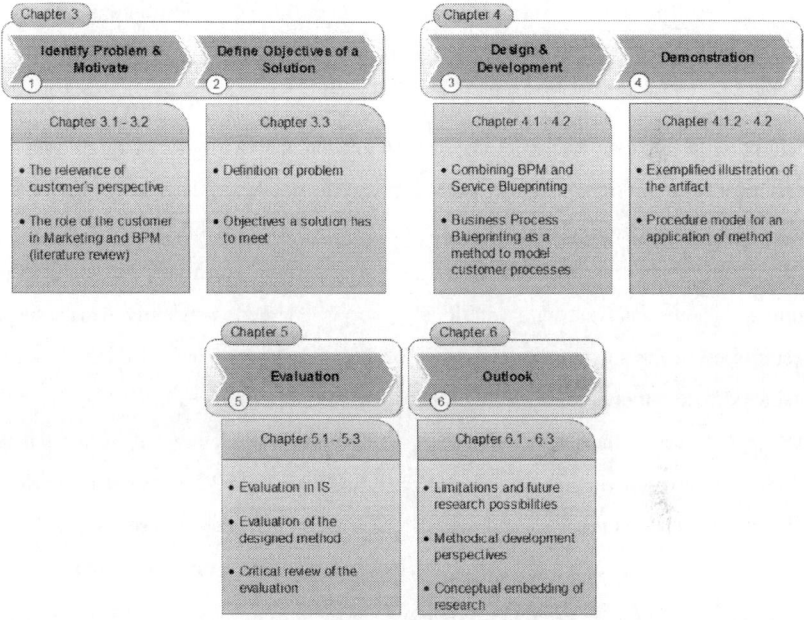

Figure 2. The research outline according to the six DSRM activities

Chapter 4 describes the design and development of an artifact and demonstrates its use by examples. Based on previous publications, the first sub-chapter elucidates the general concept behind the method and goes into detail on how the method emerged from an interdisciplinary synthesis of concepts to highlight interaction processes. Next, the method will be enhanced in order to illustrate usage processes. The expansion of the traditional perspective to the customer side is one of the key aspects of this work as it strengthens the process designers' awareness of (autonomous) customer processes. In the second sub-chapter a procedure model for the implantation of method is provided in order to minimize ambiguity. The last sub-chapter verifies by means of logical reasoning whether the artifact meets the requirements that are proposed in chapter 3.3.

In *chapter 5* the artifact is evaluated in a case study. For the sake of clarity the setting of the case study is explained in sub-chapter 5.1. The case study "BIOTRONIK Home Monitoring" resides in the field of e-health and can be seen as a prime example to show the importance of analyzing customer processes. In chapter 5.2 the artifacts deployment is described, which results in not yet considered design options. The last sub-chapter sums up the case study and its results and critically reviews the quality of evaluation.

Before the last chapter of this thesis summarizes the research process, limitations are outlined and an outlook on future research possibilities is given in *chapter 6*. The first sub-chapter considers the limitations of this research project. Further, the developed artifact can be seen as a toolkit, which provides additional instruments or a starting point for deeper analysis with additional concepts, methods and tools. This issue is exemplified in the second sub-chapter by a potential enhancement of method, which enables the determination of willingness to pay for sub-processes in BPM. Advancement is also seen in the combination of customer process modeling and Business Analytics. The third sub-chapter embeds this research to its context and relates it to principal concepts such as process landscapes that not only consider the provider and customer, but also third parties and connected networks as well as their infrastructure.

Although the outlook replaced the "communication" activity, which is already fulfilled by this thesis, it should be stated that the method has already been discussed and approved through publications on which the further explanations are based. Moreover, this thesis builds upon the lines of thought and achievements of previously published research. The artifact presented here draws on the concept and method of a working paper that presented the combination of methods (Gersch, Goeke and Lux 2006). The further enhancement of this method develops ideas from Fließ (2001) and Frauendorf (2006). However, their concepts contain certain limitations and thus invite certain perspectives for development that have been outlined throughout this manuscript and to which this research project refers. An overview of prior research in comparison to the knowledge developed by this thesis can be seen in Table 1.

Table 1. Overview of preliminary work and its advancement throughout this research project, full-page illustration in Appendix 2

No	Chapter	Focus*	Preliminary work (chronically)	State of the art*	Advancement throughout this research project*
1	3.1	Linkage of value creation and customer orientation to a process-based perspective	amongst others: Engelhardt (1996) Engelhardt/Kleinaltenkamp/Reckenfelderbäumer (1993) Gersch (2006) Vargo/Lusch (2004a)	Concepts that open up the view on value creation to the customer side	Plead for the importance of a process-based view on customer orientation by a review of the transformation from a product-over-service to an experience-oriented focus on value creation
2	3.2	Insufficient considerations of customer (modeling) concepts in BPM	Gersch (2006) Batista/Smart/Maull (2008)	First insights by conceptual discussions and an explorative analysis	Comprehensive literature review with quantitive and qualitative analysis affirms the proposition with a high level of realibility and validity
3	4.1.1	Artifact Development I: Combination of the Service Blueprinting with Business Process Modeling notations	Knackstedt/Dahlke (2004) Becker/Klose/Knackstedt (2005) Gersch/Goeke/Lux (2006) Meis/Menschner/Leimeister (2010) Coenen/Felten/Schmid (2011) Milton/Johnson (2012)	Initial combination of methods and technical explanations	Journal and conference publications with conceptual embedding, further evaluation and discussion of advantages/limitations (Gersch, Schöler, Hewing 2010; Gersch, Hewing, Schöler 2011; Hewing 2011)
4	4.1.2 4.2 5 6	Artifact Development II: Modeling of customer processes that take place beyond the direct interaction with the provider	Green/Simister (1999) Fließ (2001) Alt/Puschmann (2005) Frauendorf (2006) Eichentopf/Kleinaltenkamp/van Stiphout (2011) Heckl/Moormann (2007)	Intial reflections on and mapping of customer processes	Development of an approved method to model customer processes that has been critical reflected, considers current Business Process Modeling notations, the logic of the Service Blueprinting, evolving concepts on customer processes (in particular insight/influence) and to which further methods are applicable (Gersch, Schöler, Hewing 2011)

* detailed explanations can be seen in the relative chapters

One of the main achievements of this research project is that the concept, and its integration into Business Process Management have been seriously discussed in public and passed double-blind reviews. Articles concerning this research have been published in three highly ranked conferences, in a journal significant to the field of BPM and in a book chapter. Early publications rather explain the concept behind the method and show first evaluations of benefits (Gersch, Hewing and Schöler 2011; Gersch, Schöler and Hewing 2010). The two papers published subsequently discuss the implementation of method into Service Engineering (Rachmann et al. 2011) and its enhancement to enable the management of usage processes (Gersch, Schöler and Hewing 2011). The enhancement of method to usage processes is the other main achievement of this thesis. The most recent publication focuses on the framework and procedure model for the application of method (Hewing 2011). Table 2 lists sequentially these publications with a short note on the respective focus.

Table 2. Publications of the author that relate to this work

No.	Year	Publication	Type	Authors	Focus
1	2010	AMCIS	Conference	Gersch/Schöler/Hewing	An introduction to Business Process Blueprinting
2	2011	BPMJ	Journal	Gersch/Hewing/Schöler	BP^2 as the link between BPM and Marketing
3	2011	ISO	Book Chapter	Rachmann/Maucher/ Schöler/Hewing	Integration of BP^2 into Service Engineering
4	2011	EMAC	Conference	Gersch/Schöler/Hewing	BP^2 as a method to manage usage processes
5	2011	BPM	Conference	Hewing	The BP^2-Framework

Through this research agenda knowledge concerning a customer-oriented process management has been accumulated and advanced. The findings of this research reveal that although customer orientation is important for the creation of value, its processes are barely considered in BPM. However, through the introduction and evaluation of an enhanced method a solution has been developed that decreases this drawback and gives an outlook for possible directions for future research.

Now that the outline of research has been clarified and each activity has been allocated to the chapters of this thesis, the identification of the problem and its relevance are to be illustrated in the next chapter.

3 Customer Orientation and the Diffusion of process-based Approaches in Marketing and BPM

Interest in the creation of customer value has grown in recent years and has been discussed intensively ever since the view has shifted from product and sales to a market orientation, which implies that value originates from solutions that address and satisfy the customers' needs (Kotler et al. 2012, p. 18). Companies have to understand and meet these customers' requirements to enhance customer satisfaction and therefore level revenues.

In recent years, the approach to understanding business as a complex system of processes has gained acceptance. Process-oriented thinking is widespread for the management of organizations. Although Engelhardt already pointed in 1966 to the importance of the customer in the process of value creation, there seems little research to date on a process-based customer orientation. Slater and Narver (1994, p. 22) demand a process view when they state that the creation of "…superior value for buyers continuously requires that a seller understands a buyer's entire value chain...". Recent developments like the discussion on service-dominant logic strengthen this position by opening up new perspectives on the value creation process. Accordingly customer activities are highly relevant for the creation of value. Therefore the customer's point of view needs to be considered in Business Process Management. Furthermore, value creation happens even beyond the firm's boundaries. Customer activities outside the traditional provider interaction need to be considered. However, a customer-oriented view on value creation is insufficiently picked up from the process perspective.

In reference to activity 1 and 2 of the DSRM, this chapter explains the importance of a customer-oriented BPM and the line of thought, which led to the main research question of this thesis. In order to identify deficits in current BPM research, it is necessary to first look at customer orientation in the domestic area of marketing. Customer orientation is a principal part of marketing, which emphasizes its necessity and importance. The creation of value for the customer is an inherent element belonging to the customer's orientation. Yet, the perspective on value creation has shifted over recent decades from a product-oriented to a service-dominated logic, which exposes the analysis of customer processes and the value-in-use.

The relevance of customer orientation, its link to value creation and the evolving thoughts on value creation, which attach importance to the analysis of customer processes, will be highlighted in the first sub-chapter.

The second sub-chapter sets the focus on BPM and its lack of customer orientation. Although marketing emphasizes customer processes as a central element of value creation, Business Process Management, the scientific home of process modeling, has not incorporated their processes. In particular, there seems to be a lack of formal methods to model customer processes in a classified way. This proposition is fortified by an extensive literature review.

The third sub-chapter summarizes the research problem and its relevance and sets objectives for solutions that have to be met by artifacts that claim to provide dissolution. In this way, the origin (chapter 4) and evaluation (chapter 5) of the developed artifact can be followed more easily and whether the developed artifact pursues the identified problem can be established.

3.1 Reflections on the Customer's Perspective in Marketing

The customer focus and the identification of customer needs is one of most essential principles of marketing. In order to reflect the current status of research on customer orientation it is therefore reasonable that one takes a closer look at the achievements attained so far and considers currently evolving concepts of marketing, before focusing on its development and diffusion in BPM. To this end, the development of customer orientation, the altered view on value creation and its deriving process approaches in marketing are treated in the following sub-chapters.

3.1.1   Concerning Customer Orientation and its Relation to Effectiveness

"There is only one valid definition of a business purpose:
to create a customer."
(Drucker 1954, p. 37)

The above quotation of Drucker's proposition reveals that customer orientation has been discussed since the conceptual origins of marketing management. The creation of value for the customer is a central element within current marketing definitions. The American Marketing Association (2007), for instance, defines marketing as "the activity, set of institutions, and processes for creating, communicating, delivering, and exchanging offers that have value for customers, clients, partners, and society at large". This customer-driven definition states that marketing activities primarily serve the wants of potential consumers. Accordingly the customer develops needs that have to be satisfied by solution offers. Thus, in order to create demand for a firm's services, it is necessary to offer an added value that addresses the customers' needs.

With Shapiro's article "What the Hell Is Market Oriented?" (1988) and the subsequently published responses of Kohli and Jaworski (1990) and Narver and Slater (1990), a discussion arose on the nature and effects of customer and market orientation. The proposed conceptual frameworks accentuated the customer focus and acknowledged the customer orientation as an important element of marketing activities. In order to further contour the concept of customer orientation, the most common definitions, which are despite their year of publication still cited in recent articles on customer orientation (i.a. Brockman, Jones and Becherer 2012, p. 431; Kennedy, Goolsby and Arnould 2003, p. 68), are listed in the following. Though all definitions per se focus on customer needs, each one reflects the concept from a slightly different point of view and reveals further aspects that are aligned to the term. For instance, Narver and Slater (1990, p. 21) add a competition dimension to the term and already point to a process view by arranging the customer needs to their value chain. The definition of Deshpandé et al. (1993, p. 27) includes the stakeholders of the company, while Gatignon and Xuereb (1997, p. 78) refer to methodical issues and implementation. The definitions are as follows:

- Jaworski and Kohli (1993, p. 54) conceptualized the customer focus as "...the organization-wide generation of market intelligence pertaining to current and future customer needs...".

- Narver and Slater (1990, p. 21) state that "...customer orientation is the sufficient understanding of one's target buyers to be able to create superior value for them continuously [...]. A customer orientation requires that a seller understands a buyer's entire value chain [...], not only as it is today but also as it will evolve over time subject to internal and market dynamics."

- Deshpandé et al. (1993, p. 27) define customer orientation as the "...set of beliefs that puts the customer's interest first, while not excluding those of all other stakeholders such as owners, managers, and employees, in order to develop a long-term profitable enterprise."

- Gatignon and Xuereb (1997, p. 78) say that "a customer-oriented firm can be defined as a firm with the ability and the will to identify, analyze, understand, and answer user needs. A customer orientation also helps the firm learn a large part of the market's technical issues and provides an evaluation of possible segments, the importance of the market, and its growth rate."

Some articles limit the customer orientation in their research to the direct interaction between service employees and customers (i.a. Zablah et al. 2012). Though the salesperson's appearance and customer/provider interaction are of high importance, it has to be further stated that the customer orientation also concerns the structures, culture and systems of an organization (Bruhn 2009, p. 38; Strong and Harris 2004, p. 184).

In summary customer orientation can be seen as the driving force of marketing. Often the terms "market orientation" and "customer orientation" are used synonymously (i.a. Deshpandé, Farley and Webster 1993, p. 27). Following proposed market orientation concepts (i.a. Kohli and Jaworski 1990) and the five forces of Porter (Porter 1980, p. 4) one recognizes that there are further dimensions that need to be considered in marketing management. For instance, solutions need to be perceived as superior by the customer in comparison to relevant competitive offers (competitor orientation). Also the costs of production have to be covered (profitability). The present thesis consequently differentiates between the terms "customer orientation" and "market orientation", which incorporates all market players. Customer orientation, which concentrates on the bilateral relationship between customer and organization, should rather be seen as the central element of market orientation (Kohli and Jaworski 1990, p. 3).

All definitions relate to the creation of value that relieves the customer's needs. Yet, the question as to why their needs are so important for one's business has not yet been answered. The implication of customer orientation is that companies gain in financial worth when they create value for the customer. The "marketing process" of Kotler and Armstrong (2011, pp. 29–31) illustrate this issue in simple terms by examining sequentially five bundles of customer and marketplace core concepts, which are presented in the following:

(1) **Needs, wants and demands**: A human need can be described as the "circumstances in which something is necessary" (Oxford English Dictionaries Online 2012a) and which motivates one for action. Needs occur either through a deficit, like the necessity to eat due to hunger, or new possibilities that raise the requirements of an ideal condition, such as next generation devices. Needs, furthermore, can also be of different priority. Maslow's (1943) controversially discussed hierarchy, which offers a classification of needs, can be seen as the interface between the disciplines management and psychology (Maslow 1998). It classifies a wide range of needs according to their commonly perceived priority, beginning with needs of a physical

kind as the lowest category and ending with needs for self-actualization as the top of the hierarchy.

Once a need is formed and objectively expressed by a human's individual personality it is called a want. For instance, one may need food but want a specific dish (object). If, in addition, the person has the purchasing power to satisfy his or her wants, it is called a demand. An extensive and summarizing commentary on research pertaining to needs, wants and demand can be seen in Laß (2002).

(2) **Marketing offers**: Companies make value propositions when they promise to satisfy a specific need through a set of benefits. Marketing offers such as products or services fulfill this value proposition. As offers should be seen as tools to solve specific problems, one should rather focus on the benefits and experiences than on the offer's specification when setting up the value propositions (Kotler and Armstrong 2011, pp. 12–13).

(3) **Value, quality, satisfaction and effectiveness:** This part of the marketing process has been enhanced by the author with the concepts of quality and effectiveness. Usually customers face a wide range of marketing offers that promise to satisfy the respective need. Buying behavior is strongly affected by psychological, personal, social and cultural factors (Kotler and Armstrong 2011, pp. 192–203). The choice depends very much on the subjectively perceived added value of an offer. Customer value therefore describes the expected net benefits that remain after the subtraction of costs from benefits. It should be stated that benefits and costs in one's cognitive consideration contain highly subjective dimensions and are therefore hard to quantify (Ulaga and Chacour 2001, p. 529).

How customers perceive a marketing offer is the basis of the customer-oriented quality concept. Quality is a complex concept, inviting a wide range of interpretations. The International Organization for Standardization (2005), for instance, defines the quality in their standard 9000:2005 as the "…degree to which a set of inherent characteristics […] fulfils requirements…". Therefore the quality of a marketing offer is affected by a wide range of characteristics, which are mutually dependent and weighted differently. Moreover, it is a measure that shows the degree to which requirements are fulfilled and can be therefore seen as a relational benchmark. By differentiating between five approaches Garvin (1988, pp. 39–48) provides a classification scheme for quality definitions. The first approach is related to the production, in which an acceptable internal quality level is given that needs to be met through inspection and testing. The production-oriented approach defines quality by physical criteria that have to be fulfilled. The absolute approach contains a quality concept in which a specific minimum expectation is set. Quality can be seen as the performance, which is either good, medium or bad. The value-oriented quality concept is determined by the price-performance ratio (value for money), which puts the quality in relation to the price. Quality is given when the performance is worth the price. The last approach is the customer-oriented quality concept. As mentioned above, quality is understood as the degree to which the marketing offer fulfills customer expectations. In contrast to the product quality, the quality measurement relies on subjective criteria. Quality is determined by the subjectively perceived characteristics and the performance. The opinion of the customer specifies the degree of fulfillment. Because the quality concept will be described in more detail in chapter 3.1.2.2.2, the next paragraph shortly presents the basic thought of customer perceived quality concepts.

Thus, quality itself is determined by customer satisfaction and is the outcome of a subjective comparison between the expected and actually perceived performance (over time). According to the confirmation/disconfirmation model (i.a. Churchill and Surprenant 1982; Oliver 1980, 1993; Tse and Wilton 1988; Westbrook 1987) the result of the comparison process can be either a confirmation (performance = expectations), positive disconfirmation (performance > expectations) or negative disconfirmation (performance < expectations). In analogy with this model, the customer is satisfied with the marketing offer in the first two scenarios, while the last case leads to dissatisfaction. Customer satisfaction is connected to post-purchase behavior and strongly influences future purchases. A post-purchase conflict due to discomfort would most likely result in a switch to other marketing offers. Customer satisfaction is key to the development and retention of relationship to the customer that is necessary to receive revenues from the customer in the long term.

Related to customer satisfaction is the effectiveness, which describes the degree to which the desired results or (as in this case) expectations have been met (Keh, Chu and Xu 2006, p. 266). Due to its customer orientation, effectiveness is an external performance measure. The objective of effectiveness is to live up to the expectations of the customers by pursuing a high quality of marketing offers.

Accordingly, quality, satisfaction, effectiveness and value are all closely linked. Due to the focus of this work further explanations rely on the customer-oriented quality concept. As effectiveness expresses how much the expectations of the customers have been met, customer perceived quality can serve as an indicator of the effectiveness.[1]

(4) Exchange, transactions and relationship: Exchange labels the process of satisfying wants through trade relations. Customers obtain a marketing offer by giving something in return. The transaction describes the trade, which is specified by the assets of exchange. Profitable customer exchange relationships are indispensable for the company's survival. Thus, customer relationship management is essential.

(5) Markets: The market is the place where exchanges are performed. Deriving historically from local areas of commerce, markets describe nowadays the buyers and sellers of a specific class of products and/or services. These classes can be determined by the particular needs the marketing offer addresses and include all potential (market potential) and actual (market volume) buyers.

The marketing process strikingly points out the importance to orient one's business to the customer needs and to create appropriate values. Thus, satisfaction of customers needs by meeting their expectations on performance and quality fortifies a profitable

---

[1] In order to avoid confusion on terms an informal list of description can be seen in Appendix 3.

long-term relationship to the customer. A similar line of argumentation has also been illustrated by Johnson (1997, p. 103) and Bruhn (2011, p. 11).

Figure 3. Profit chain of customer orientation (modified from Bruhn 2011, p. 11)

A lot of research focuses on the validation of customer orientation, the links between the relative concepts (i.a. Anderson, Fornell and Lehmann 1994; Appiah-Adu and Singh 1998; Brady and Cronin 2001a; Brockman, Jones and Becherer 2012) and the drivers of customer orientation (i.a. Strong and Harris 2004). Johnson (1997, pp. 2–4) translates the underlying core concepts of marketing into three sequential goals of customer orientation. First, one needs to acquire information on the customer needs and establish the extent to which they are currently served. Next, these gathered insights must be spread throughout the organization and transformed into actions, which are subsequently implemented in a third step in order to satisfy the customer's needs. In sum, understanding customers' needs is the first and essential step to long-term economical success.

3.1.2 Transformation of Value Creation and the increased Awareness of the Importance of Customer Processes

According to the explanations above the creation of customer value is an important and foundational element of customer orientation, which implies that a company should create offers that are positively perceived (high quality) by the customers and that satisfy their needs. One's buying behavior depends very much on the subjectively perceived added value of an offer, which is conceptualized in quality models. Therefore this chapter reflects the changing view on value creation over time, corresponding quality concepts and the increasing awareness of the customer processes' relevance in those concepts. Thus, the need of a process-based view in customer orientation is best explained by a review of the transformation from a product-over-service to an experience-oriented focus on value creation, such as value-in-use.

3.1.2.1   Product Orientation: an internal View

In its early stages the formal marketing discipline focused the analysis merely on tangible goods by relying on the statement that economic exchanges are based on goods and their (industrial) production (Vargo and Lusch 2008a, p. 2). In order to maximize profit, economic activities should define targets to efficiently produce and subsequently distribute units of output. The product's value was mostly determined by the nominal price of exchange (value-in-exchange). From the provider's point of view the creation of value was therefore completed with the product delivery and transfer of ownership, while the customer solely received and consumed this value. As the process of value creation was limited to internal activities, customer processes have not been considered in the concept of value creation.

The industrial revolution and evolving thoughts on economic science, especially Adam Smith's (2010; first published in 1776) book on the "Wealth of Nations", can be seen as important promoters of this view. Value was considered a property of goods. The product-oriented approach defines quality on the basis of the good's characteristics. This economical doctrine strengthened a rather production- and sales-oriented philosophy in the origins of management, which concentrated on product specifications, mass distribution and efficiency. This resulted in a focus on product attributes and features. Added value, in contrast, tended to emerge from a higher number and quality of features. Profit maximization was pursued by a price that reflected the supply and demand equilibrium and the optimization of the supply chain. The task was to market products through promotion.

The focus of quality on internal operational sequences and processes set the provider's view to the production and efficiency with the aim of cost reduction. One of the main objectives of companies is the maximization of profit, which implied at these times that profit increases by economically efficient work processes. In accordance with the economic principle of profit maximization and due to the scarcity of goods, agents put the required input in relationship with the outcome and therefore try to realize the highest possible benefits with the lowest input of resources for a process. Thus, to be economically efficient means achieving the most favorable ratio of inputs and benefits (i.a. Fried, Lovell and Schmidt 2008, p. 8). This ratio can be pursued in two different ways (i.a. Endres and Radke 2012, p. 17). The minimum principle implies that one reaches a fixed output with a minimal amount of resources. In contrast, the maximum principle means that the output of a process is maximized under the restriction of a fixed amount of input. So while one of the two parameters is fixed, the other needs to be either minimized or maximized. Hence, the quotient between input and output is the measure of economical efficiency. It has to be stated that efficiency is a relative measure and rather interpretable when one compares measurements to reference values such as the ones of other companies or earlier periods. The term "efficiency" also adapts to the respective theories of specializations in business administration. In the field of marketing the term describes the maximization of target achievement under a given allocation of resources (Bush, Smart and Nichols 2002, p. 343). Often the question is raised as to whether things are done right. Effectiveness, in contrast, asks whether the right things are done. Whereas the first question points to operative activities, the second refers rather to a strategic level. The key to efficiency, on the other hand, is the question of how a particular aim can be reached as economically as possible. The goal is to attain a maximum output with few resources. This thesis is based on a quantitative efficiency concept that implies that an increase of the input-output ratio, which results in lower quality, still applies as efficiently.

However, such an inward looking approach might lead to market myopia (Levitt 1960), which means that providers most likely narrow their focus on the company's needs and operations instead of on the customers'. A product orientation can result in an improper definition of a company's purposes and accordingly to a decline in demand. This becomes even more evident in affluent societies and with the shift from sellers' to buyers' markets, which contain a supply surplus. Here the company primarily aims to stimulate customers' interests and establish a preference for their products (Kotler et al. 2012, p. 78).

3.1.2.2   Services Marketing: the Customer as Value Creation Participant

Services have mostly been seen as extra benefits that additionally enhance the value of goods. Adam Smith (2010, p. 314 ; first published in 1776) regarded services as not contributing to a nation's wealth as they do not produce a surplus of commodities. In

1884, Bastiat (i.a. 1995) opposed the importance of services by stating that services are exchanged for services and, therefore, the basis of economic. He also pointed to the value-in-use and to the perspective that products solely render value. However, due to the fact that the materialistic view was more compatible with the mathematical models of natural science, an economical view on services (i.a. Malthus 1820; Say 1855) was neglected and the goods-dominant logic (GDL), which basically comprises product orientation, established itself as the main approach (Vargo and Lusch 2008a, p. 255).

With the beginning of the post-industrial societies in various countries around 1970 (Bell 1973), in which economic wealth and value derives to a large degree from services rather than from the industrial and manufacturing sector, research on service-based value creation began to grow. In European countries the common gross domestic product consists commonly of an approximately 30/70 product-service ratio and is reflected in a similar employment rate (Kotler et al. 2012, p. 8).

While the production of goods has been examined closely and automated meanwhile to a large extent, further research on services such as logistics or commercialization was necessary to distribute and vend products. Coming from economics, service-related research has been increasingly incorporated in various disciplines such as marketing, operations and IS (Spohrer and Maglio 2011, pp. 168–171)

3.1.2.2.1   On the Nature of Services

Service marketing started in the 1960s as one of the earlier research streams on services. It focuses on the nature of services and outlines managerial implications. Judd (1964, p. 1) called for a clear redefinition of services in order to raise attention to this subject in marketing. Shostack (1977, p. 74) was to strengthen this position by stating that service marketing needs to break free from product marketing. This would be achieved when research explored its structural definitions, which hint to the special managerial implications of services.

To understand the service-based view on value creation it is recommendable to highlight the special characteristics of services. With this purpose in mind, this chapter gives a short explanation on the nature of services. The term service is a multifaceted notion with a wide range of ideas and concepts behind it. The problem of defining its characteristics reflects this circumstance. Definitions should therefore not be seen as wrong or false but rather as appropriate constructs that represent the prospect of a subject (Kleinaltenkamp 2001, p. 29). Discussions on the special characteristics of services can be very well structured and described by looking at the procedure of service production.

Engelhardt (1966) provided an early reflection on the special characteristics of services. His essay on the process of service rendering pointed to an important aspect of value creation. Accordingly, services can be characterized by special circumstances in the value creation process, which can be very well discussed along the integrative value chain that is illustrated in Figure 4. The production of a service passes through two stages and results in a specific outcome (Engelhardt 1995). Thus, value does not only arise from the outcome, but also from preceding activities.

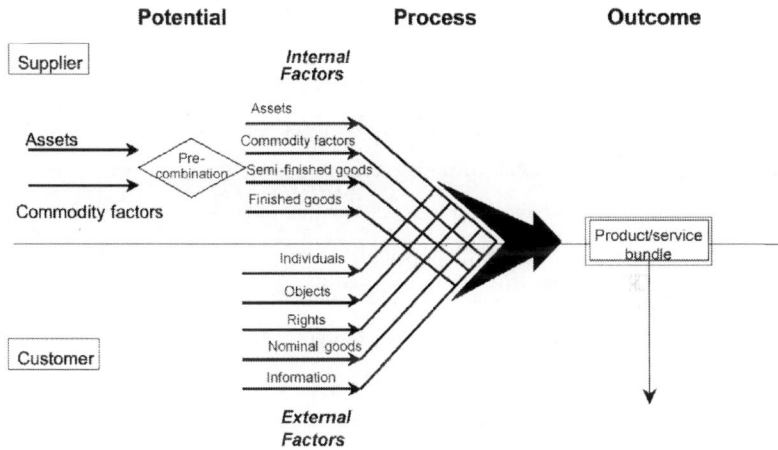

Figure 4. Integrative value chain (Fließ and Kleinaltenkamp 2004, p. 394)

The first stage is the *provider's potential* (Engelhardt and Freiling 1995; Engelhardt 1966, p. 168). As services cannot be produced in advance due to the necessity of external factors, providers can only show the willingness and ability to perform and deliver the service as desired. In order to do so, appropriate infrastructure needs to be arranged. The potential of performance derives from assets and commodity factors, which are transformed customer-independently in combination with finished or semi-finished goods to internal factors. Thus, the infrastructure gives the supplier the potential to perform appropriately. Furthermore, immaterial internal factors such as human labor and capacities decline when they are not consumed in a specific amount of time and cause substantial costs. Classic examples are vacancies in hotels or a surplus of flight capacities. Keeping up the performance potential at low costs requires capacity management. This is even more important for services than for products, which can be stored and distributed at a later date. Yet, as standardized services can be prepared to a certain extent in advance, this characteristic alone is not appropriate to distinguish between goods and services. In fact, one can already recognize that the discussion is rather on the implications for the provider (see Figure 4). Although it might be also of interest how the customer's potential stage does look like.

The second stage involves the service operations, which can also be labeled as the service production *process*. As a follow up to the concept of his publication in 1966, Engelhardt (1989) introduced und discussed at the Annual Meeting of German Academic Association for Business Research in Münster one of the most distinctive characteristics of services. In order to initiate production the customer needs to integrate him or herself. External factors, such as information, objects or a person, are given to the provider so s/he can combine them with the internal factors and conduct the service operation sequence. Without an external factor the provider cannot perform and deliver the service. For instance, if one does not present oneself for physical examinations or consultation, a doctor can hardly provide his or her service. Hence, by integrating additional and necessary resources the customer contributes to the service operation (i.a. Kleinaltenkamp, Fließ and Jacob 1996). A managerial implication of the customer integration is the uno-actu-principle, which implies that the production and consumption of services takes place at the same time (i.a. Herder-Dorneich 1978, p. 3). Provider and consumer need to get together in space and time. Direct contact and interaction between provider and customer is required. Due to the external factor the service provider does not have autonomous control over the production process. The service outcome can thus very much vary depending on the properties and conditions of the external factors. The doctor's consultation, for example, is based on an anamnesis for which the patient has to provide information (e.g. documents). Thus, services can be seen as heterogenic, unique and difficult to standardize (irrespective of services delivered through software or Information Technology, see Gersch 1995, p. 30). Nevertheless, for the distinction of services it is critical that every customer order contains a minimum of external factors.

The *outcome* describes the result of the previous activities, which the customer receives in the end. In comparison to goods, services are not constituted by an object, do not have a physical presence and cannot be touched. As a result of this intangibility, it is difficult to evaluate the service quality. The customer's quest for information about the quality is more easily complied with tangible products as they mostly contain search attributes that can be evaluated before the purchase. However, most services are rather high in experience or even credence attributes that make it difficult to evaluate the performance. According to Nelson (1970) attributes of goods and services can be divided into three dimensions. Search attributes are the ones whose quality can be checked by the customer a priori. Experience attributes only allow an evaluation of performance during or after the production process (e.g. haircut, eating out). Finally, credence attributes cannot be evaluated at all. Returning to the example of a medical consultation, evaluating the quality of the advice a patient receives presents him or her with a challenge (Fließ 2009, pp. 67–70). Due to their immateriality and the uno-actu-principle such services involve a high proportion of experience and credence attributes. A managerial implication of such attributes is that providers increasingly have to create confidence through brandings and trademarks (i.a. De Chernatony and Segal-Horn 2003, p. 1098). Further, intermediaries and distributors are almost not involved (except of barter slips such as tickets) (i.a. Donnelly 1976, p. 55). A major criticism of this approach is that due to the wide variety of existing goods/service bundles, it is hard to draw an objective dividing line between products and services. Depending on the share of tangible products, immateriality should be rather seen on a continuum (Engelhardt, Kleinaltenkamp and Reckenfelderbäumer 1993).

All three phases of the integrative value chain are considered essential. Yet, none provides a distinctive demarcation between goods and services. However, the critics on service definition concepts of each stage (i.e. potential, process and outcome) can be resolved by integrating concepts of the other two stages. Thus, one can speak of a service when the respective specifications of each stage are predominantly met. Zeithaml, Parasuraman and Berry (1985) condensed the special characteristics of services explained above to the four categories intangible, heterogeneous, inseparable and perishable (IHIP characteristics) by reviewing relative literature.

An unique approach was suggested by Engelhardt, Kleinaltenkamp and Reckenfelderbäumer (1992, 1993), who intentionally gave up the separation between services and goods. Because every offer requires a minimum of customer integration such as ordering information, a selective definition is not feasible (Kleinaltenkamp 1997, p. 85). This approach can be seen as a prequel to the service-dominant logic, which is explained in chapter 3.1.2.3. In order to include all the implications that have been mentioned above they set up a two axis continuum on which the degree of intangibility and customer integration of an offer can be classified. Accordingly, almost all the other implications can be deduced from these two characteristics.

Instead of products with attributes, benefits are marketed in the form of service offers. This aspect questions established and rather product-oriented marketing approaches such as the marketing mix (Borden 1964), which usually classifies a market offer by determining the components' price, product, promotion, and place (4P's) (McCarthy 1960). As these categories do not seem to be appropriate for services anymore, the marketing mix has to be modified to adapt the special characteristics of services (i.a. Booms and Bitner 1981; Dev and Schultz 2005). Promotion is not merely connected to price but also has to do with the value delivery and instead of the supply chain of production the integrative value chain thereby comes to the fore.

The service-based value creation process relies to a large extent on the co-production of the customer, who needs to participate in the operation sequence by integrating external factors. With the integration of the customer a first hint is given to the relevance of the customer processes. Firstly, s/he needs to integrate him- or herself to actually enable value creation and can thereby influence the quality of service delivery. Secondly, customers evaluate the created value differently compared to tangible products.

In order to design customer-oriented services properly, one thus needs to understand the altered perception of service quality that derives from customer integration. This becomes especially important for the method that is introduced in this research manuscript. The next chapter therefore gives an overview of service quality models.

3.1.2.2.2 Dimensioning the Service Quality

One major research stream of service marketing is the identification of service quality dimensions. As already outlined in chapter 3.1.1 the customer's perception of service quality is very subjective and varies according to the personal preferences. Important factors can be, for example, the friendliness of the sales personal or the atmosphere of the environment. As service is a highly complex concept, there are numerous approaches to aggregate quality attributes to dimensions. In contrast to products, most services are not predominantly measured by objective criteria, such as durability or number of defects. The immateriality, heterogeneity and simultaneous production and consumption lead to the fact that service quality is an elusive and abstract construct.

Models on service quality often base on the previously introduced confirmation/disconfirmation-paradigm. Because the price constitutes part of the performance evaluation, which takes place after the quality appraisal, it is not usually incorporated in the service quality models. In order to point out the relevance of a process-based view on value creation a short outline of service quality models is represented in the following. An overview can be seen in Spohrer and Maglio (2011, p. 163).

One of the earliest service quality models comes from Grönroos (1984), who deduces two dimensions for the assessment of services. Technical quality is the outcome that the customer retains at the end of the service production process. This could be, for example, a successful treatment of a medical problem in the hospital or the transport of the customer to a specific place. This dimension is intensively affected by the know-how of the company, its technical possibilities and the expertise of its employees. Yet, this dimension alone does not determine the entire quality of a service. The perception of the customer is also affected by the way s/he receives the technical quality. Because the customer participates in the production process, the customer perceives a wide range of attributes, which impact the perceived quality. Examples are, inter alia, accessibility, parking facilities, appearance, staff behavior and expertise. Grönroos aligns these attributes to the functional quality. Basically the technical dimension relates to "what" the customer receives and the functional dimension asks "how" s/he receives it. The technical quality may be assessable by objective criteria, but the functional quality is strongly influenced by subjective perception. However, in order to be competitive in the long term, a high level of customer satisfaction must be achieved in both dimensions. Thus, customer orientation in the production process seems equally important.

Rust and Oliver (1994) extended the model by explicitly adding the service environment dimension. In their model they differentiate between the value creation process on the one hand, which is allocated to a particular action and behavior the customer expects, and the physical environment on the other. For the environment they refer to Bitner's (1992) Servicescape Framework, which combines the terms service and landscape. According to the explanations the physical environment influences the cognition, emotions and physiology of the consumer. The customer may memorize a specific image of the restaurants', hospitals' or banks' premises, which in turn impacts his or her further behavior. For example, in the publication by Leister (2011), the influence of the physical environment on confidence building is empirically analyzed. As service delivery and consumption coincide, the environment and ambience determine (depending on the nature of the service) the perceived quality to a large degree. In the case of fully automated services, such as in the telecommunications service Voicemail, for instance, the (rather technical) environment is not of such high importance as it is in shops which involve a high degree of self-service and little interaction with the staff. Through the design of the environment one can develop strategies that will have a positive impact on the customer satisfaction and attractiveness of a service offer. A pleasant environment, for example, can lead to a longer duration of stay in which more money is spent. A number of factors, such as interior design and temperature, will determine the service environment. The framework encompasses three dimensions, which strongly influence the customer. Firstly, there are the ambient conditions to which all factors belong that one can sense (e.g. air quality, temperature, noise, music, odor or lighting). Further, there is the functional space, which describes the composition of the furniture, equipment and their supportive attributes for the service process. The other dimensions can be summarized under the heading "signs, symbols and artifacts", which explicitly or implicitly send signals. Signs are, for example, a type of explicit communication. All three dimensions are moderators for the customer's cognitive (e.g. categorization), emotional (e.g. mood) and/or physical (e.g. comfort) response. Management should therefore use the design of the premises to promote customer satisfaction in order to establish a viable foundation of business.

One of the most representative researchers in the field of service quality are Parasuraman, Zeithaml and Berry (1985), whose approach to identifying typical gaps between expectations and assessment of service delivery became prominent in service marketing. Through explorative research, they identified ten dimensions of service quality, but because these dimensions overlapped they further refined their SERV(ice)QUAL(ity) model to include five dimensions (Parasuraman, Berry and Zeithaml 1991; Parasuraman, Zeithaml and Berry 1988). The first dimension relates to the perceived convenience of the tangible environment. This dimension includes the appearance of the premise and employees. Secondly, whether a company performs as consistently and accurately as promised refers to its reliability. Third, responsiveness reflects whether the company is able to immediately react to the wishes of the customers. This addresses the company's capability and speed. Fourth, expertise expresses the politeness, expertise and trustworthiness of the service provider. And finally, empathy describes the ability to recognize and comprehend the customer's needs. SERVQUAL considers a questionnaire with 22 items to measure the expected and perceived quality of the five dimensions, which pushed the diffusion of the service quality model due to its practical applicability. This unified survey enables comparisons between companies and trend analyses over time. Although the methodology is widespread and has been received positively, there have been critical responses that point to problems in form and content (Smith 1995). For instance, in studies in which the questionnaire was used, items had to be replaced or removed in order to conform to the specific situation. Often, the five dimensions could not be confirmed and additional dimensions have been identified. Thus, it would appear that the model is not applicable to all services.

Critics state that the SERVQUAL model is inapplicable on combinations of goods and services, which are, for example, important to retailers (Dabholkar, Thorpe and Rentz 1996; Finn and Lamb 1991). As a consequence, Dabholkar, Thorpe and Rentz (1996) developed a new model, whose dimensions are structured in a three level hierarchy, which is also part of a unifying model that is described and illustrated in the following paragraph. The top level describes the service quality in its entirety. This is composed of several dimensions from the middle level. Depending on the complexity, sub-dimensions can be aligned to the relative dimensions on the lowest level. Thus, dimensions that have a high inter-correlation can be assigned to a higher dimension of the middle level. In this manner, inter-correlations between the dimensions can be explained. Moreover, the approach enables a more detailed analysis of the service quality. Although the authors state that the development of a generally valid instrument for the measurement of service quality is not feasible, they acknowledge the presence of basic dimensions in all kinds of services.

The last model that is described in this chapter combines the basic ideas and dimensions of each conceptualization. Brady and Cronin (2001b) introduced an approved model that consists of three dimensions with three sub-dimensions respectively. The reliability, responsiveness, and empathy of the SERVQUAL concept can be seen as a parameter of each sub-dimension. With regard to SERVQUAL, the "interaction quality" dimension contains the sub-dimensions attitude, behavior and expertise. "Physical Environment Quality" describes the tangible environment, which is often taken as an indicator of quality. Servicescape can be divided into the sub-categories ambience, design, and social factors. Ambience includes the environmental conditions exposed by Bitner (1992), such as odor, heat and all of the other factors that are received by means the senses. Design describes the aesthetic and functional interior decoration. Social factors specify the number of people involved and their behavior. For instance, unpleasant people in the environment or crowded rooms can influence the perception of quality. Outcome quality involves the sub-dimensions waiting time, tangibles and valence. Waiting time exerts a high impact on this dimension. Long queues, as well as delays in service delivery have a strongly negative correlation to the outcome quality. Transaction and transfer time are also included in this sub-dimension. Tangible items are an important indicator for performance due to their search attributes. Physical quality is an explicit feature and easier for the customers to process. Another determinant of the result quality is the valence. This includes attributes that affect the perceived quality regardless of previous and actual performances. Valence describes factors that are out of the company's influence range but influence a person's perceived experience. For instance, while a case of irreparable damage may not in fact reflect an inability of the repair shop, it may have a negative effect on the perceived service quality. Figure 5 represents the hierarchical dimensioning of service quality.

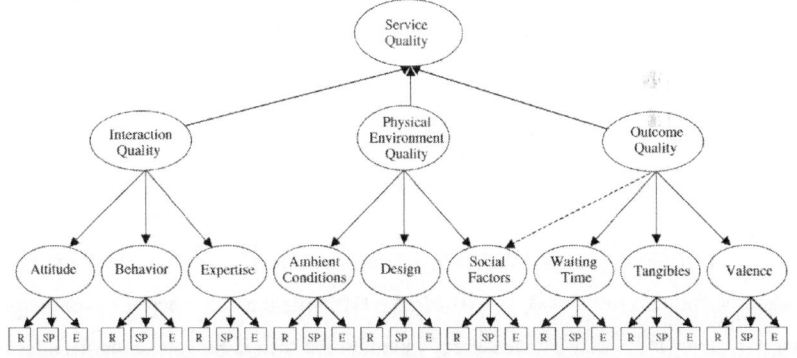

Note: R = a reliability item, SP = a responsiveness item, E = an empathy item. The broken line indicates that the path was added as part of model respecification.

Figure 5. Hierarchical conceptualizing of service quality (Brady and Cronin 2001b, p. 37)

Although the model seems to contain a comprehensive view of the various dimensions of service quality, Brady and Cronin point out that it has only been tested in a few industries and a generalization should not be considered uncritically. If one reflects the importance of the functional quality dimension that necessarily derives from customer integration, the relevance of designing and supporting customer processes becomes all the more clear.

In order to have a customer-oriented value creation it is not enough to provide a specific outcome quality. Customer participation requires a widened view on value creation to include interaction and the perceived environment. One of the first methods that emphasizes this circumstance is Service Blueprinting (Shostack 1982), which visualizes a service process and its activities from the customer perspective in a flowchart. In this way the provider can simulate the customer's view on the service production process and identify important points of interaction, so called "moments of truth", that have a high influence on the perceived quality (Grönroos 1990). The method has been very much accepted and is widespread beyond the service marketing community. As it is part of the designed artifact of this research, it will be explained in further detail later on. In this chapter it merely serves to underline the rising importance of customer processes for the value creation in services.

3.1.2.3   Service-Dominant Logic: Co-Creation, Value-in-use and Usage Processes

With their article, "Evolving to a new dominant logic for marketing", Vargo and Lusch (2004a) revived the discussion on economic exchange and the creation of value, which is often seen as a shift of paradigm in the marketing community. The service-dominant logic (SDL) has been debated at length in a number of dedicated conferences and special issues of journals such as the *Journal of Marketing* (2004, Vol. 68, Nr. 1) and *Marketing Theory* (2006, Vol. 6, Nr. 3). Of particular relevance for this thesis is that SDL, which has gained widespread international recognition and support in recent years, acknowledges the idea that value creation needs to integrate the specifics of usage processes on the customer's side ("value-in-use").

3.1.2.3.1 Foundational Premises of the Service-Dominant Logic

Vargo and Lusch (2004b) argue that definitions of services on the basis of constitutive characteristics are rather a negative definition of tangible products. In analogy to this, the view on value creation is still goods-centered and "services" a term that can be aligned to the good-dominant logic as it implies units of output. Their remarks are supported by explanations that disapprove the IHIP characteristics of services (see chapter 3.1.2.2.1). The intangibility is denied as a distinctive characteristic because services often have tangible results (as seen in the service quality model of Brady and Cronin). Furthermore, goods often render intangible benefits. They do not, for instance, admit heterogeneity as a distinguishing factor, because goods can also be very non-standardized (e.g. production of an airplane) and services can be homogenized (e.g. information from databases such as internet platforms). By looking at the entertainment industry such as the film industry, in which production and consumption is quite separated, they state that inseparability between these two dimensions is not always given in services. Lastly, the benefits that derive from goods are also perishable (e.g. fashion trends), while services often have longer lasting benefits. Due to the fact that the IHIP characteristics are not mandatory defining a service, Vargo and Lusch (2004a) call to rethink marketing and adopt a new perspective, a service-dominant logic on economic exchange, in which skills and knowledge are the basis of exchange.

The SDL should be seen as a pre-theoretic and rather paradigmatic mindset (Vargo 2011, p. 4). Vargo and Lusch (2004a) distinguish between operand resources, which can be treated as objects that receive an effect, and operant resources that produce the effect. These operant resources, which basically consist of knowledge and skills, are seen as primary, because they produce the effect on operand resources. Operand resources are rather tangible objects that solely serve to embody and transmit the value of operant resources. In order to highlight the operant resources they use the singular form "service" instead of "services".

Accordingly they define a service as a "…process of using one's resources for the benefit of another entity" (Vargo and Lusch 2008b, p. 2). To encourage this view, ten foundational premises outline the implications of this new perspective on economic exchange (Vargo and Lusch 2008b, p. 7), which are shortly described for sake of a better understanding:

(1) "Service is the fundamental basis of exchange": A service is determined by the operant resources, which are seen as the basic value of exchange.

(2) "Indirect exchange masks the fundamental basis of exchange": Because operand resources transmit operant resources, the value the operant resources render is not always apparent.

(3) "Goods are a distribution mechanism for service provision": Benefits do not arise by owning operand resources. They derive from the service they render.

(4) "Operant resources are a fundamental source of competitive advantage": The ability to drive changes derives from operant resources.

(5) "All economies are service economies": As service is the basis of every economic exchange, the distinction between economic sectors is obsolete.

(6) "The customer is always a co-creator of value": Value can never be created unilaterally as it requires a combination of the participant's resources. This becomes especially apparent when one considers that the value does not derive from exchange but from usage.

(7) "The enterprise cannot deliver value, but only offer value propositions": Companies can only offer their resources to create value in combination with other participations of exchange.

(8) "A service-centered view is inherently customer-oriented and relational": The value of a service is determined by the benefit for the customer (customer-oriented), who is necessarily co-creator of value (relational).

(9) "All social and economic actors are resource integrators": Everyone who is affected by the exchange can be seen as a resource integrator. Furthermore, the created value is embedded and connected to networks of resource integrators, such as Consumer-to-Consumer networks.

(10) "Value is always uniquely and phenomenologically determined by the beneficiary": As already described in the marketing process, value is a highly subjective construct with individual dimensions.

In summary, it is not so much about the differences between a particular good and a service, as much as about the relationship between them. From the article authors' point of view "service is exchanged for service" (Vargo and Lusch 2008b, p. 7), which implies that goods only transfer a service. They see "service as a process – doing something for another party" (Vargo and Lusch 2008a, p. 3). Whether the service is provided directly, through education or through goods does not matter, because activities and things only render service. That this rather paradigmatic concept of economic exchange is already established and lived in real, can be seen in examples such as the "Collaborative Consumption" movement (i.a. Botsman and Rogers 2010), in which the community organizes the sharing and renting of goods via IT-systems. Instead of individual consumption, which is very much based on the ownership of a property, the focus in this case is on the temporary benefits of goods that in turn stimulate only a short-term usage and subsequent interexchange.

3.1.2.3.2 The Co-Creation and Usage Processes of the Customer

The implications of the shifted view on economic exchange from services- to resource-based service are a major concern of this thesis. Of special interest is the sixth premise, which states that the customer is always a co-creator of value. Although the view on pure co-creation networks is not seen without reservations and other authors like Grönroos and Voima (2012) tend to differentiate between a provider and customer, who share a connecting joint sphere, the proposition promotes the importance of customer processes. Contrary to those who believe that value already is embedded and created in the service production process, Lusch and Vargo (2006, p. 284) see the usage of the provider's operant resources by the customer as fundamental for the value creation when they argue that "…value can only be created with and determined by the user in the 'consumption' process and through use or what is referred to as value-in-use." Just in combination with the skills and knowledge of the customer the offers unfold their value. A comprehensive list of co-creation definitions can be seen in McColl-Kennedy et al. (2012).

An important element of the definition mentioned above is the process view on the customer's co-creation. Such a perspective is also affirmed by Grönross (2008, p.

307), who says "…adopting a service logic makes it possible for firms to get involved with their customers' value-generating processes…", and by a statement of Xie, Bagozzi, and Troye (2007, p. 110) saying that "…prosumption is a process rather than a simple act…". This line of thought is condensed by the term "value-in-use", which implies that value only emerges when benefits arise for the customer in his or her usage processes. The value-in-exchange known from the GDL only anticipates this usage (Lusch, Vargo and O'Brien 2007, p. 13). For instance, Dev and Schultz (2005) relabeled the dimensions of the previously mentioned marketing mix to "Solution", "Information", "Value" and "Access" (SIVA). Naming these aspects shifts the focus onto the solution the marketing offer delivers. The company Apple Inc. already considers these aspects when focusing in commercials on practical scenarios, in which the promoted product is presented as very useful in various situations, such as detailed directions on their smart-phone via voice commands when one searches a specific location or the manageability of a videoconference in private and professional surroundings without any complications.

Closely linked to value-in-use are also new approaches to model the perceived quality, which consider the overall experience over time instead of merely the result of a single transaction. Recently proposed experience models with such a holistic viewpoint are among others Grewal, Levy and Kumar (2009), Lemke, Clark and Wilson (2011), Maklan and Klaus (2011), Payne, Storbacka and Frow (2008), Verhoef et al. (2009) and Voss, Roth and Chase (2008). It is assumed that customers do have a longitudinal perspective for the evaluation of experience. For instance, Arnould and Price (2003) and Shaw and Ivens (2004) propose a multi-stage model of customer experience. Turnbull (2009) even replaces the term value-in-use by value-in-experience to cover all phases of customer experience. Hence, research ought not only to consider service encounters where a direct interaction between provider and customer occurs, but also take into account the customer's experience before and after contact with the service provider (Verhoef et al. 2009, p. 32). It is supposed that experience is not determined by a single episode, but rather arises and solidifies over time by numerous encounters across diverse channels. For example, Payne, Storbacka and Frow (2008, pp. 90–91) differentiate between communication, service and usage encounters. These three encounters are also part of the conceptual model of Lemke, Clark and Wilson (2011). Communication encounters describe activities such as advertising to connect with the customer. Communication activities already have been considered in the GDL. Service encounters refer to the interaction between provider and customer, which has already been elucidated along with the service quality models in chapter 3.1.2.2.2. The usage encounter concerns the use of a product and/or service. However, research on usage processes is only now emerging. Eichentopf, Kleinaltenkamp and van Stiphout (2011, pp. 650–651) state that because "…value creation lies in both co-production and usage, firms need not only a precise image of how customers use the processes of co-production but also an understanding of how they navigate through them."

Accordingly, a result of the discussion on co-creation and experience quality is the affirmation that the usage processes significantly impact the quality perception. They are seen a crucial part in shaping overall satisfaction (Lemke, Clark and Wilson 2011, p. 4). The usage as an integral part of overall value creation is a relatively new perspective (Grönroos 2011, p. 242). A major part of the utility expected by the customer usually emerges after traditional value activities of the provider. Usage plays an important role in shaping overall customer satisfaction. Usage process quality is, for example, an important element of the study done by Macdonald et al. (2011), who affirm in reference to goal theory (i.a. Paulssen and Bagozzi 2006) that the usage process quality significantly impacts a person's perceived value-in-use (the customer's goals). The papers of Kleinaltenkamp, Macdonald and Wilson (2011, 2012a, 2012b) explore the concept of value co-creation in usage centers and propose a model that contains nine processes that have an influence on the customer's quality perception. However, research on usage processes is still at an early stage. Nevertheless, first concepts and findings have been introduced and discussed. For instance, a Special Interest Group on "Usage Processes and Value-in-Use" discussed relevant research at the 40th Annual Conference of the European Marketing Academy (Kleinaltenkamp and Macdonald 2011).

Usage processes can be labeled as autonomously coordinated customer activities that usually emerge after interaction with the provider. They are therefore traditionally outside the provider's perception. Usage processes are not to be confused with after sales services, which are provider related offers whose purpose is to ensure the functional reliability of a purchase as part of an add-on to the interaction (Weiber and Hörstrup 2009, p. 296). Because of their important role in overall value creation, usage process-es provide valuable information about the customer's behavior and perception of the preceding provider process. The challenge and opportunity for the provider is to use these findings to enhance and redesign future offers in order to match customers' or customer groups' expectations and requirements with appropriately tailored process designs. As such a proceeding may increase customer satisfaction, it can result in more effective processes (Lemke, Clark and Wilson 2011, p. 860). On the provider side, efficiency gains are also possible, e.g. by extending process standardization in accord-ance with a better understanding of homogenous customer segments (Gersch, Hewing and Schöler 2011, pp. 744–745).

A rather simple and catchy example is the case of ARM & HAMMER®'s Baking So-da (i.a. Datta 1996; Park, Jaworski and MacInnis 1986). Once the company discovered their product's versatile application spectrum (e.g. baking soda as soap powder or cleanser), and how it goes far beyond the realm of cooking, they actively began to communicate the various usage possibilities in the form of guidelines on the product's packaging, and promoted these on their website (Arm & Hammer 2013) too resulting in an increase of their sales. The company even went on to enhance their line of prod-ucts to include soda-based refrigerator deodorants and toothpastes.

However, forthcoming (technological) possibilities to influence previously autono-mous usage processes open up new potentials of value creation for the provider. Usage can be supported to improve customers' overall perception of quality and their satis-faction. Also opportunities to influence and control these processes arise, which blur the line between interaction process and usage. Payne, Storbacka and Frow (2008, p. 91) list helpful guidelines to support the usage encounters, such as 'good-to-know' information and check lists.

The following example illustrates the importance of supporting usage processes, which are especially relevant in outpatient care. At present, a therapy service often consists of a periodical consultation with the physician only. So after direct interaction with a health consultant, the patient is on his or her own and has to be self-reliant without any or only weak support from the outside. Yet, the success of a medical therapy is to great extent related to the compliance, the cooperative behavior of the patient. Further information on co-creation in health care can be seen in McColl-Kennedy et al. (2012). An inadequate regard of medical advices can in fact worsen a patient's quality of life by resulting in increased symptoms. There can also be a higher mortality risk. In addition, it causes rising costs in the health sector (i.a. due to more hospital stays), whose funding reaches its limit in a certain amount of time. Referred to the WHO (2003, p. 7), only 50% of all patients follow their therapy correctly. In this context, the maximization of compliance seems to be of great importance. The main reasons for inadequate compliance are forgetfulness and a negative perception of health improvements. However, further support by the medical service providers is hardly feasible. With recent innovations in the field of telemedicine, a potential evolves to get insight into these autonomous patient activities. After direct interaction between the physician and patient, activities that are relevant for the therapy are mostly outside of the care provider's perception and therefore beyond his or her area of influence. By collecting data of telemedicine solutions, patient's processes become visible and can thus become easier to support. Treatment can be optimized by monitoring (residential) activities in terms of health and safety using sensor technology. Also web portals for people concerned, for instance, with diabetes mellitus may support therapy by means of an option to record and analyze medical parameters. If approved by the patient, intervention in the usage process can enhance efficiency through increased compliance and may have a positive influence on the effectiveness of therapy by enabling a better perception of the (positive) course of a disease and providing a higher sense of security.

Providers therefore need to extend their process-related analysis to develop an enhanced perspective on process performance. Usage processes on the demand side need to be understood, aiming to support these normally autonomous processes. Moreover, a guided redesign of the overall value creation process would help to improve efficiency and effectiveness, taking the complete overall process of value creation into account, even beyond the provider's traditional perception. It is apparent that the chance to open up new potentials of value creation is offered to the provider. Thus, usage processes that used to take place beyond the provider's perception need to be analyzed in greater detail.

3.1.3 The Need for a substantiated Process View on the Customer

Before moving on to the field of Business Process Management, it is advisable that we sum up the consolidated findings and highlight the line of argumentation so far. Table 3 compactly illustrates the shift of concepts and highlights the rising importance of customer processes.

Table 3. Conceptual transitions (modified from Lusch and Vargo 2006, p. 286)

Goods-dominant logic concepts	Transitional concepts	Service-dominant logic concepts
Goods	Services	Service
Products	Offerings	Experiences
Feature/attribute	Benefit	Solution
Value-added	Co-production	Co-creation of value
Profit maximization	Financial engineering	Financial feedback/learning
Price	Value delivery	Value proposition
Equilibrium systems	Dynamic systems	Complex adaptive systems
Supply chain	Value-chain	Value-creation network/constellation
Promotion	Integrated marketing communications	Dialogue
To market	Market to	Market with
Product orientation	Market orientation	Service orientation
Internal processes	Interaction processes	Customer and usage processes

In the first sub-chapter the author elucidated the importance of customer orientation for a company's long-term profits. The concepts of customer value, perceived quality, customer satisfaction and effectiveness are closely linked to each other and have a high impact on customer retention and economic success. Yet, in the early years of marketing management the focus was exclusively dedicated to the production of physical goods, its efficiency and the delivery to the customer. The quality of a marketing offer tended to be evaluated in terms of the technical quality involved and the number of features of a product. Customer activities were largely left unconsidered. Instead, internal processes were the subject of analysis.

With the emerging research stream of service marketing, articles began to draw attention to customer activities in the service production process, which implies a necessity of direct interaction between the provider and customer. As the customer needs to integrate him- or herself in the process, s/he becomes a co-producer of value. Interaction processes become an important element of analysis. Quality models adopted this circumstance and added dimensions of functional quality to the outcome quality, such as interaction and the physical environment. Methods like Service Blueprinting point to the fact that a process view on the value creation is indispensable.

With the almost paradigmatic shift to a service-dominant logic and its accentuation of the immateriality of value, the perspective on value creation completely opened up to the customer side. The customer is treated as a co-creator of value and as a consequence his or her processes are considered to be fundamental. As a consequence, quality models have begun to widen their focus to include overall experiences between a provider and customer in communication, service and usage encounters. Thus, these models integrate the usage processes of the customer as a major dimension of quality perception. As already stated above the importance of the customer's usage processes has been underlined by Grönross (2008, p. 307), Lusch and Vargo (2006, p. 284), Payne, Storbacka and Frow (2008, p. 85) and Xie, Bagozzi, and Troye (2007, p. 110).

Some researchers even go one step further and see the driving element (process leadership) in the customer processes. Potts (2010, p. 43) postulates a (literally) customer-centered approach by saying that it is actually the customer who has a process. The company needs to reflect on which part of this process they play a part and how they participate in delivering contribution. Firms have to picture the whole relationship of exchange to comprehend the customer's process chain, which can be grouped into three sections: pre-purchase, interaction (with the provider including after sales services) and usage (Blackwell, Miniard and Engel 2005, p. 67). Slater and Narver (1994, p. 22) stated that the creation of "…superior value for buyers continuously requires that a seller understands a buyer's entire value chain, not only as it is today but also as it evolves over time." In reference to Behara, Fontenot and Gresham (2002) customer processes are defined by Heckl and Moorman (2007, p. 113) "…as the entire procedure customers pass through to meet a desire or to solve a problem. Such a process comprises every single step until a specific wish has been fulfilled or the solution for a problem has been found." Thus, customer processes refer not only to direct interaction with the provider, but to all activities that are conducted by the customer such as pre-purchase, interaction, usage and latent (provider independent) processes.

Weiber and Hörstrup (2009) call for a swift of perspective from customer integration, which sees the customer as an external factor that is incorporated to the provider processes, to provider integration that mirrors this issue. This position is fortified by research from Arnould and Price (2003), Shaw and Ivens (2004), Turnbull (2009) and Verhoef et al. (2009).

Thus, understanding customer desires and the creation of appropriate value propositions require that one comprehend the customers' entire value chain (Narver and Slater 1990, p. 21). To understand customers' needs and create customer value, it is beneficial to granulate their value chain into processes in order to take up the customer's point of view, understand the quality of the customer's experience and design appropriate marketing offers.

In order to do so, appropriate methods and management tools are necessary. As research in the area of customer processes is still in its early stages, only a few methods have been presented and proposed. For instance, Service Blueprinting, which will be elucidated in detail along with the developed artifact in chapter 4.1.1.2, can be used to highlight the interaction processes. Frauendorf (2006) picked up the idea behind the method and with reference to Fließ (2001, p. 48) pointed to the idea of extending the Service Blueprinting to the buyer's side in business-to-business (B2B) service transactions. The conceptual framework of these publications is based on transaction cost theory (i.a. Coase 1937; Williamson 1979) and scripts (i.a. Schank 1975), which can be seen as describing the whole interactive value creation processes that are implicitly expected by the customer. Based on these publications, together with Kleinaltenkamp and Eichentopf (Eichentopf, Kleinaltenkamp and van Stiphout 2011; Kleinaltenkamp, van Stiphout and Eichentopf 2010) she resumes the discussion on scripts and presents a suitable typology.

Furthermore, with reference to the three types of encounter, Payne, Storbacka and Frow (2008, p. 92) mapped the customer, supplier and encounter processes. A similar approach from a rather practical view is presented by Richardson (2010), Creative Director at the innovation firm frogdesign, in the Harvard Business Review Blog. His customer journey map illustrates in a diagram the steps a customer goes through. In the discussion on provider integration, Weiber and Hörstrup (2009) present a "usage print" of the customer. Further concepts, which can be considered interesting, are the "Customer activity chain" (i.a. Sawhney, Balasubramanian and Krishnan 2003) and "Customer Experience Modeling" (Teixeira et al. 2012) both of which propose to set the focus of process analysis to the customers' side.

Much as these methods contribute to structuring process elements, they lack a complete, clear and consistent way of how to model and manage processes. Most illustrations can be seen as rudimentary, containing a high level of abstraction. The syntax of process illustrations differs between the methods listed above. It is even incoherent in the same method. For instance, the elements of the Service Blueprint method vary in the articles of Fließ and Kleinaltenkamp (2004), Kingman-Brundage (1995) and Shostack (1982). This can lead to misunderstandings and misinterpretations.

Certainly it is not one of the main tasks of the marketing discipline to develop a substantiated and comprehensive modeling language. However, the level of detail of current methods makes it rather difficult to illustrate and manage complex and intertwined processes. As the marketing community does not possess tools and software instantiations for the illustration of processes, it is challenging to store further information pertaining to the process elements without losing clear arrangements. A discipline, which particularly deals with this issue, is Business Process Management. It seems that research on customer processes in marketing can very much benefit from the integration of BPM approaches.

In conclusion, chapter 3.1 can be summarized as a recognition of the fact that value creation is a principal part of customer orientation, which is important to sustain economic success. The view on value creation has shifted over recent decades to a service-dominated logic, in which customer processes as part of the value creation have become central. Yet, there still seems to be a lack of formal methods for modeling customer processes.

3.2 The Role of the Customer in Business Process Management

With its focus on processes and corresponding modeling methods, BPM is a discipline which shows great promise with regard to evolving an appropriate approach to solve the deficit of research mentioned above. This chapter therefore describes the basic principles and reviews to which degree customer processes are already considered in this field of Information Systems.

3.2.1 Business Process Management in Information Systems

Business Process Management is basically an approach to structure and redesign activities. Economic performances are the result of combining multiple activities or in other words "any work is process work" (Hammer 2010, p. 11). Business processes organize these activities with control flows that coordinate their relation to one another. Though the definitions of business processes vary, there is a given consensus. Most definitions describe similar key characteristics. Davenport (1993, p. 5), for instance, defines a (business) process as "…a structured, measured set of activities designed to produce a specific output for a particular customer or market." Hammer and Champy (1994, p. 38) state that a business process is "…a collection of activities that takes one or more kinds of input and creates an output that is of value to the customer." Accordingly, business processes coordinate and organize a collection of activities. Management comprises the planning, directing and controlling of an organization. Hence, BPM includes "…concepts, methods and techniques to support the design, administration, configuration, enactment, and analysis of business processes" (Weske 2009, p. 5).

According to Harmon (2010), BPM is based on three traditions. Coming from Taylor's (2001; first published 1911) concept of work simplification, which implied a division of labour, segmentation of processes and specialisation on a specific activity, the first tradition is that of Quality Control, which includes concepts that focus on the technical quality of internal processes such as Total Quality Management and Six Sigma. The second tradition is Business Management, which failed to emphasize process approaches for a long time. Yet, important process related conceptions such as Porter's Value Chain (1985) and Balanced Scorecard (Kaplan and Norton 1996), which comprises measurements of internal business processes, have been established. The last tradition is Information Technology, which in its early phase focused on the assistance and automation of activities with the help of IT-systems. Considering the fact that BPM also contains other traditions, it ought to be stated that business processes are independent of IT-systems that are used to autonomously conduct or support performances. For the sake of distinction, the (partial) automation of business processes by Information Technologies is therefore nowadays called workflow management (Georgakopoulos, Hornick and Sheth 1995). However, the main focus was on software methodologies and IT-architectures. The 1990s gave rise to Business Process Reengineering (BPR), which drew on the management tradition to advocate companies to reflect and see their businesses within comprehensive processes (i.a. Davenport and Short 1990; Hammer 1990). Along with the BPR approach, Business Process Modeling tools and techniques have been developed. Today BPM is an inherent part of the IS community (Laudon and Laudon 2012, pp. 515–518), which studies in general components that handle information to support the management in an organization (see chapter 2.1). BPM has become a substantial subject in IS journals and conferences. In summary, BPM emerges from all three traditions and incorporates their approaches. This is why BPM involves a wide range of aspects. An overview of the elements included in BPM is given by Rosemann and vom Brocke (2010, p. 112), who identified six core elements with respectively five capability areas that are critical to BPM and to which most aspects can be aligned. Process design and modeling constitute central aspects in this context.

3.2.2 A Literature Review on Customer Processes in Business Process Management

According to the explanation of chapter 3.1, marketing considers customer processes as an important part of value creation. However, its process approaches lack formal methods. BPM with its modeling techniques is a discipline that may bridge this gap.

As a first step, a study on the current state of customer-oriented BPM research has to be performed. In order to review the extent to which customer processes have been incorporated in BPM and which formal method exits to model them, an extensive literature review is required. However, it is often stated that BPM tends to focus on optimization the process of production within a business unit and comprises only little or poor customer intelligence (i.a. Batista, Smart and Maull 2008, pp. 536–538). The proposition of this review is that though customer needs and their processes seem relevant to sustain and level revenues, current methods in Business Process Management provide a rather inside-out view on processes. As the customer's perspective is of great importance, it is interesting to review the extent to which the management of customers and their processes is picked up and illustrated in BPM related publications. A literature review shall reveal the current state of research regarding customer process concepts in BPM. Because the objective of this review is to provide an overview of existing research in this area, the question of interest is as follows:

What is the current state of research on customer processes in Business Process Management related literature?

In order to answer this question one needs to highlight current key concepts and ideas on the customer and reflect the major issues and debates. Therefore this chapter reviews and analyzes relative articles that have been found in relevant databases. The next three sub-chapters follow the framework of literature reviewing by vom Brocke et al. (2009) and give detailed insights on the review process (background, design, analysis and discussion). The concluding sub-chapter summarizes the findings.

3.2.2.1   Reviewing customer-related Concepts in Business Process Management

3.2.2.1.1   Rigor of Literature Reviews

Research needs to incorporate and ground on the existing knowledge of the relevant research areas. In order to identify relevant concepts a literature review is often conducted in the early phase of research (Baker 2000). A literature review can be described as the summary and discussion of previous research that has already been published, exploring the strengths and weaknesses of current knowledge. It helps to organize, integrate and evaluate the present progress of research regarding a specific research question. In this way, inconsistencies, contradictions and gaps in literature can be identified. Furthermore, it emphasizes the value of research that closes these gaps and points with concluding proposals to the next steps that have to be taken. An overview of further reasons for reviewing literature can be seen in Hart (1998, p. 29).

The task of a literature review is to raise relevance of research by preventing reinvestigations on already known knowledge, as well as to fortify rigor by showing that the respective and current knowledge has been very much incorporated into one's research process. As a literature review with high rigor strengthens the reasoning of the research's relevance, the rigor of the review can be seen as essential part of the overall rigor of the research project. Rigor in a literature review is given when it contains validity and reliability (vom Brocke et al. 2009, p.4).

The validity element questions the degree to which a review operationalizes the specific research question. This concerns particularly the selection of keywords, databases, the journals they contain and the accuracy of the search process. For instance, a review of concepts in BPM should include a revision of the central publications like "Business Process Management Journal".

The reliability element describes the replicability of the review process and its results. Reliability is given when, irrespective of the investigator, equal results are achieved through a repetition of the search process under the same conditions. This can be obtained by a comprehensive and detailed documentation of the search process, which gives the reader a deep insight into the proceeding, showing every step that has been taken.

3.2.2.1.2   The Review Design

Even though rigor is most important for scientific literature reviews, publications often contain insufficient documentation of the search process, which in turn gives little insight on the validity and/or reliability of the review. For instance, vom Brocke et al. (2009) showed that most review articles that have been published in ten major Information Systems (IS) journals do not document the procedure adequately. They therefore call for more rigor by providing further information about the literature search process and present a guideline to do so. The guideline considers and incorporates relevant publications on how to conduct literature reviews. As this guideline represents the state-of-the-art of literature reviews in the IS domain, the design of the present review follows its principles. This review can therefore also be seen as yet another confirmation of this guideline, illustrating its approach. The guideline presents a framework that contains five phases for literature reviews. Figure 6 illustrates this course of actions. In addition to the guideline of vom Brocke et al. (2009), the author considered IS related publications that provide further information on how to conduct a literature review (Levy and Ellis 2006; Randolph 2009; Vanwersch et al. 2011; Webster and Watson 2002).

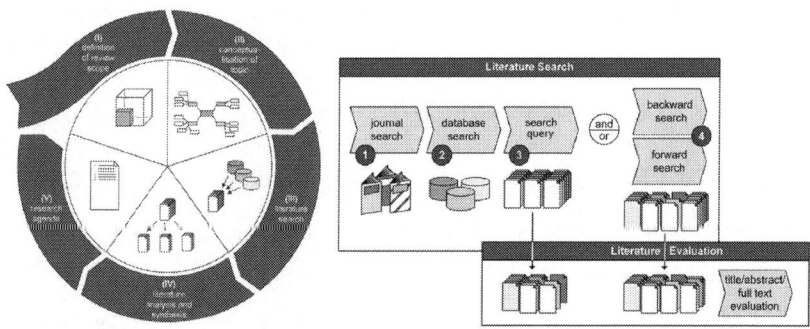

Figure 6. Framework of literature reviewing (modified from vom Brocke et al. 2009, pp. 8-9), full-page illustration in Appendix 4

Definition of Review Scope

In a first step the scope of the review needs to be defined. For the description of the review's characteristics the taxonomy of Cooper (1988, p. 110) can be consulted. According to Cooper literature reviews can be classified on the basis of the six characteristics "focus", "goal", "coverage", "organization", "audience" and "perspective".

The focus of most literature reviews is on research outcomes, research methods, theories and/or applications. Research outcomes refer to the findings and conclusions of studies, methods to the body of techniques and theories to the underlying principles.

Finally, applications describe how a certain practice has been applied. This review explores the integration of customer process concepts in BPM. As concepts can be considered the building blocks of methods, the primary focus of this review can be attached to this category.

The goal of many reviews is the integration and generalization of findings. Further goals can be the critical analysis of current research and the identification of central issues. Often the integration of findings requires additional critical analysis and may point to central issues. This is why reviews often contain multiple goals even though there may be a primary one. The goal of this review is to explore the degree to which BPM has included customer process concepts and to identify gaps. It can be seen as a critical analysis of the body of knowledge.

The coverage of reviews can range from "exhaustive" over "exhaustive with selective citation" or "representative" to "central" or "pivotal". Exhaustive reviews consider every publication about the topic of interest, while a pivotal coverage would examine central articles only. Because this review is a comprehensive one but mainly focuses on journal articles and conference papers and only marginally on books, it can be classified as an exhaustive review with selective citation. The coverage will be illustrated in detail in phase 3, which describes the literature search.

The organization of a review describes its structure, which can have a historical, methodological or conceptual format. This means that the review is either organized chronologically, methodologically or around a concept. Though this review also illustrates the progression and changes of concepts over time, the review is organized around concepts.

The two remaining characteristics are the audience the review is written for and the perspective revealing pre-existing biases. The review addresses mainly scholars within the field of BPM and process-related research fields, but might be of interest for scholars in the IS discipline and marketing as well as for practitioners who are familiar with or interested in customer concepts and/or BPM. Though the reviewer already had the feel that customer process concepts are insufficiently picked up in BPM, the review can be seen as neutral as it contains to a large extent a quantitative dimension and objective criteria in the qualitative selection of relevant articles.

Conceptualization of topic

Now that the scope of the review has been described according to the six characteristics, a conceptualization of the topic is necessary in order to gain a broad overview. A common technique to identify key concepts is concept mapping – the creation of a conceptual map on the basis of synonyms and related concepts. The result is a diagram that organizes and represents the concepts that are considered important. These concepts are the basis for the selection of keywords in the search process. Therefore the listed concepts can be seen as a guiding rail for the search process.

The question of this review is to which degree the customer and his or her processes are conceptually considered in BPM. With this in mind the author created a suitable concept map. As a first step keywords of related publications, like the ones in BPM, marketing and service management, have been consulted and summarized. This also includes other subjects that include aspects of customer orientation, such as New Product Development, Operations Management and Customer Relationship Management. The intermediate concept map has been presented and discussed in two research colloquiums with field-related experts. Before and in between these colloquiums the author discussed in several consultations with colleagues further revisions. Minor changes have been incorporated through this iterative process. Figure 7 visualizes the course of events.

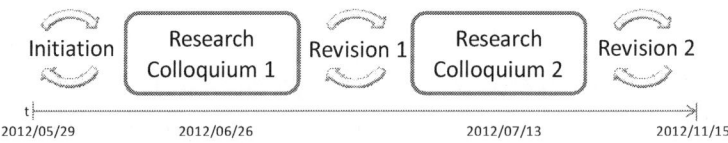

Figure 7. Time bar regarding the revision of the concept map

The last version of this concept map can be seen in Figure 8. The central concepts of the research question are "customer" and "Business Process". As they are elementary for the concept map, these two concepts rank highest. The right side of the figure illustrates the concept of "Business Processes" and its acronym as well as the most common optional complements. Customer concepts and keywords of related publications have been incorporated to the left with sub-concepts like "customer activities" or "service-dominant logic" (SDL).

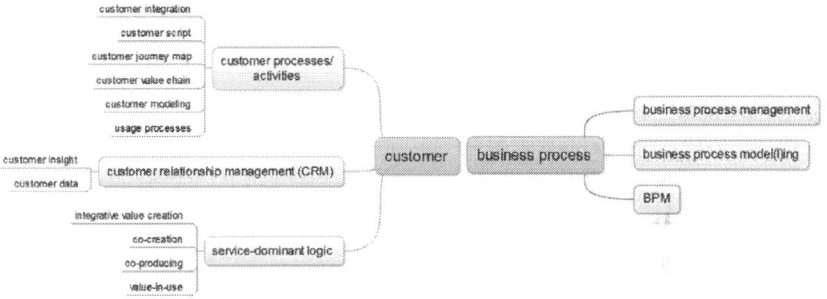

Figure 8. Conceptualization of the review's topic

Literature search

Now the scope of the review has been declared and the topic conceptualized, the actual search for literature has to be structured. For the literature search process vom Brocke et al. (2009, p. 9) refer to four steps (see Figure 6).

A first step considers which publications are essential in the field of interest and therefore need to be included in the literature search. This review is resident in the field of BPM and should accordingly include its top-tier sources. Especially journals and proceedings should be considered as they usually contain peer-reviewed articles. Important journals and conferences can be identified in academic rankings like those in the "Journal Quality List". Some rankings even contain a subdivision into specific areas of research. Of particular significance in BPM are the top-ranked publications "Business Process Management Journal" (BPMJ) and "International Conference on Business Process Management" (BPM). These two sources also have been identified as central by vom Brocke and Sinnl (2011, p. 361) in their literature review on culture in BPM. Yet BPM topics are also picked up in special issues of journals in the domain of IS or in tracks of various conferences, like the "International Conference on Information Systems" (ICIS), "European Conference on Information Systems" (ECIS), "Americas Conference on Information Systems" (AMCIS), "Australasian Conference on Information Systems" (ACIS) and the "Pacific–Asia Conference on Information Systems" (PACIS). Though a closer look and special attention needs be given to the publication channels BPMJ and BPM, those further sources should also be included in an extensive review.

For this reason the second step, the selection of databases, is of further interest. The identification and choice of proper databases determines the coverage of publications. One needs to assure access to the sources that have been considered essential in the first step. In order to have a wide and comprehensive foundation for the literature search, and after perusing other reviews in the domain of IS, the author decided to browse five different databases. The choice of databases is illustrated in Figure 9 and will be explained subsequently.

The centre of the graph highlights the two most important publication channels in the field of BPM. While the BPMJ is included in the database of Emerald, the articles of all BPM conferences to date (2003-2012) can be found in the digital version of the conference proceedings, which are published in the SpringerLink series "Lecture Notes in Computer Science".

Emerald Group Publishing Limited (2013) is known as the worldwide leading publisher of scholarly journals and books in the domain of business and management and should therefore be considered. Further it is home of the BPMJ and other IS specific publications.

Business Source Premier (2013), which is hosted by EBSCO Publishing, is the most commonly used database for business research. Full texts of more than 2100 journals and contains 1100 peer-reviewed titles are provided. It considers four fifths of the top 50 MIS journals in the ranking of the Association for Information Systems (AIS, 2013) and outperforms its competitor ABI/Inform that includes little more the half of them (Levy and Ellis, 2006, p. 186). Further, it includes publications on various business disciplines such as marketing, service management and management of Information Systems. Thus, this database covers a fair part of the two domains of this review.

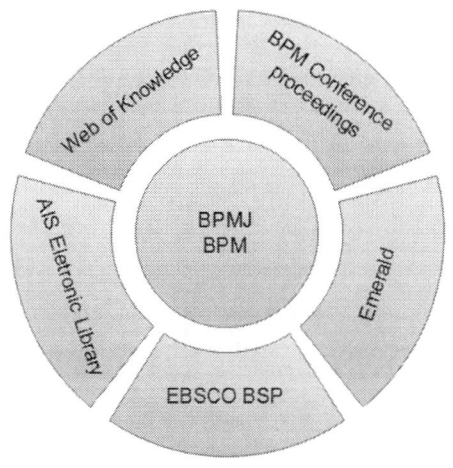

customer*
usage process* | service dominant logic | sdl
integrative value creation | co-creation | co-producing | (value-in-use)

AND business process* (management) | bpm | process model(l)ing
in ABSTRACT/TITLE/SUBJECT/KEYWORDS

Figure 9. Considered databases and keywords for the review

The fourth database is the Electronic Library of the Association for Information Systems (AISeL). This library includes highly ranked academic journals like the "Information Systems Journal" and "Management Information Systems Quarterly" as well the previously named conferences ICIS, ECIS, AMCIS, ACIS and PACIS. It is seen as the central repository of IS relevant publications.

In order to cover a broad range, the Thomson Reuters (formerly ISI) platform Web of Knowledge has been included too in this review. The attached Web of Science database includes the Conference Proceedings Citation Index, which contains 3440 proceedings of IS conferences. However, the main argument for integrating Web of Knowledge is that its database is not focused on the business discipline only and therefore opens the view to other sciences. For instance, one article in the search results that has been considered relevant has been published in a medicine journal. Moreover, the database considers pre-published content and monographs such as books and theses.

In phase 3 of the literature search process the search query will be initiated. Since the query specifies how close meshed the "save all" of the search is, the author sees this step of capital importance. Yet, explanations on the search query are in most reviews not existent. One can see this by looking at the literature reviews found by vom Brocke et al. (2009, p. 6). Because this step is picked up by vom Brocke et al. (2009, p. 9) rather briefly, the author would like to extend the third step of the procedure model by highlighting the aspects that need to be considered for the search query. This concerns especially the keywords, fields and operators that need to be determined in order to generate the algorithm the database is queried with and further the search mode as well as limiters and expanders of the search. For this reason the author changed the label of the literature search's third step in Figure 6 from "keyword search" to "search query".

The keywords for the search algorithm emerge basically from the terms that have been identified in the conceptualization of topic. In this case this would be on the one hand "Business Process Management", "Process Modelling" and the acronym "BPM", which is not only the shortcut for "Business Process Management" but also sometimes for "Business Process Modelling" (i.a. Aguilar-Saven 2004; Giaglis 2001). In the case of "Process Modelling", special attention must to be given to spelling variants between American English and British English. Therefore both variants have been included in the query's algorithm. When the results of the search have been too little, some terms have been trimmed. That is the reason why "Process Model(l)ing" instead of "Business Process Model(l)ing" was chosen. Also, the term "Business Process Management" is reduced to the words "Business Process". Only the algorithm for the Web of Knowledge database contains the full term in order to identify which other sciences directly refer to BPM.

For the customer concepts the word "customer" is almost sufficient because beside "usage processes" and the special terms of the service-dominant logic, all sub-concepts contain the word "customer". Additionally the terms "usage process", "service-dominant logic", its acronym "sdl", "integrative value creation", "co-creation", "co-producing" and "value-in-use" have been integrated. The capitalization of words is irrelevant as upper and lower letters are treated the same in all five search engines.

Now the keywords for the search have been selected, one needs to reason which fields of the articles' meta-information should be scanned. Many reviews concentrate on the abstract and title, arguing that relevant publications should at least consider the concept of interest in these two fields, otherwise it is not of central relevance. The review follows this approach, but in addition to the abstract and title, it queries the fields "subject" and "keywords" (if procurable).

The last elements that are needed for the algorithm are the operators to which beside Boolean operators like "AND", "OR", "NOT" also quotation marks, parentheses and wildcards ("*", "$", "?") belong. The algorithm of this review consists of two conditions that articles of relevance need to meet. First, it must compromise at least one of the terms "Business Process Management", "Process Modeling", "Process Modelling" or "BPM". Second, it needs to contain one of the customer related words listed above. Parentheses and the "AND" operator have been used to distinguish between these two requirements. "OR" operators have been applied to separate each search term. Further, the asterisk wildcard has been used for truncation of words. This is particularly relevant for inclusion of the terms' plural form such as "customers" or "processes". A hyphen is mostly treated as a wildcard (e.g. value?in?use). However, some search engines like EBSCO BSP seem to misinterpret wildcards on phrases, but with the "apply related words" option, plural forms can be included without wildcards.

Due to the fact that some terms consist of two or more words and the query builds on Boolean operators, the search mode has been set to "phrase/Boolean" when this option was available. The author tried to include all expanding options like lemmatization, which includes further synonymies.

Figure 9, which has already been illustrated above, summarizes the decisions that have been made throughout phase 2 and 3. The complete algorithm can be seen together with the hit results, limitations and expanders in Table 4. The restitution of the algorithm extremely levels the reliability of the review. Critics can check the algorithm for errors and even repeat the search query, which in turn allows for a verification of hit results.

Table 4. Settings of the search query for the databases including hit results, full-page illustration in Appendix 5

Database	Hits	Algorithm	Search mode	Limiters/Expanders
BPM	7	(customer, service dominant logic, usage process, sdl, integrative value creation, co-creation, co-producing, value-in-use) in titles and abstracts of the digital conference proceedings	-	-
Emerald	195	("business process*" OR "BPM" OR "process modelling" OR "process modeling" in All except full text) AND ("customer*" OR "service dominant logic" OR "usage process*" OR "integrative value creation" OR "SDL" "co-creation" OR "co-producing" in All except full text)	Any/Any	All content; incl. Backfiles
EBSCO BSP	424	(AB "business process" OR TI "business process" OR SU "business process" OR KW "business process" OR AB bpm OR TI bpm OR SU bpm OR KW bpm OR AB "process modelling" OR KW "process modelling" OR TI "process modelling" OR SU "process modelling" OR KW "process modelling" OR AB "process modeling" OR KW "process modeling" OR TI "process modeling" OR SU "process modeling" OR KW "process modeling") AND (AB customer* OR TI customer* OR SU customer* OR KW customer* OR AB "usage process" OR TI "usage process" OR SU "usage process" OR KW "usage process" OR AB "service dominant logic" OR TI "service dominant logic" OR SU "service dominant logic" OR KW "service dominant logic" OR AB sdl OR TI sdl OR SU sdl OR KW sdl OR AB "integrative value creation" OR TI "integrative value creation" OR SU "integrative value creation" OR KW "integrative value creation" OR AB "co-creation" OR TI "co-creation" OR SU "co-creation" OR KW "co-creation" OR AB "co-producing" OR TI "co-producing" OR SU "co-producing" OR "co-producing" OR AB "value-in-use" OR TI "value-in-use" OR SU "value-in-use" OR KW "value-in-use")	Boolean/Phrase	Document Type: Article, Books Apply related words
AISeL	15	(abstract:("business process*" OR "BPM" OR "process modeling" OR "process modelling") OR subject:("business process*" OR "BPM" OR "process modeling" OR "process modelling")) AND (abstract:("customer*" OR "usage process*" OR "service dominant logic" OR "sdl" OR "integrative value creation" OR "co-creation" OR "co-producing" OR "value-in-use") OR (subject:("customer*" OR "usage process*" OR "service dominant logic" OR "sdl" OR "integrative value creation" OR "co-creation" OR "co-producing" OR "value-in-use") OR (title:("customer*" OR "usage process*" OR "service dominant logic" OR "sdl" OR "integrative value creation" OR "co-creation" OR "co-producing" OR "value-in-use")	-	All Repositories
Web of Knowledge	80	Topic=("business process management" OR "bpm" OR "process modelling" OR "process modeling") AND Topic=("customer*" OR "usage process*" OR "service dominant logic" OR "sdl" OR "integrative value creation" OR "co-creation" OR "co-producing" OR "value-in-use")	-	Lemmatization=On, All databases, Timespan = All Years
Duplicates	62			
Total	**659**			Date of query: 2012-11-15

One shortcoming of all used search engines is that they do not have a uniform interpretation of algorithms. Therefore adjustments in the algorithm to the databases' specifics are inevitable. For this reason the algorithm is slightly different for each database. The algorithm for the conference proceedings and AISeL need to be commented on due to special circumstances. The conference proceedings are digitally available in PDF format and have been scanned via the basic search function of Adobe Acrobat. As the proceedings were already BPM related, only marketing and service management related words were entered one after another. Lastly, the AISeL search engine cannot handle large queries. With this in mind, the database was queried three times with variations in the search fields.

Final words shall be given to the practical aspect of data aggregation. All databases allow a transfer of results to reference management software. In this case the online platform RefWorks was chosen for the collection of results. It allows the export of the complete bibliography to a formatted txt-file, which can be opened easily with spreadsheet applications like Microsoft Excel. As a result one possesses a comprehensive database that contains most of the meta-information on the detected articles. Table 5 illustrates an excerpt of the database this literature review relies on.[2] The detailed information that is given in the database not only eases the qualitative review of relevant articles but is also very useful for explorative and quantitative analyses such as the one in the next chapter. Moreover, it can be handed to reviewers and interested parties. This way, the analysis of data becomes more comprehensible and reliable.

Table 5. Database of the literature review

Authors, Primary	Year	Periodical	Title Primary	Abstract	Keywords	...
A.H.M. Shamsuzz	2011	Business Pro	Modular pro	Purpose: The aims of	Customizatic	
Abdinnour-Helm	2000	Production &	Time-Based	This article illustrate	MANUFACTL	
Agarwal,Ritu;We	2012	MIT Sloan M	The Benefits	The article looks at tl	BUSINESS pla	
...						

3.2.2.2   Analysis of Data and Results

3.2.2.2.1   Quantitative Analysis

The literature search was performed on the 15th of November 2012. The search in the five databases resulted in a total of 721 publications that fitted the requirements of the search query (see Table 4). After the elimination of duplicates a list of 659 articles remains, covering a range from year 1992 to 2012. 102 of those articles are published in the BPMJ and seven in the proceedings of the BPM conference. The subsequent analysis of data and results can be related to the phases 3 and 4 of the review framework (see Figure 6).

In order to get a first overview a quantitative analysis was conducted. First the keywords of the publications were collected and arranged according to their frequency of appearance. Figure 10 shows the Top 20 of the most used keywords in the result list. First conclusions can already be drawn from this summary. It reveals the most common topics and themes when articles refer to the concepts of "customer" and "business process". First there is the group of customer concepts "customer service", "customer satisfaction" and "customer relations", which are highlighted in the graph and will be analyzed in detail subsequently. Another main topic seems to be the production of

---

[2] In case of interest please contact the author for complete data files and further information.

physical goods. The production is represented by the concepts "industrial manage-ment", "supply chain management" and "manufacturing processes". The terms "organ-izational change", "contracting out" and "business process outsourcing" approve that also organizational aspects are often picked as a central issue. Despite the terms that are directly connected to BPM, "electronic commerce" appears to be also discussed quite frequently. So, beside the customer concepts, especially aspects concerning the production, organization and the electronic commerce are outlined. Further keywords below the Top 20 in the ranking are, amongst others, "total quality manage-ment/TQM" and "knowledge management".

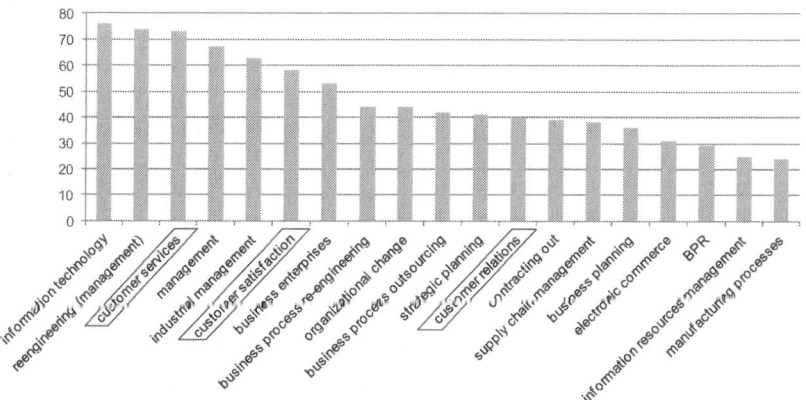

Figure 10. Top 20 of the most used keywords in the result list

After corresponding topics have been accentuated, the concepts "customer service", "customer satisfaction" and "customer relations" will be analyzed in detail in order to get a differentiated view of their development. With this in mind, their appearance in articles (title, abstract and/or keyword) has been illustrated sorted by the years in a se-cond step. Figure 11 visualizes the absolute frequency of selected terms arranged by the year in which the relative article was published in. The wildcards behind the terms imply that the plural forms count too. Also all articles that have been detected in the search query are represented in this graph. One can see that an increasing amount of publications contain the concepts of "customer" and "business processes" in the title, abstract and/or keywords. Customer services and the customer satisfaction have been discussed with growing attention but still on low level since the early 1990s. Customer relations have been connected to business process and picked up in this field more intensively in the first years of the 21th century.

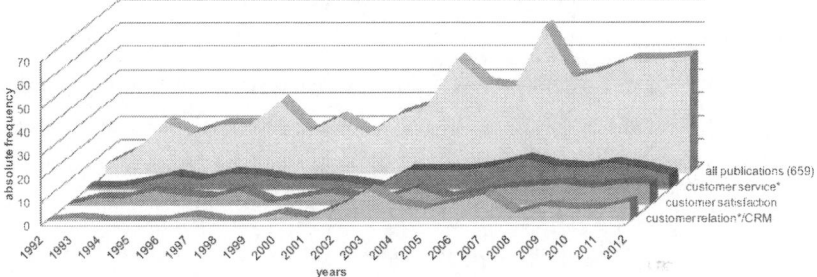

Figure 11. Frequency of selected terms sorted by years

3.2.2.2.2   Qualitative Analysis

After the quantitative evaluation of results, a qualitative review was conducted on the 659 identified articles. In order to get a deeper insight into the extent to which the customer perspective has been discussed in BPM related literature, the titles and abstracts of all 659 detected articles were studied in detail in several sessions. Articles published in the BPMJ and BMP conference proceedings were reviewed twice. In order to attest that this procedure was conducted and to keep record of the extracted information of each article, the main sentence or phrase of the article has been highlighted in the abstract cell of the results list and duplicated into an own column. This sentence or phrase of the abstract explains the purpose of the article to the reader in a few words. The investigators' review of the abstracts confirms the findings of the quantitative analysis. Many of the articles focus on Manufacturing, Supply Chain Management, Process Outsourcing, Total Quality Management as well as on Knowledge Management.

Contrary to the quantitative evaluation, which had a broad focus of analysis, the personal review of articles concentrates on customer processes and their activities. This means that articles of interests are those that refer to the customer's side and perspective. In reference to the review of Vanwersch (2011), an inclusion criterion has been defined for an unbiased screening of relevant articles. The criterion can be deduced from the research question of the survey and is expressed in form of a question, for which a positive answer results in an inclusion and a negative one in an exclusion of the relative article. The question that determines whether an article is selected for closer review is "Does the article relate to customer processes?". Terms of special interest and therefore of particular importance for the screening were, among others, "customer process", "customer activity", "customer action", "interaction", "service", "perspective" and "point of view". In total the term "customer process*" constitutes part of the meta-information of four articles. No article referred to the term "customer activit*". According to this method, the meta-information (title, abstract, keywords) of every article has been checked whether it responds positively or negatively to the question.

Table 6. List of identified articles that relate to the field of interest, an extended version including journal titles can be seen in Appendix 6

Nr.	Author	Year	Title
1	Alt/Puschmann	2005	Developing customer process orientation: the case of Pharma Corp.
2	Barua et al.	2004	An Empirical Investigation of Net-Enabled Business Value
3	Batista/Smart/Maull	2008	The systemic perspective of service processes
4	Behara/Fontenot/Gresham	2002	Customer process approach to building loyalty
5	Bolton	2004	Customer centric business processing
6	Dorgianni/Caschi/Rottri	2010	Process value analysis for business process re-engineering
7	Coenen/von Felten/Schmid	2011	Managing effectiveness and efficiency through FM blueprinting
8	Gersch/Hewing/Schöler	2011	Business Process Blueprinting - an enhanced view on process performance
9	Gersch/Schöler/Hewing	2010	Service Dominant Logic and Business Process Blueprinting
10	Gossain	2002	Cracking the Collaboration Code
11	Green/Simister	1999	Modelling client business processes as an aid to strategic briefing
12	Heckl/Moormann	2007	Matching Customer Processes with Business Processes of Banks
13	Huang/Zhu/Wu	2012	Customer-Centered Careflow Modeling Based on Guidelines
14	Kim	1995	Process Modeling For BPR: Event-Process Chain Approach
15	Milton/Johnson	2012	Service blueprinting and BPMN: a comparison
16	Rajala/Savolainen	1996	A framework for customer oriented business process modelling
17	Tseng/Qinhai/Chuan-Jun	1999	Mapping customers' service experience for operations improvement

The screening of the 659 abstracts resulted in a selection of 16 articles that relate positively to the questioned criterion and thus discuss to a minimum extend the field of interest. A list of the selection can be seen in Table 6. The small number of articles can be explained by the fact that most papers referred to the customer, but did not discuss his or her processes. Once the relevant articles were collected, a backward search was conducted, so that related references of the articles are also included in the qualitative analysis (step 4 of the literature search). One reference (Behara, Fontenot and Gresham 2002) in the bibliography of identified articles, which was not already been detected by the literature research, is regarded relevant. So in total 17 articles are considered related.

Yet, process models are the foundation of BPM and crucial to understand, analyze and design processes (Polyvyanyy, Smirnov and Weske 2010, p. 149). Thus, in order to gain an overview of current modeling techniques, another criterion was included in a next step. This time the question was "Does the article discusses methods to model customer processes and/or contains models of customer processes?". Full paper versions of the 17 articles were read and examined in detail. The extent to which the relative article focuses on customer models was evaluated.

Stating that the whole business needs to built on customer needs, seven articles mainly focus on strategic approaches that align processes and service to customer requirements (Bolton 2004; Borgianni, Cascini and Rotini 2010). They relate to topics such as electronic data interchange (Barua et al. 2004; Gossain 2002), customer loyalty (Behara, Fontenot and Gresham 2002), customer-centered health care (Huang, Zhu and Wu 2012) and statistical analysis (Rajala and Savolainen 1996).

Ten publications debate the processes of customers on the basis of process models. The first hint of customer processes in the detected IS related literature derives from Kim (1995), who dealt with the concept of cross-functional flowcharts like Wang's Process Flow Diagram and Andersen's Process Map that contain swimlanes to separate between organizations like the customer and service provider. With the differentiation between organizations, customer processes can be clearly localized. Tseng, Qinhai and Su (1999) strengthened this approach by considering the marketing method Service Blueprinting, which provides an additional focus and further information with its structured layout. Especially in recent years the incorporation of this method and its effect on process performance has been discussed (Coenen, Felten and Schmid 2011; Gersch, Hewing and Schöler 2011; Gersch, Schöler and Hewing 2010; Milton and Johnson 2012). Other publications in the field of BPM, which also refer to the Service Blueprinting but have not been detected by the literature search, are among others

Becker, Beverungen and Knackstedt (2009), Gersch, Goeke, Lux (2006), Klose, Knackstedt and Becker (2005), Knackstedt and Dahlke (2004) and Meis, Menschner and Leimeister (2010). By combining Business Process Modeling languages and Service Blueprinting, the customer processes of direct interaction with the provider can be considered. However, the autonomously performed activities of the customer are not incorporated in these approaches. Only Gersch, Hewing and Schöler (2010, 2011) hint in their publications to model with Service Blueprinting the customer processes that take place beyond the direct interaction of service delivery.

Merely four publications discuss approaches that explicitly establish as the primary subject of analysis those customer processes that are also performed outside the provider's perception. Batista, Smart and Maull (2008) argue that there is a gap between the customer-oriented approach of CRM and BPM and call for an extended review of the customer experience over time. The remaining three publications even go a step further by modeling the customer processes in a simplistic way. Green and Simister (1999) postulate a strategic understanding of clients' business processes by bubble diagramming their primary activities. The basic needs of different customer segments have been visualized by Alt and Puschmann (2005) in the form of processes. Heckl and Moormann (2007) model the processes of banks' clients in order to anticipate their needs.

Thus, it is clear that research regarding customer processes currently evolves. Most illustrated customer processes are within a B2B context. Here the provider often has further knowledge about the customers' activities. Yet, B2C relations are not considered. Further, the process models of these articles map the customer side in a very aggregated way. In a process hierarchy they can be aligned to the process area in which the generic business activities are modeled (Scheer and Bräbander 2010, pp. 256–257). However, established Business Process Modeling notations are barely considered. Therefore, research on the integration of established modeling approaches is necessary. Furthermore, process models in their current form merely represent the as-is state of processes. Methodical fortification and guidance is required for the redesign of these processes. As the analysis of customer processes is rather new to the community, guidance on how to manage these processes seems necessary. Besides further reflection on the concept of customer processes, the development of applicable methods by which to model and analyze these processes in more detail would seem beneficial for research and the concept's diffusion in practice. In summary, although preliminary approaches are currently evolving, there is still a need for a methodical fortification of the customer process concept that supports the BPM community in order to better model and subsequently analyze these processes.

3.2.2.3   Limitations and Discussion

The last phase of the review framework refers to limitations and the research agenda, which is given with this chapter. By using the concepts "customer" and "business process" the literature search bases on a search algorithm that takes into account a very broad spectrum of publications. Still, some articles that could be interesting and relevant to the topic may not have been detected by the search. Reasons for this could be that they have been published in channels that are not covered by the extensive databases, use different terms in the meta-information instead the common expressions or are written in another language than English and/or do not contain an English abstract. This is, for example, the case for articles of Caesar et al. (2005), Kagermann, Österle and Jordan (2010) and Österle and Senger (2011), to which this manuscript refers in the outlook. Further, documents or manuals (e.g. Integration Definition for Function Modeling [IDEF]) have not been included in this review as they have been considered rather technical.

Nevertheless, the comprehensive literature review points out that the customer perspective and his or her point of view has only rarely been discussed in BPM related literature. Research in the field of customer processes is limited. Most articles focus on strategic approaches to integrate customer needs into process performance. The fact that aspects concerning production and organization are one of the most stated keywords reveals that the focus of articles still lies primarily on (inter-)organizational processes. Efficient consumer-response (i.a. Wood 1993), for instance, considers information of the retailer such as sales volumes, but the data is still based on the provider's and not on the customer's perspective. As they do not directly consider customer processes, one may rather label those approaches as demand-oriented.

By comparing the quantitative and qualitative analysis, one may recognize that more and more publications consider the customer, but still disregard his or her processes. Although a few publications reflect the interaction between service provider and customer, the qualitative review showed that only few articles provide a model of customer processes. A formal method to model the customer's processes is still lacking. Especially with CRM and the digitalization of customers' activities more opportunities arise to get insights and information into his or her processes or even be able to form process fragments out of patterns that are detected by data analysis. This knowledge could be used to support the customer in his or her processes by anticipating proactively yet unrealized needs and/or process design alternatives. In order to do so one has to understand and illustrate the actual as well as conceivable processes of the customer.

Therefore further research is necessary on the management of customer processes. Artifacts like constructs, methods, models and instantiations (e.g. software) need to be designed to capture, document and analyze customer processes as part of Business Process Management. Furthermore, extended research is necessary on the behavioral effects when using Information Technology for the management of customer processes. As models are the foundation of BPM, the primary question of interest is how customer processes can be managed and modeled. Due to synergies with other disciplines (i.a. Service Engineering, marketing) an interdisciplinary approach seems most promising to answer this question.

3.2.2.4   Summary of the Literature Review

The purpose of the review was to screen to which degree customer processes have been considered in Business Process Management related research. By querying five comprehensive databases, 659 articles have been detected that contain concepts of "customer" and "business process" in their meta-information. The quantitative analysis of these articles revealed a trend towards customer aspects, but mostly still in connection with a production-related or organizational and therefore rather internal "inside-out" focus as it has been described in chapter 3.1.2.1. The term "customer process" appeared merely in four articles. The qualitative analysis considers 17 of the articles as related to the specific field. However, just a few publications primarily focus on customer processes or activities. Further research and discussion on the management of customer processes seems necessary.

In addition, the review extended the framework model for literature reviewing of vom Brocke (2009) by adding information on the search query. In order to raise reliability of the review, the search query is explained in detail and visualized in clearly arranged graphs and tables. As such a detail is not given in current reviews, this review may help researchers to fortify the reliability of their reviews by giving an example of how one can specify and clearly illustrate the search procedure.

3.3 Problem Definition and Solution Objectives

Before we move on to the artifact that has been developed to bridge the research gap, which has been identified throughout chapter 3, this section summarizes (as is recommended by the DSRM) the line of thought until now, defines the problem and expresses the objectives and specifications that a problem solving artifact has to meet.

Chapter 3.1 reflected the importance of customer orientation for economic success and sets the creation of customer value as its essential element. The shift from product-over-service to overall experience quality, which comprises value-in-use, is attended by the rising awareness that a process-based view is indispensable. The SDL and concepts of customer experience state that value is not only created by means of interaction with the provider, but also in the more or less autonomous customer processes that emerge after direct contact (value-in-use). As research in the area of usage processes is still at an early stage, only few approaches have been proposed to date. In particular, formal methods to model interaction and usage process are nonexistent.

Consequently, chapter 3.2 focuses on BPM – a discipline that deals with the planning, management and control of processes. It has to be stated that although BPM is a holistic approach with diverse elements (Rosemann and vom Brocke 2010, p.112), process models are especially crucial to understand and design processes or in other words

"...to enable their analysis business processes are represented in models" (Polyvyanyy, Smirnov and Weske 2010, p. 149). Accordingly, process models can be seen as fundamental. The literature review revealed that not only marketing, but also BPM lacks formal methods to model customer processes. Until now BPM merely picked up (with a delay of almost two decades) the special characteristics of the interaction between the provider and customer in the service production process. The SDL and correspondingly usage processes have not yet been considered in BPM. Though BPM is the domain of Business Process Modeling and has accordingly the potential to illustrate these processes in a structural way, it does not currently consider customer processes.

Summarizing the explanations of chapter 3.1 and 3.2, the identified problem is that there is so far no method to capture, document, analyze and design customer processes in Business Process Management. Winter et al. (2012, p. 405), for example, calls for an extension of current methods to capture the dynamics of customer processes. The arising question is how these processes can be modeled in order to illustrate, analyze and (where applicable) support them. The objective for a solution corresponds to the development of a method that facilitates to model customer processes. Deriving from the explanations above there are four specifications an artifact has to meet. The profile of requirements contains:

- *Requirement 1 – Capability to integrate existing approaches and methods of the Business Process Management:* Of greatest importance is that the artifact is based on the well-established modeling techniques BPM offers. As process modeling is the foundation of BPM, a lot of research has been put into this aspect, which has in turn resulted in extremely well-founded and empirically approved approaches and artifacts. Moreover, the compatibility of the artifact to existing approaches is likely to help build up and maintain acceptance in the relative research community.

- *Requirement 2 – Capability to integrate marketing concepts on value creation:* The second requirement emerges from the identified research gap. Recently emerged concepts on value creation have only barely been considered in BPM. By looking at the special characteristics of services and the service-dominant logic, it is apparent that special attention needs to be given to the interaction and usage processes. Therefore the artifact should provide the ability to model either interaction or usage processes. Most suitable would be a modeling method capable of modeling both kinds of processes.

- *Requirement 3 – Promote the awareness of customer processes:* As customer processes have hardly been considered in current BPM research, it seems preferable that the artifact promote the existence of customer processes in a straightforward fashion. This means that through the application the user of the artifact becomes aware of usage processes and anticipates the value-in-use concept.

- *Requirement 4 – Classification of process elements:* A plain and simple illustration of customer processes may already help to analyze their properties. However, current modeling languages provide additional information by aligning process elements to a grid of levels and functions, so called swimlanes, which reflect specific criteria. Novel modeling artifacts should consider this aspect of process illustration. So, instead of merely drawing interaction or usage processes, it would be beneficial to add at the same time further information throughout gridlines that categorize the process elements corresponding to criteria of interest. By a segmentation of process elements according to specific issues, the processes are put into a managerial context. For the planning and management of customer processes this could be, for instance, the explicit reference to concepts and design options that concern effectiveness (e.g. internalization/externalization, support of usage processes)

In reference to activity 2 of the DSRM, this profile of requirements turns the problem definition into a definite form. Thus, it is easier to understand why the developed artifact takes specific aspects into account and to approve whether it pursues the identified problem.

4 A Blueprint of the Customer – Design of a Method for an extended View on Customer Processes in BPM

After the problem is identified, the motivation for research described and the objectives of a solution defined, the DSRM next schedules the design, development and demonstration of the artifact (activity 3 and 4). As the activities of the DSRM build upon each other, they should be considered of similar value from a scientific point of view. However, the designed artifact is often seen as the centerpiece of research projects. This is most probably due to the added value that is intended to arise from the artifact in practice.

Because the design of artifact seems central, the development process and a procedure model for application are documented in detail. Thus, this chapter deals with the design of the artifact and its application. Sub-chapter 4.1 describes the basic idea behind the artifact, its origin, development process and demonstrates emerging implications. Sub-chapter 4.2 addresses the artifact's employment and proposes a conceptualization of a customer-oriented (multi-stage) procedure model for the analysis of customer processes. Before we move on to the artifact's evaluation in chapter 5, the last section of this chapter approves whether the requirements that have been proposed are met by the artifact through logical reasoning.

4.1 Business Process Blueprinting: the Combination of two Disciplines

Chapter 3 already highlighted the diverging point of views that dwell between marketing and BPM. The difference between those two perspectives becomes even clearer when one looks at the performance measurements that evolve from their diverse concepts of quality. Evaluating and improving process performance is a core theme of both disciplines. Performance can be defined as the action of performing a task and is often quantified in suitable measurements (i.a. Lebas 1995, p. 24). Yet, marketing tends to focus rather on the effectiveness of a particular marketing offer with its customer-oriented quality constructs. Effectiveness is the external part of performance – describing how well the company achieves the customer's requirements from the customer's perspective. The strong accentuation of the customer orientation emphasizes external measurements such as perceived satisfaction. The matter in question is whether one is doing the right thing (Drucker 1974, p. 45). BPM, on the other hand, comprises a rather product-oriented definition on marketing offers and concentrates on the optimization of internal processes. The quality control of processes can be aligned to efficiency, which considers whether things are done right. Efficiency can be defined as a more internal part of performance – describing the relation between input and output from the company's point of view. Measurements of efficiency are, among other aspects, cycle time and capacity utilization. The literature review confirmed that many publications consider aspects concerning efficiency in the production and organization such as TQM and Six Sigma.

The rival question is whether the pursuit of effectiveness or efficiency is of primary concern. Efficiency is often considered as a sub-goal of effectiveness (Lasshof 2006, p. 16). Whilst effectiveness reflects the target achievement, efficiency describes the input-output ratio. One argument for the priority of effectiveness claims that efficiency alone does not create value for the customer (Brown 1987). A company with a high effectiveness can stand despite inefficiency, but a company will not be able to survive without effectiveness. Looking at concepts of market orientation (i.a. Kohli and Jaworski 1990), which also include, beside the customer, competitor orientation, one recognizes that the long-term existence of a company is dependent on the pursuit of both criteria. To successfully maintain a competitive advantage requires that an organization's marketing offers contain a higher net benefit than the competition (Porter 1985). This can be accomplished by achieving higher effectiveness or efficiency. Effectiveness expresses the benefits that have been created. Efficiency reflects cost advantages that can be passed on to the customer (price advantage). Both elements need to be considered. Only in combination can a lasting success be guaranteed. Yet, competitive relationships can arise between the objectives of the two criteria. For instance, literature on project management points to the "iron triangle", which describes the tensions between quality, time and cost factors (Atkinson 1999; Babu and Suresh 1996; Khang and Myint 1999). Limited by the given resources of the company, effectiveness and efficiency can often not be maximized at the same time, so that trade-offs have to be considered (i.a. Porter 1996). Depending on the company's ambition the tracked targets have to be ranked. However, as both criteria are necessary to stay in business, a company cannot concentrate on one set.

As each discipline represents one of the two measurements, a combination seems obvious. However, research in both disciplines is largely done in parallel and independently from each other, although they would very much complement one another. Exchange between both disciplines seems underdeveloped (Gersch 2006, p. 9). Exchanging ideas and concepts between the fields is difficult. For example, Brady, Saren and Tzokas (2002) identify misinformation and misunderstandings regarding the adoption of IT developments into marketing practices. Both fields approach processes from different points of view. Service marketing focuses on the external view of the customer and aims to improve effectiveness and perceived quality. On the other hand, BPM limits the scope on process efficiency, i.e. the internal view of the enterprise. A combination of efficiency- and effectiveness-based approaches seems most promising to achieve a competitive advantage. Accordingly, criteria for performance measurement have to address both perspectives.

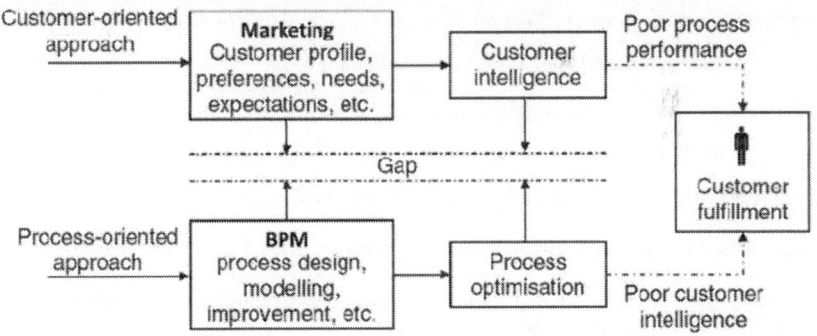

Figure 12. Business approach gap (modified from Batista, Smart and Maull 2008, p. 538)

Reconsidering the explanations of chapter 3.1 and 3.2, it seems like both disciplines, marketing and BPM, would benefit from each other. Batista, Smart and Maull (2008, p. 537) also get to that point, when they state that "…a customer-oriented mindset should lead process-oriented actions." They generated an easily interpreted graphic image of this issue that can be seen in Figure 12.

Marketing provides an extended perspective on value creation, but lacks a comprehensive process view. BPM in contrast incorporates powerful and well-established process approaches and syntaxes, but has still a rather product-oriented and internal focus on value creation and process optimization. Though the importance of a customer focus on processes is occasionally mentioned, there is still more work to be done to embed the perspective into Business Process Modeling. So, the core idea is to bring the customer orientation to BPM and BPM-knowledge to marketing.

This research proposes to close the gap between the two disciplines by combining their approaches. As the work is associated with the IS community and the BPM discipline, the developed artifact bridges the gap by exceeding the range of BPM approaches to concepts of service marketing. As criteria of efficiency are very much discussed and common in BPM, the focus of further explanations is rather on effectiveness.

The artifact that has been developed to cover the lack of structured customer process models is a method to illustrate those processes, which in turn enables their analysis. With the "Business Process Blueprinting" the author points to an integrated approach that enhances well-established process modeling methods.

To reflect its basic idea and initial conceptualization, the first sub-chapter describes the fusion of the disciplines by merging two of their major approaches. The second sub-chapter enhances and extends the concept to usage processes.

4.1.1 Deriving a Method for a customer-integrated View on Processes

As already hinted in the last section, the basic idea, which has been outlined in the working paper of Gersch, Goeke and Lux (2006), derives from a combination of two approaches. The first one is Business Process Modeling, which comprises models, methods and techniques to illustrate and visualize abstractions of business processes and the information they contain. The second marketing-based approach is called Service Blueprinting. It provides a way for the operator to illustrate processes of provider/customer interaction from the customer's point of view. By combining the two approaches, the so called Business Process Blueprinting bridges the existing gap between disciplines and incorporates the respectively other point of view into their familiar perspective as a valuable aspect to gain new insights without needing to completely abandon well established constructs. Therefore, it can serve as a "lingua franca" between the two disciplines.

4.1.1.1 Principles of Business Process Modeling

The developed method is based upon Business Process Modeling, whose principles are explained in detail in this chapter. Stachowiak (1973, pp. 131–133) describes the concept of a model with reference to the three characteristics mapping, reduction and pragmatism. Accordingly, models are a shortened (reduction) representation of an original (mapping) for a specific purpose (pragmatism). So, as models illustrate via declared languages a part of the original in a subjective manner for a specific purpose, they are not to be criticized as true or false, but can be seen as more or less contextually valid, consistent or helpful (Winter 2003, p. 89). Drawing on an extensive literature review, Leist (2002, pp. 7–9) identifies diverse purposes of a model, which she categorizes into four groups:

- **Instructions:** The abstraction of a subject into a model can be very useful to impart knowledge. For instance, new employees can familiarize themselves faster with their working processes and operating activities.

- **Communication basis:** A model can serve as a basis for internal and/or external communication. Internally it can be used as a common viewpoint on the subject of interest in discussions across every division (Dubberly, Evenson and Robinson 2008, p. 61) and between different research disciplines (e.g. marketing and IS). Furthermore, an issue that has been put into graphs may simplify communication with external interlocutors.

- **Analysis:** Besides providing a communication basis, a model may also serve as a foundation for structured analysis, such as process controlling or audits. In BPM, for instance, business processes are often checked for weaknesses with methods like the failure mode and effect analysis (i.a. Stamatis 2003).

- **(Re-)Design:** Design is very much based on models. They formalize the changes that need to be implemented. Generic activities in BPM include, among other aspects, the modification, combination, rearrangement or elimination of process elements. All these variations can be captured in models. One may differentiate between the creation of all new designs and the re-organization/optimization of existing ones.

As mentioned before, due to the complexity of the original issue, models are reduced to only a selection of reality (Ludolph 1997). When only relevant elements are taken into account, the subject matter becomes more transparent and controllable. However, to avoid losing valuable information, enterprise models mostly provide multiple model layers and views. The subject matter is subdivided into different views. Each view homes in on an aspect with distinct notations and is connected to the other views via interfaces. Scheer's (2000a) Architecture of Integrated Information Systems (ARIS) is a widespread tool for Business Process Modeling and one of the leaders in this sector (Blechar 2010). Due to the multiple perspectives on the subject matter, the area of interest is specified and pictured in this tool comprehensively. ARIS includes an organization, functions, data and control view.

The benefits of a process model are a better understanding and increased perception of economic activities. Process models can be differentiated between "as-is" and "as-should" models. While the first of these visualizes the process at present, the second illustrates the desired process layout to which the first has to be adapted. A common task is to find potentials of improvements in the process layout such as the elimination, merging, parallelization and automation of activities. The amount of interfaces can then be reduced and redundancies avoided. A list of such generic activities can be seen in Malone et al. (1999, p. 436). Process models reflect these generic activities. Thus, the identification of problems and potentials in the "as-is" process layout and the implementation of solutions via the "as-should" model drives process efficiency (and if considered effectiveness).

Normed modeling languages, which basically illustrate a diagram, are used for abstraction. An overview of modeling languages is given by Gadatsch (2010, p. 71), who differentiates between data flow-oriented (i.a. IDEF), control flow-oriented (i.a. eEPC, BPMN, Petri net) and object-oriented (i.a. UML) diagram methods. This thesis is based on control flow-oriented modeling methods and alternates between the "(enhanced) Event-driven Process Chain" (eEPC) (Scheer 2000b) and "Business Process Modeling and Notation" (BPMN) (OMG 2011).

The basic concept behind the languages hardly differs. They simply use diverging elements that consider special aspects and are aligned to specific Enterprise Resources Planning and Enterprise Architecture tools. Since the ARIS framework that uses eEPCs has a leading position in the market (Blechar 2010; Peyret 2009), the concept of process modeling will be exemplified in this modeling language. An eEPC consists of two central elements and additional supporting components, which are connected by lines:

- Functions represent the active element of the eEPC. They illustrate a sub-process or an individual activity.

- Events are the passive element of the eEPC. They represent the environmental conditions and circumstances as results of one or more activities. Events are the connecting elements between functions.

By connecting events with functions, a linear representation of the process's sequence is generated. To illustrate complex processes with parallel or cyclic activities, logic connectors can be used. More information can be illustrated by adding further components (e.g. organization units or documents). Since these elements have been added to the syntax of the language at a later date the EPC is labeled as enhanced. Those elements are sufficient to describe a complete process. Attributes can be aligned to those elements to add further information. Figure 13 shows an overview of the most important EPC elements.

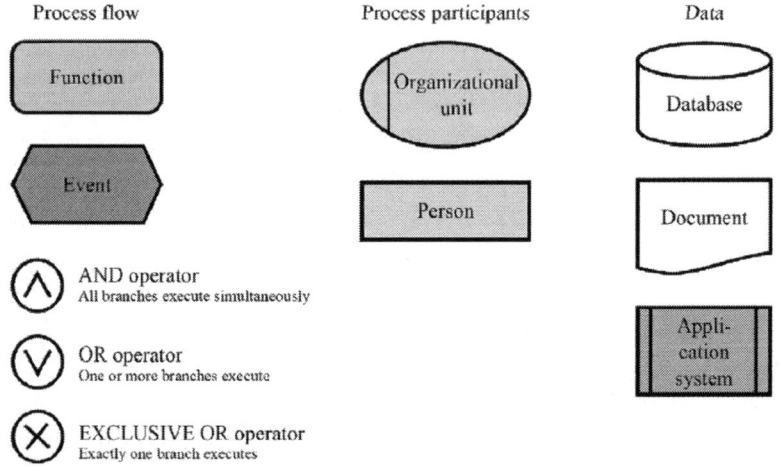

Figure 13. Core elements of an eEPC (Gersch, Hewing and Schöler 2011, p. 737)

The eEPC specifies which event a function is triggered by. Functions are initiated by an event and run by organizational units, persons or systems that generate an output, which in turn triggers a new event. The control flow connects the two elements together, so that an ordered sequence is given. The level of detail depends on the purpose. One may first model overall processes with little detail and subsequently add subprocesses with further information, which are then organized into a hierarchy. This makes it possible to scale from process landscapes through core processes to partial or even elemental functions.

Operators can be used to represent more complex processes that are not linear. The AND-connector, for example, creates sequences that run parallel. OR operators point to process alternatives. With the EXLCUSIVE OR operator, which is often shortened to XOR, only one branch of the process alternatives is executed. Due to the bilateral alteration between events and functions, the temporal process logic is visualized in a process flow diagram. Appendix 7 represents a version of such a process in eEPC.

Business Process Modeling focuses on the activities within the company. As the literature review revealed, BPM still has an inside-out view and so do Business Process Modeling methods. Process mapping, analysis and designs are used in particular to improve the process flow and to drive efficiency.

Yet, the customer perspective, which becomes even more important for service processes and his or her deriving co-creation, are almost neglected. Business Process Modeling needs to incorporate customer-oriented concepts. This requires the integration of mature methods from marketing into Business Process Modeling and Management.

4.1.1.2   Service Blueprinting in Marketing

Concepts relating to customer experience are numerous in service marketing. Service Blueprinting can be considered as one of the most established process-oriented approaches, especially for the design of interaction processes.

The term "Blueprint" originates from engineering and describes the process of contact printing on light-sensitive sheets, which is called diazotype. The result of this process is an illustration of technical drawings, which, due to the chemical process, is in the shade of blue. This technique was often used for architectural photo-reproductions (Kissel and Vigneau 2009). Although the term "blueprint" describes a technical process, it is interpreted as an allegory in other disciplines and describes in common speech a master plan.

Service marketing uses Service Blueprinting to visualize, analyze, and design service processes. In analogy to architectural blueprints, G. Lynn Shostack (1982, 1984) identified the deficit of such an objective and formal plan for services. Managers often use subjective descriptions to outline the concept of operation, which is mostly not accurate enough. Although services do not have a tangible form, the need for further rigor and an objective manner to describe them seemed obvious. In order to make procedures explicit and communicate details Service Blueprinting was introduced. Taking the basic example of a corner shoeshine, Shostack represented a molecular model approach to illustrate the basic elements of a marketing offer, which are (in reference to bundles) products and services. By visualizing these elements in a flowchart and separating them by a "Line of visibility", which distinguishes between activities the customer can and cannot perceive, one can already draw a basic Blueprint of the service procedure.

This method was later developed by various authors. Kingman-Brundage (i.a. 1989, 1993, 1995) picked up Shostack's concept, adding three further lines that increased the possibilities of classifying process elements and aligning correspondingly important SERVQUAL-dimensions to these lines. This enhanced Blueprint, which was labeled "Service Mapping", has been applied to the case study "SkillsLink". It has to be stated that though some researchers differentiate between Service Blueprint as the illustration of not yet realized services (planning) and Service Mapping as the visualization of already existing processes (redesign), both terms are treated equally in this thesis (Fließ and Kleinaltenkamp 2004, p. 396). In reference to Langeard et al. (1981), who state that service managers not only need to consider products, but also the customer, technical and employee perspective, Kingman-Brundage, George and Bowen suggest (1995) having three views on the service map. Further they state five propositions on the benefits of the technique.

Fließ and Kleinaltenkamp (2004) reflected on efficiency management and the balance between production and market risk. They extended the method by appending an additional line, which is important as it separates customer-induced from customer-independent activities. It sets the focus to the question to which degree the offer should be standardized and how internal and external factors shall be directed. In general, much research on Service Blueprinting has been conducted and subsequently published by Fließ (i.a. 2001, 2006), who analyses customer integration from a process-based perspective that draws upon production and transaction cost theory (i.a. Coase 1937; Williamson 1979).

Service Blueprinting eases the identification of service activities, which involve the customer, shows where the interaction between customer and provider takes place and illustrates where the customer exerts influence within an overall process architecture. All service activities and required processes are chronologically ordered on the horizontal axis of the diagram. The vertical axis is divided into activity levels, in which the activities are arranged depending on where the major part of actions takes places. As of today the concept has been through three phases of development (Fließ and Kleinaltenkamp 2004, p. 397). Most of the latest Service Blueprinting versions consist of six activity levels that are separated by five parting lines:

- The "Line of interaction" separates the activities of the customer and provider. All following lines are a further differentiation of provider activities.

- The "Line of visibility" divides the visible (Onstage) from invisible (Backstage) activities from the customer's point of view.

- The "Line of internal interaction" divides activities of the customer's personnel (front-office) from back-office activities, which support the process flow of the front office (support activities). Thus, activities above this line are conducted by employees with customer contact.

- The "Line of order penetration" refers to the dividing line between individual integrative value creation processes and autonomous preparation activities. Activities that can be conducted autonomously without the intervention of the customers and without external factors are arranged below this line. As this line divides integrative activities from autonomous activities, which can be very much standardized, special importance is attached to this line (i.a. Gersch 1995; Jacob and Kleinaltenkamp 2004).

- The "Line of implementation" splits these autonomous activities into preparation activities, which are necessary for direct preparation of the service process, and facility activities, which integrate potential and consumption factors. Activities concerning general preparation include the pre-combination of internal factors, the maintenance of the machines and further training of the staff. Facility activities describe the allocation of resources that are necessary to run the service at all.

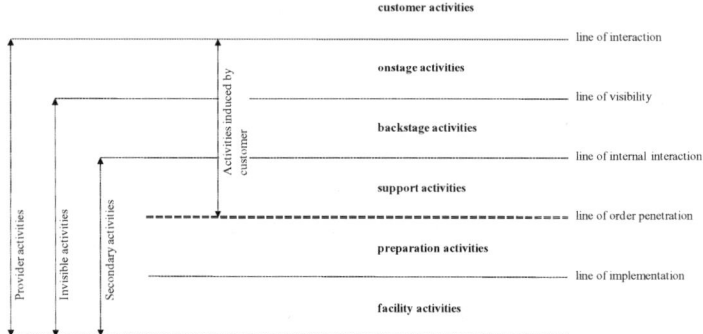

Figure 14. Structure of a service blueprint (Gersch, Hewing, et al., 2011, p. 738 modified from Kleinaltenkamp 1999)

Figure 14 provides a detailed overview of the Service Blueprinting's structure. When reading from top to down one takes the perspective of the customer (Kingman-Brundage 1989, p. 33). The reversed view reflects the view of the supplier. Because the activities below the "Line of order penetration" are conducted autonomously and independent of orders, a temporal sequence of activities is only given above this line. Hence, the "Line of order penetration" can be seen as the timeline.

A common scenario for using a Service Blueprint to describe a service process is illustrated in the form of eating out in Figure 15. Each task is put into one of the activity levels. Tasks below the "Line of order penetration" prepare and support multiple processes, but are not part of the individual value creation process. Therefore they have no connection to the individual process above the "Line of order penetration". This concerns, for instance, the preparation of food and the cleaning of the tables. The activities above the "Line of interaction" such as the placing of an order are performed by the customer. One activity level below corresponds to all the activities that can still be perceived by the customer. As it can be seen clearly, the focus of a Service Blueprint is on structuring processes into activity levels rather than providing a complete, clear and consistent way of modeling processes.

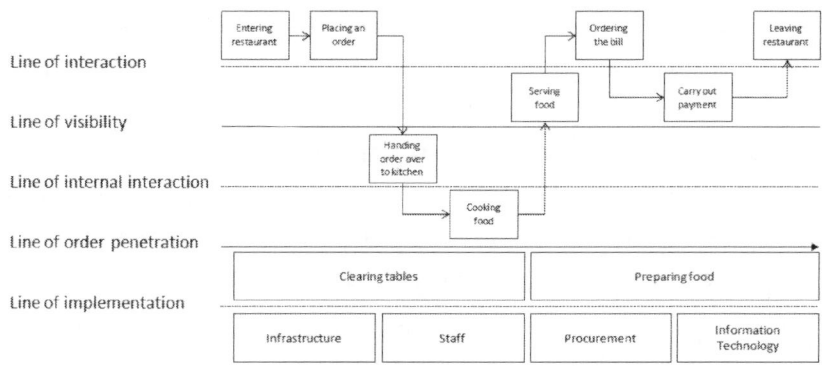

Figure 15. Example of a service blueprint for eating out (Gersch, Hewing and Schöler 2011, p. 738)

With reference to service scripts, the Service Blueprinting provides a design layout of the production process. For each activity level specific aspects have to be considered (i.a. Fließ 2008, pp. 193–244). Each line poses a specific question of how to design a process.

Activities above the "Line of interaction" are performed by the customer. It is of special importance that the customer knows how and when s/he needs to integrate him- or herself (i.a. Möller 2004). An explanation of the steps that need to be taken in the process could increase the customer's involvement and lead to a better understanding. One design option that arises at the "Line of interaction" is the question of whether activities should be externalized or internalized (i.a. Fließ 2008, pp. 206–221). Externalization means that activities that have been conducted before by the provider are now performed by the customer. Internalization is the very reverse. Externalization could lead to cost reduction, but also increases the risk of inappropriate customer activities that might lead to poor outcome quality or reduce customer satisfaction when the externalized processes contain bothering elements (Gersch 1995, p. 98). An example of externalization would be self-service in snack bars. Another is when a customer assembles furniture s/he bought at IKEA. The degree of customer integration can also be labeled as customer intensiveness.

Onstage activities take place above the "Line of visibility" and are therefore within the visual field of the customer. There is a necessity for a corresponding qualification of the customer's personnel and an effective design of the interaction interfaces. Especially dimensions of the physical environment quality play a decisive role. The ambience of a restaurant may affect the perceived quality to a large extent. McDonalds, for instance, with its open kitchens allows a sneak peek into the food preparation. This may give the customer the sense of things being prepared properly.

The distinction between front and back-office activities at the "Line of internal interaction" points to a risk of complications between these two divisions. Horizontal differentiation involves issues regarding organization theory and transactions costs.

Preparations activities below the "Line of order penetration" bring up the design question as to what degree and how the service offer should be standardized. Thus, the line helps in deciding to what degree a process should be standardized or rather individualized. An assembly postponement (i.a. van Hoek 2001) may increase the flexibility and reduce costs but can have a negative influence on the consumer's perception due to minor individualization. A comprehensive discussion on service standardization can be seen in Gersch (1995).

Facility elements below the "Line of implementation" point to capacity decisions. Customer integration can cause fluctuation in demand. With a lack of customer orders, resources (like human labor) are wasted despite creating costs. Hence, a well-adjusted and balanced capacity management is required.

Though design changes can have an (indirect) impact on the effectiveness at every activity level, alterations at the "Line of interaction" or "Line of visibility" do have a direct effect. Design decisions for activities attached to the "Line of interaction" or "Line of visibility" have a profound impact on the perceived service quality. For example, depending on the brand the customer sees, different prize expectations are assumed. This especially concerns services delivered in a cross-organizational manner. In the customer's perception some brands are linked to all-inclusive services with no extra charges for additional performances. Others are considered as discount brands with low price expectations. Thus, it might be worth considering how the involvement of the different service providers should be communicated to the customer.

Service Blueprinting serves as a technique for planning and analyzing service interaction process, i.e. for the redesign of existing processes and the basic conceptualization of novel processes. Through its gridlines the service process is illustrated in transparent and clearly arranged manner. Encounters with the customer can be easily identified and subsequently analyzed with further methods. The Blueprint can also be used as a foundation to justify changes in the process design. In addition, such a representation of the process serves general understanding and may be useful for briefing new employees. Thus, Service Blueprinting is an appropriate method for mapping and designing the interaction processes of services. A practical description of how to develop a Blueprint can be seen in Lovelock and Wirtz (2006, pp. 232–245). An enumeration of exemplary applications in management books is listed by Shahin (2010, pp. 4–5). With the current growth of web 2.0 technologies, which multiply the possibilities of customer co-creation (Fließ, Jacob and Fandel 2011), recent research reflects on the applicability of Service Blueprinting for electronic services that operate to a high extent in a virtual manner (Breithaupt 2005, pp. 95–96; Fließ and Völker-Albert 2002). Also worth mentioning is the procedure model of how to conduct a Blueprinting by Randall (1993, p. 8).

4.1.1.3 Combining both Approaches for a Comprehensive View on the Service Interaction

After the introduction of two concepts, it seems that the gap between the two disciplines could be covered by a combination of both approaches. Shostack already hinted (1982, pp. 56–57) to a combination of service marketing and engineering concepts such as time/motion engineering, PERT charting and Systems/Software Design. However, so far a homogenous form of process models like in BPM has not been established.

For the sake of clarity, it must be stated that the artifact that merges the approaches and is introduced throughout the next chapters is to be classified as a method. Methods determine a sequence of activities that need to be conducted to reach a particular result

(Winter 2003, p. 88). Procedure models specify this course of action by arranging these activities and giving further instructions with regard to the relative tasks. Although
the plain layout of Service Blueprinting looks much like a model that illustrates an
extract of reality, the artifact is assigned to method that describes the generic activity
to model customer processes by using lines that divide specific process elements.
Thus, the outcome of this activity is a distinct (process) model. Further, Service Blueprinting has also been considered a method by most of the authors that participated in
its development. The classification of the developed artifact as a method is further confirmed by a procedure model described in chapter 4.2.

However, Business Process Modeling notations as of today provide a well-founded
syntax and measurements for internal processes. Service Blueprinting would include
the customer's point of view, which is connectable to marketing concepts on effectiveness. This way the weaknesses of both approaches, i.e. the deficit of the customer's
point of view and missing criteria of effectiveness in Business Process Management as
well as the lack of syntax and corresponding modeling tools in marketing, can be
bridged. Table 7 summarizes the features of each approach and points out the academic void.

Table 7. Characteristics of Business Process Modeling and Service Blueprinting
(modified from Gersch, Hewing, et al., 2011, p. 736)

Concept	Discipline	Point of View	Orientation	Perspective	Analyzed Process Participants	Focus	Common methods
Business Process Modeling	Business Process Management/ Information Systems	provider	product-oriented	rather internal	provider (unilateral)	efficiency (e.g. cost, time)	event-driven process chain, unified modeling language
Service Blueprinting	Marketing	customer	customer-oriented	rather external	provider, customer (bilateral)	effectiveness (e.g. quality)	target pricing, service quality management

By enhancing Business Process Modeling with the marketing concept Service Blueprinting, the firm's and customer's perspective can be visualized and analyzed within a
single integrated approach. Incorporating the swimlanes outlined in Service Blueprinting into Business Process Modeling integrates two worlds and offers a conceivable

"lingua franca" between traditionally separated perspectives with different concepts, methods and tools. The idea of combining the approaches and elucidating the advantages was first put down in writing in a working paper by Gersch, Goeke and Lux (2006). Initial applications have been carried out in three research projects with industry partners (Gersch 2006, p. 11). Further conceptualization, details on the integration of Service Blueprinting into BPM, and an evaluation of the benefits and development perspectives have been published in several articles by Gersch, Hewing and Schöler (see chapter 2.3). In this thesis the artifact's rigor is strengthened by means of a detailed and structured development process and relevance extended by the enhancement of method to usage processes.

The developed method that is described in these publications has been entitled "Business Process Blueprinting". Considering the words the two approaches have been labeled with, this denomination reflects the unification of concepts. Because the initial letters of "Business Process Blueprinting" keep repeating, the name can be shortened to BPBP or even BP^2, which in particular emphasizes the added value that derives from the synergy of concepts and implies that the combination is more than just the sum of individual parts.

The two approaches can be combined by adding Service Blueprinting lines (which arrange process activities) to the flowchart of common Business Process Modeling languages. Thus, to close the research gap, the marketing concept Service Blueprinting is incorporated into Business Process Modeling. Basically, therefore, BP^2 consists of a normal business process diagram with an additional customer-related dimension. Processes in BP^2 are illustrated in a two-dimensional graphic. Process elements are arranged in chronological order from left to right – not from top to bottom as in usual business process diagrams. The six Service Blueprinting activity levels determine the vertical dimension. Each element of the eEPC (functions, events and information objects) is aligned to one of the activity levels according to its content.

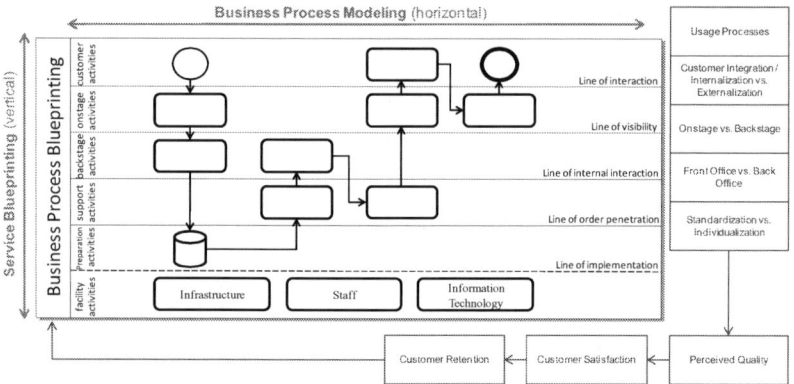

Figure 16. Business Process Blueprinting Framework (modified from Hewing 2011,
p. 3), full-page illustration in Appendix 8

Figure 16 visualizes the basic layout of such a BP² and the design options for each
line, which have already been explained in the chapter on Service Blueprinting
(4.1.1.2). The most probable design options have a high influence on perceived quality
and consequently on customer satisfaction and retention (see Heskett, Sasser and
Schlesinger 1997, p. 12 and chapter 3.1.1 for the links between the constructs). Once
specific design options have been chosen, regular evaluation of the process performance (effectiveness and efficiency) and corresponding adjustments seem beneficial.

As this concept promotes a customer-oriented way of thinking, it contains more than
six "swimlanes" in a "pool" (swimlanes are the short-form of swimming lanes and refer to areas of responsibility). In BP², the customer view is methodologically integrated into the modeling approach. When designing and implementing processes with BP²,
the customer perspective is taken into account as an inherent component of the design
and implementation process. For process measurement and improvement, BP² provides
the basis to create a measurement system that overcomes the current narrow focus on
internal efficiency measures. With BP² process management can be linked to effectiveness, which, combined with criteria of efficiency, enables an overall rating of processes performance.

Because BP² is an extension of the modeling syntax without changing its basic logic, it is compatible and adaptable to most modeling tools. For example, it seamlessly integrates into the ARIS framework and to modeling suites like iGrafx or MEGA. This is also true for process modeling techniques, which include modern extensions of a flowchart such as the Unified Modeling Language, Business Process Modeling and Notation or (as in this case) eEPC.

An explorative case study from one research project, which has been published in the BPMJ (Gersch, Hewing and Schöler 2011), demonstrates the application of BP² in practice. Although many health care institutions recently implemented process management, there is still a lack of awareness concerning the patient's point of view. Most processes in health care fulfill the old-established characteristics of services like the intangibility and customer integration. For example, a medical consultation and attendance is based on specific know-how to a great extent. The specialized knowledge can lead to a solution that is of immaterial nature and can only be realized with the cooperation of the customer. Production and consumption of the consultation take place at the same time – the service is used up, so to speak, in the very same moment it is produced. Activities in health care are perfect examples for services with high customer integration and therefore useful to demonstrate the advantages of BP². Due to its compactness, the following case study was chosen to illustrate the basic idea of BP². A similar setting can also be seen in Strametz et al. (2012).

The whole process is illustrated in Figure 17. For a better insight and a comparison between the usual process modeling and BP², both visualization alternatives can be seen full-page in Appendix 7 and Appendix 9. By comparing both versions one may recognize the added value that emerges from the structured layout of Service Blueprinting. In order to ensure an easy understanding of the process illustration, trivial events have been omitted. For example, the event "patient's documents are checked" does not appear between the functions "check patient's documents" and "enter patient data". However, this event only marks the completion of the preceding function and does not add any additional information. Similarly redundant events were omitted in order to ensure a concise and clear graphical display (Becker, Delfmann and Knackstedt 2007, p. 33).

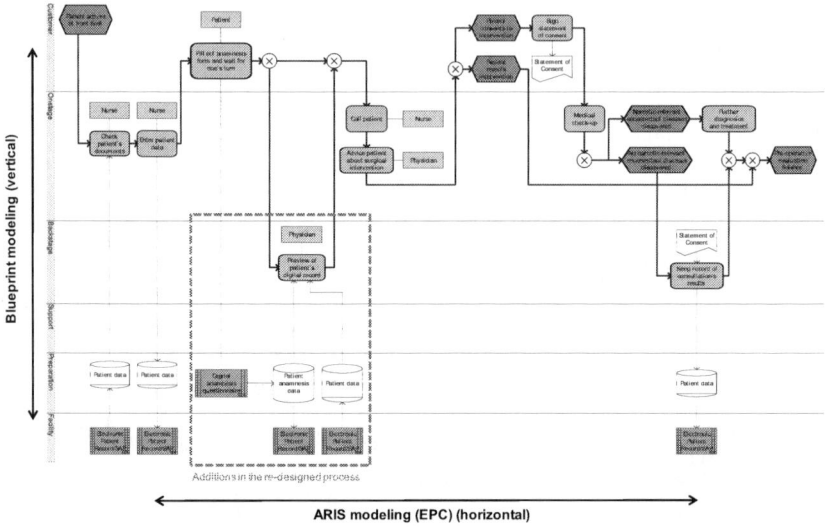

Figure 17. Case study of a BP² in health care (Gersch, Hewing and Schöler 2011, p. 739), full-page illustration in Appendix 9

The case setting is the pre-operative evaluation in one of Europe's biggest hospitals, which is at the same time one of Europe's most important scientific medical facilities. Prior to surgery the anesthetist interviews the patient to define the required dosage of anesthetics with reference to the patient's medical history. The sample is based on real processes. The task was to redesign the processes in order to improve process performance. Initially, data was collected through direct observations of staff and customers, followed by semi-structured interviews with twelve patients, two nurses, one assistant doctor and the senior physician. By using flowcharts the respondents commented on the process activities sequentially. Additionally, a survey based on the quality model of Brady and Cronin (2001b) was carried out among 30 patients in order to measure the perceived service quality. The results of the interviews and the survey show that one main problem in this setting was the very long waiting time. The durations of the consultations vary, which makes fixed appointments hardly possible.

The main activities of the pre-operative evaluation can be summed up in two processes: the admission of the patient and the anesthetic consultation. The patient admission process contains all administrative activities run by the staff. It begins with the arrival of the patient at the reception desk resulting in the registration of the patient and his or her data. The entire process takes a few minutes. Afterwards the patient is asked to complete the anamnesis sheet (including questions about his or her medical history) while waiting for his or her turn in the foyer. Waiting is a typical example of a "bothersome activity". From a service marketing's point of view the customer expects a fast and efficient fulfillment of such activities (Gersch 1995, p. 49).

The main service is the anesthetic consultation. It begins when the patient enters the examination room. The physician reviews his or her anamnesis form. Accurate and honest answers are prerequist for a proper selection of anesthetic. Further inquiry in order to gather more detailed information about the patient's medical history is common. The physician then explains options for narcotic treatments and potential risks. The medic chooses the preferred treatment together with the patient. Physical examinations are advised if there is anything to suggest narcotically-relevant concomitant disease or when infants, elderly persons or pregnant women need to be narcotized. If any related disorders are revealed, further diagnostic and treatment may become necessary. If no concomitant diseases are visible, the patient is asked to sign a consent form for legal reasons. Finally the patient leaves the room and the health care professional keeps a record of the results of the consultations with a standardized form so that the information is available on the day of intervention. The main process results include: choice of narcotics, information of the patient and legal protection for the medicating anesthetist. The average duration of this process is about 20 minutes (excluding waiting time). However, this measure can vary, because it is based on the completeness of the anamnesis form and the patient's behavior. Anxious patients, for example, require more time. The longest amount of time is taken up in explaining the procedure and its risks as well as by any further inquiry into the person's medical history.

After data on the process and its perceived quality had been collected, three physicians were collectively asked to identify IT-improvable areas in the process notated in eEPC. Afterwards they were asked to repeat this task using BP². As the process was modeled with BP², they decided in less than five minutes to transfer activities to the patient. A digitalization of the anamnesis was discussed most intensively.

A digital version of the anamnesis sheet could support the patient comprehension by adding more information and using audiovisual contents. At the same time the waiting period can be enhanced with service elements. The anamnesis could be more precise by specifying the questions through a multi-level query design. Further information to questions or multilingual options could lead to a better understanding. An automatic evaluation of the anamnesis sheet would be conceivable in order to make a guideline available at the beginning of the consultation. The process could be shortened substantially by omitting the evaluation of the anamnesis sheet. Although the additions in the redesigned process lie partially beneath the "Line of visibility", all the changes have a direct impact on the customer. Through further externalization of the anamnesis, the perceived waiting time can be reduced. Without the customer-related dimension the physicians did not consider an externalization of activities in such an explicit way. Kingman-Brundage (1995, p. 141) referred to this phenomenon when she said that the lines of the Service Blueprinting make "...explicit the taken-for-granted ways of doing things that under normal conditions remain implicit..." and it "...changes forever the way in which people in service systems view their customers...". Thus, the focus of process designer seems to open up to the customer's point of view in the service interaction. The additional lines with their relative design questions raise the attention to customer concepts in marketing. Because the elements of the interaction process are now classified and visualized in structure, it is easy to keep the design options in mind.

It has to be stated that the idea to highlight interaction processes is already considered in current modeling languages. The eEPC syntax, for instance, contains symbols for organization units and persons to illustrate process participants. In BPMN 1.1 the Object Management Group introduced so called swimlanes to distinguish different activity levels. BPMN 2.0 comprises "choreography" symbols to visualize the interaction between two process participants. Nevertheless, there is still no consistent way of labeling these swimlanes. As a result, the design options of Service Blueprinting are not considered. Although the literature review revealed that other (rather short) publications in BPM have also considered Service Blueprinting (i.a. Becker, Beverungen and Knackstedt 2009; Coenen, Felten and Schmid 2011; Klose, Knackstedt and Becker 2005; Knackstedt and Dahlke 2004; Meis, Menschner and Leimeister 2010; Milton and Johnson 2012), they hardly discuss or evaluate (apart from Knackstedt and Pellengahr 2007) the influence and employment of the Blueprinting's integration into Business Process Modeling. Most articles focus on the technical part and do not describe the design options of each activity level. Some even omit several lines of the Service Blueprinting, which in turn drops important design questions concerning marketing and management concepts, such as the trade-off between standardization and individualization at the "Line of order penetration". The unique feature of BP^2 is that its conceptual foundations and the deriving implications have been very much highlighted, its employment is described in further detail and its benefits have been evaluated in practice. Most importantly, BP^2 is able to take the usage processes of the customer into account.

While BP^2 in its current state concentrates on direct interaction between customer and provider, the next section turns the focus to customer processes that follow after the value creation process is concluded, showing how the logic of BP^2 can be transferred to gain more transparency concerning customer processes that are out of the usual operation distance.

4.1.2 Capturing Usage Processes: Enhancement of Business Process Blueprinting towards Customer Activities

As already mentioned, current research efforts concerning the customer in BPM tend to mainly focus on a detailed understanding and the design of the integrative value creation process, which ends with the buying transaction for a product or the completion of a service production process. But this is only one part of the customer process, which also includes usage and pre-purchase activities. A key result of the previously described SDL discussion is that especially subsequent usage processes significantly impact the performance of the customers' activities, because they are a crucial part in shaping overall satisfaction (Lemke, Clark and Wilson 2011, p. 4). A major part of the benefits expected by the customer usually emerges after traditional value activities of the provider. For example, the value of knowledge provided in university or through-out seminars may evolve later on. Usage has an tremendous impact on the overall effectiveness and efficiency. However, providers do not have adequate instruments to observe usage. This is partly evident with regard to the difficulty of gathering data relating to such autonomously performed customer processes. However current developments in Information Technology such as the digitalization of customers' activities are leading to a rapidly changing situation. Especially Web 2.0 applications as well as the (mobile) internet provide new possibilities to analyze, influence and shape usage processes. Coming back to the example of learning processes, courses that are supported by computer-mediated activities such as web-based trainings or modifiable web pages (i.e. wikis) facilitate a tracing of the usage of content and performed tasks. Gathered information can be used to adjust the structure and format of the course and its content according to the requirements and characteristics of each participating individual in order to support them in their relative learning processes (Fink et al. 2011; Gabriel, Gersch and Weber 2008, 2009; Lehr 2012, p. 52).

In reference to the typical stages in industries' e-transformation (Deise, Wright and Nowikow 2000), three stages of design alteration concerning usage processes can be addressed from a conceptual design perspective. The stages should be rather seen as marks on a continuum. The three design stages are:

- **Redesign of current offers:** Usage processes that take place beyond the provider's perception need to be analyzed in greater detail. Because of their important role in value creation, they contain valuable information about the customers' requirements, behavior and their perception of the preceding interaction process. Thus, the provider may gain further insights on the customer, which may results in a possible redesign of pre-purchase, interaction or usage processes (and if given also of tangible elements) to match to a larger extent the expectations of relative customer groups and provide higher customer satisfaction.

- **Transformation of usage processes:** While the first issue addresses the adjustment of process details to drive satisfaction, the second stage relates to large-scale changes of value creation. The possibility to influence previously autonomous usage processes opens up new potentials of value creation for the provider. Opportunities arise to influence and support these processes, which blur the line between the traditional service production process and usage. A profound variation would be an additional interaction or even complete takeover of activities the customer normally performs autonomously. The music streaming service Spotify, for instance, collects information on one's playlists, which is used for collaborative filtering (i.e. the identification of behavioral patterns of user groups that allows conclusions to be inferred about an individual's preferences). As a result one gets very accurate recommendations that fit a person's listening taste. It is also possible to follow and discuss playlists of participating artists, which gives the supporter further insight and thus reduces the distance between artist and his or her fan base.

- **Establishment of new value chains:** In an extreme case, the analysis of customer activities may uncover not yet realized potentials to create benefits for the customer, which could result in completely new structures of value creation. Examples are business models like the Infomediary (Rappa 2010) or Information Broker (Timmers 1998, p. 7) in Electronic Markets, which base on the collection and vending of information on costumers and their habits. In the B2B sector market research institutes can sell valuable information about the customer's usage processes to the industry. The service offer "Dynamic Insights" by Telefónica S.A. (2013), for instance, provides real-time useful information on the customers' current positions. However, now the gathered information of the customer activities can also be used to create value for the end customer. An example of a completely new value chain regarding customer activities is Personal Life Systems (Rosemann 2013a), which aims to support and ease via IT specific areas of life by converging and orchestrating (Gersch and Hewing 2012, pp. 12–13) all required devices and process-es such as taking charge of a person's finances or organizing their health examina-tions or restoration.

Although the three levels of design alteration point out the benefits of analyzing usage processes, research in this field is still limited. No scientifically substantiated concept exists in BPM that analyzes usage processes. Given the fact that the Business Process Blueprinting method already concentrates on management and the evaluation of inter-action between provider and customer, it seems appropriate to use it as a conceptual basis and to extend it to usage processes. Drawing on this enhanced BP², the aim is to analyze usage to improve future offers in accordance with customer requirements and to realize new potentials of value creation by supporting or controlling usage process-es. While there is no concrete formulation of lines for customer activities, this chapter accentuates the need for such a concept and proposes potential swimlanes for the anal-ysis of usage processes. The key theme here is a methodology-based extension of the relationship between provider and customer to usage processes. Figure 18 visualizes the idea of mirroring Service Blueprinting in the Business Process Modeling language cEPC to the customer's side.

In 2006, Frauendorf (2006, pp. 49–52) picked up the idea (in reference to research on scripts and Fließ 2001, p. 48) of expanding Service Blueprinting to the customer side. The focus of analysis is here on B2B service transactions. Because clients also possess production activities, a simple duplication of Service Blueprinting is applicable. If in-formation on the backstage activities of the business customer is available, one can model them on the Service Blueprinting. However, this approach is not adaptable to all kinds of service transactions. Firstly, it requires a full insight on customer activities, which is mostly unavailable in great detail, particularly in the case of rather anony-mous B2C transactions. This issue would make the mapping of secondary customer activities obsolete. Secondly, the title of her publication already points to the fact that the concept still focuses on the interaction between the provider and customer. Citing Edvardsson's (1997, p. 34) article on customer participation in the service production process, customer processes are defined as "…activities or part-processes that the customer participates in either passively or actively by carrying out certain activities…". The customer process concept of this thesis considers a rather holistic viewpoint, which includes all activities that are conducted by the customer to meet a specific desire – including pre-purchase, interaction, usage and latent (provider independent) processes.

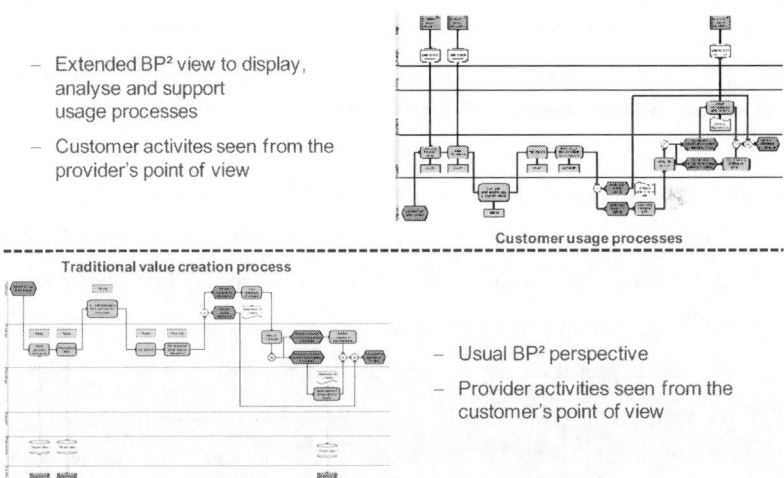

- Extended BP² view to display, analyse and support usage processes
- Customer activites seen from the provider's point of view

Customer usage processes

Traditional value creation process

- Usual BP² perspective
- Provider activities seen from the customer's point of view

Figure 18. Basic idea behind the enhanced Business Process Blueprinting

The BP² approach can be seen as a first step towards modeling such processes. In the first instance, the lines of Service Blueprinting, which have been expanded by Business Process Modeling notations, have been substituted by lines that facilitate the illustration of the customers' usage processes. An enhanced BP² can be seen as a step towards a concept that extends traditional analysis of value creation processes to usage. In BP² traditional value creation is usually presented from an outside-in perspective. Provider activities are seen from the customer's point of view. In usage processes however the provider wants to gain insight into customer activities. In analogy to Service Blueprinting, the basic idea is to mirror its gridlines to the customer's side. Thus, the grid-logic requires a turnaround of perspectives for an extended view on customer's usage processes. Customer activities are now seen from the provider's point of view in order to visualize the degree to which the company can gain insight into and influence customer processes.

The lines for an extended BP² are developed according to the procedure model of Knackstedt and Pellengahr (2007, pp. 735–744), who propose five phases for the development of perspectives in BPM. First, one needs to define the perspective one wants to model, which is in this case the provider's point of view. In the next three steps, the perspective's aspects (matter of analysis) have to be declared, which are subsequently separated by a specific scheme (i.a. lines of the Service Blueprinting). For on overview of possible schemes to differentiate processes see Gersch, Goeke and Lux (2006, pp. 19–23). Here the objects of analysis are the customer processes and the extent to which the provider can insight or even influence these processes. The logic of the Service Blueprinting is applied for the differentiation of process elements. The last step of the procedure model calls for an evaluation of the developed perspective, which is conducted in chapter 5 of this thesis.

The extended grid begins at the upper line of the traditional BP² and can be set up on top of the existing lines. Although the idea of extending Service Blueprinting has been around for some time, it has not yet been developed in concrete terms. As the idea to model customer activities from the provider's point of view is almost unexplored, no publication has been discovered that can be used as a reference for the denotation of customer swimlanes. Because the lines of the traditional Service Blueprinting consider to a large degree internal aspects, they are due to limited insight and restricted information on the customer's "internal processes" not applicable to the customer's side. For this reason, the author looked about the lines of the Service Blueprinting that have direct impact on the customers' satisfaction and perception of quality, which are namely the "Line of interaction" and the "Line of visibility". The main concepts behind these two lines are the participation of the customer, which refers to the question of extern- or internalization, and the perception of the environmental quality. These two concepts have also been considered for the compilation of new swimlanes for usage processes. The proposed lines of the enhanced BP² focus on the visual range and participation of the provider on the customer's usage processes. The enhanced BP² adds three additional lines to the Service Blueprinting, which results in a total of eight lines and nine swimlanes. An exemplary template of a BP² that considers provider and customer activities can be seen in Appendix 10. However, for the sake of clarity and due to the different focus of analysis, an independent illustration is recommended. Figure 19 shows the basic structure of an enhanced Business Process Blueprinting. It should be mentioned that the following explanations differentiate between the terms traditional and enhanced BP², when the issue is just on one of the two versions. If a differentiation is of little importance or the issue concerns both types only the label BP² is used.

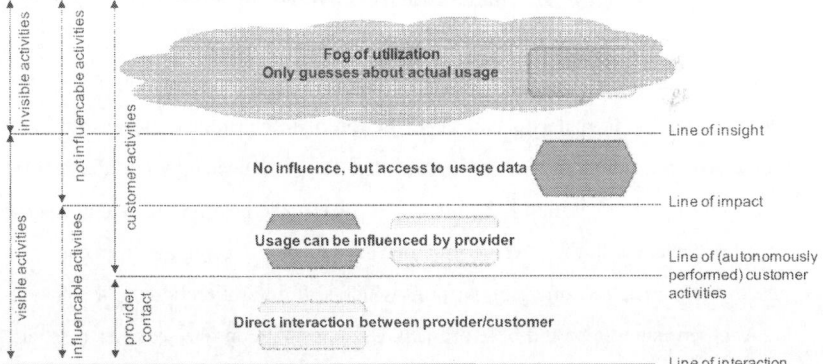

Figure 19. BP² for usage processes

The first and second additional lines refer to the possibility of influencing the usage activities of the customer. The third line separates still visible but not suggestible process elements from not perceivable activities. With the "Line of interaction" the enhanced Business Process Blueprinting consists of four lines. In the following each line will be described in further detail:

- The grid starts at the upper end of the BP² – the "Line of interaction". This line splits customer from provider activities and therefore includes all those elements, which derive from a direct interaction between the provider and customer. Process elements above this line belong to the customer process. Yet, these elements still relate to the direct interaction between provider and customer. The design question referred to the "Line of interaction" is whether provider or the customer leads the relative activities.

- The "Line of (autonomously performed) customer activities" winnows the activities that are autonomously performed by a customer from those involving provider interaction. In contrast to direct interaction, which can be labeled as the service encounter, every element above this line relates to usage encounters (Payne, Storbacka and Frow 2008, pp. 90–91). Thus, autonomously performed customer processes initiate above this line. Customer activities in-between the "Line of (autonomously performed) customer activities" and "Line of impact" can still be influenced remotely. The contact via Information and Communication Technology (ICT) allows the provider to impact the action of the customer. Because the customer does not integrate him- or herself physical, data exchange is rather considered as a virtual integration, which can also take place beyond the spatial interaction. For instance, in the internet provider influence may originate from the structure of the provider's software platform, which still gives directions to the customer. Another example would be a pro-active support. When one searches a specific solution regarding a company's software, it should be possible for customers to sent useful data to the provider, who can then analyze the information, which subsequently leads to a recommended course of action or even remote intervention.

- Following up, the "Line of impact" divides those customer activities, which still can be influenced by the provider, from activities that are not tractable anymore. Activities above this line can no longer be influenced, merely examined. Indirect contact through ICT allows the provider to gather data about the usage and aggregate it into useful information. This information can be used amongst others to re-define one's customer segments according to their usage profiles. By doing this, communications such as commercials or recommendations can be more precise.

- The "Line of insight" finally separates visible activities from untraceable once. All activities above this line are invisible to the provider leaving behind a fog, in which anything related to actual usage can only be guessed. The term "fog" refers to "…a state or cause of perplexity or confusion" (Oxford English Dictionaries Online 2012b). Therefore the "Fog of utilization" symbolizes the addressed issue vividly. Simon and Long (2011, p. 40) presented a similar term (fog of uncertainty) concerning learning analytics.

Because unknown processes cannot be mapped, the need for such a swimlane may be deemed unnecessary. However, it is important to keep this swimlane for three reasons. First, not all process activities in this area are necessarily unknown. From a high aggregated point of view some elements of the main usage process are familiar, they just lack insight and details. Second, this activity level indicates that even though the usage processes of the customer have been analyzed there can still be a lot of covered types and activities of usage, which lead to further inquiries and (as the case may be) to new insights. Last, this swimlane is useful for the ex-post reconstruction of the course of events, i.e. the visualization of the shift of process elements, which have been first undetected and afterwards discovered, from the highest swimlane to a lower one. Such an example will be given later on in the demonstration.

With the BP² for usage processes and more acute awareness of the degree to which the provider can gain insights into customer processes, a structural foundation and a starting point for reshaping usage can be acquired. In order to gain control, the basic aim is to lower activities from higher swimlanes without affecting the customer's perception adversely. Whereas traditional Service Blueprinting questions whether a process element should be above or under a specific line, the main task is to drop process elements from the swimlanes above. Elements above the "Line of insight" ought to become visible. Depending on the added value from the customer perspective it may also be reasonable to move process elements that cannot be influenced via process redesigns below the "Line of impact", where customer activities are supportable, or to even lower them to the deepest activity level, which is beneath the "Line of (autonomously performed) customer activities".

By applying this method to usage processes one creates a process model, which can be used for all the purposes that have been described at the beginning of chapter 4.1.1.1 (i.e. instruction, communication, analysis and redesign). The method also suits the three steps to enhance provider integration by Weiber and Hörstrup (2009, p. 298), which are namely identification of potentials, analysis and design. The enhanced BP² provides several unique benefits:

- The enhanced BP² spatializes the concept of usage processes vividly, which makes the issue more tangible. What Kingman-Brundage (1995, p. 141) said about Service Blueprinting is also transferable to the enhanced version. It makes a rather implicit concept explicit and it may change or extend the way in which providers view their service offers. With this method the focus is very much set on customer processes. Even if one does not regard the lines as important, they certainly encourage one to put thought into customer processes. It is now easier to realize that one should look on and gain control over those processes in order to shape and coordinate usage processes on the demand side.

- It can be used to structure gathered information about the usage process and identify potential new contact points. By applying the logic of activity levels to the customer side, important and useful information can be collected with regard to usage. In analogy to Service Blueprinting one can easily separate at a glance autonomous customer activities from those still involving the provider. As each element is aligned to one of the activity levels it is possible to identify the extent to which the provider can perceive or even influence customer's activities. Thus, it can now be mapped what the provider perceives or impacts and which activities are out of the provider's sphere (Grönroos and Voima 2012).

- Further, it can be used as instrument for the documentation and illustration of further proceeding, visualizing the "as-is" and "as-should" process layout in order to extract necessary modification on the arrangements. It is also appropriate to reconstruct already conducted changes in the usage process layout and to reconsider and illustrate graphically the course of events.

Thus, the enhanced BP^2 can be used to achieve Johnson's (1997, pp. 2–4) goals of customer orientation that are in particular to attain customer information, disseminate customer information in the organization and implement appropriate actions. Altogether, the enhanced version is suited to modeling usage processes, which in turn facilitates management, i.e. planning, application and control, of usage processes.

With the help of a practical example the explanations above and the artifact's benefits shall be illustrated and made concrete. An example of tracking the customer's location is the community platform for runners, provided by one of the major sportswear suppliers in combination with their GPS-integrated watch or smart-phone add-on, which keeps track of a person's jogging workouts. The collection of route data as well as other information like distance or pace is automatically analyzed after being uploaded through the company's software platform. While runners are now able to review their progress, the provider gains a lot of insight into their behavior. This information might help the provider to search for specific patterns, which can be factored into customer segmentation or advertisement placement. Furthermore, the provider shapes customer activities in the form of training recommendations and pushes platform usage through an included bonus system that rewards the customer. The watch has recently been enhanced to all day activities, which exceeds the collection of information beyond jogging. Recalling the three different stages of redesign at the beginning of this chapter, one could align this variation of processes to the stage of "transformation of usage processes".

The case shows that jogging, workout and all day activities were not traceable by the provider prior to the innovation. Through the new service offer these activities are now visible and can be influenced. Thus, related process elements moved from the highest swimlane to the next lower line or even to the activity level with provider impact. Figure 20 shows a common training process (white process elements). Now, with the watch, important data can be evaluated to support the customer in his or her workout.

The watch can also give the athlete useful information on the run. Further, the advanced process ends with the analysis of training. The customer can thus improve his or her running behavior, so for instance, a break is no longer necessary.

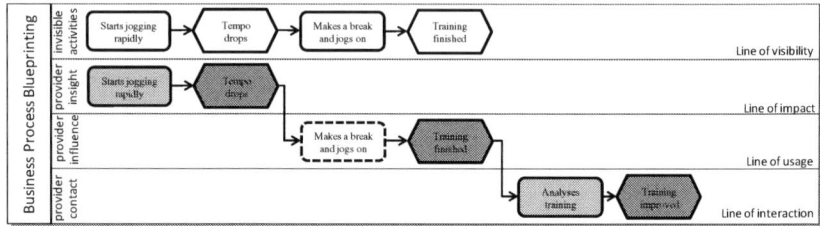

Figure 20. Basic example of the redesign of an autonomous customer process

With the enhanced BP² this procedure can now be explicitly visualized and explained in detail. This basic example shows that the artifact is suitable for the reconstruction of design changes and their deriving implications. It further illustrates that the main question the artifact poses is which design changes have to be conducted to shift process elements to a lower swimlane and therefore reduce the proximity to the customer and his or her processes.

As usage processes derive from every economic exchange, the BP² is applicable to all industries and sectors (i.a. Business-to-Business and Business-to-Consumer). Information on the customer processes can be collected through diverse channels, such as primary research, which refers to the collection and subsequent analysis of new data (field research), or secondary research, i.e. the analysis based on already existing data collection (desk research).

Interviews, observations and surveys are typical methods of primary research. For this method the contextual inquiry (Beyer and Holtzblatt 1997) seems especially appropriate. Another interesting approach for collecting information on encounters that are outside the perception of the investigator is in particular mobile-phone text messaging, which enables one to capture customer experiences in real time (Baines et al. 2011; Macdonald, Wilson and Konus 2012). A transfer of the approach to usage processes seems very promising for the collection of usage data.

Sources of secondary research are among others user-generated data that has been published on Web 2.0 platforms such as blogs, forums or comment fields. A very well known example of such data is the rating of products via comment fields of the online retailer Amazon. Another treasure of information about the customer is passively generated data that is tracked by software or hardware and subsequently transferred via ICT to the provider. Smart phones, cookies that track one's navigation through the World Wide Web or sensors in the private and public infrastructure (e.g. Ambient Assisted Living, traffic) are examples of such passively generated data. These human-computer interactions are an important link between the provider and customer's usage processes. Industries that depend to a high degree on ICT are therefore most suitable for the application of BP^2. However, considering the current e-transformation in many industries, the spectrum of automated data collection is widening to other branches, especially when technologies keep evolving such as the Internet of Things or Ubiquitous Computing (i.a. Atzori, Iera and Morabito 2010), which promote information feedbacks to the provider. Technologies like radio-frequency identification, near field communication or smart grids link artificial intelligent products together and connect them to the internet. It is predicted that in the near future, most products will include a digital interface for the exchange of data. The huge amount of data collected via ICT such as the internet or mobile phones can be analyzed for patterns with approaches like Business Intelligence and Analysis. Such a procedure is highlighted in the outlook of this thesis (chapter 6.2.2).

It is important to mention that data about usage processes is very sensitive. An intervention should be handled carefully. In order to prevent misuse, data collection and application must respect current laws on consumer and privacy protections (i.a. Winn and Wrathall 2000) as well as legal practices on customer data. Although technology serves a specific aim, it is free of values. Thus, the (potential) users of a technology create an affinity and must determine whether its application is appropriate. It is important for the analysis of data that the customer holds the data authority, so s/he is informed and can determine what data and information the provider is given to process. Besides legal issues, the customer may otherwise see those actions as an intrusion into privacy. A cautionary example is the tracking-function of smart-phones (i.a.

Gerpott and Berg 2011). The revelation of a non-contracted recording of the mobile's position had an extremely negative influence on some of the providers' reputation (Marzilli 2011). It is therefore important to keep the customer's perception in mind while gathering further insights.

4.2 Proposition of a (multi-level) Procedure Model as a Guideline for an Application of Method

For the sake of clarity and in order to strengthen a customer-oriented perspective in the design of services, it is reasonable to merge the Business Process Blueprinting and its enhanced version into one approach. In the early 1980's, first scientific papers began to deal with Service Design (i.a. Shostack 1982), a field of research concentrating mostly on the marketing perspective of how to develop a service. As the research of this thesis advocates a rather inter-disciplinary approach through the combination of IS and marketing methods, it is convenient to refer to current research in this area such as Service Engineering, which includes both perspectives. Service Engineering deals with the systematic development and design of services using models, methods and tools adopted from engineering science enriched by well-established marketing concepts (Bullinger, Fähnrich and Meiren 2003, p. 276). One principal aspect in this field of study is the definition of a reference model specifying the aspects that should be considered and the activities that are necessary for the development of a service (i.a. Schneider et al. 2006, p. 134). Even if many procedure models are proposed with different foci like waterfall or spiral flows, most of them contain similar phases of project schedule (i.a. Edvardsson and Olsson 1996; Ramaswamy 1996; Scheuing and Johnson 1989). Also Shostack and Kingman-Brundage (1991), the main developers of Service Blueprinting, consider such a procedure model as important and propose their own reference guideline. Their model begins with the design phase, which contains the steps "Definition", "Analysis" and "Synthesis". This sequence keeps repeating until a rough general arrangement plan evolves from this iterative course of action. Once a master design is certain, the implementation of operative procedures follows. The whole service process should be documented like a guidebook for employees before the service is finally introduced into the market. The procedure model ends with loop of final design audits and relative design modifications. Service Blueprinting, like Business Process Blueprinting, perfectly fits the requirements of the design phase as it provides with its intuitive visualization of the service operation a basis for discussions and thus can substantiate parts of the definition and synthesis processes. The Blueprint further can be a foundation for the implementation, documentation and recurring adjustment of the service offer.

As far as the author knows none of current procedure models include recent research on value-in-use and usage processes. Therefore the author proposes to incorporate the enhanced BP^2 to support an enhanced view. This way the designer may pay greater attention to the customer experience models and the SDL mindset, which resonate from the enhanced BP^2 that builds upon these concepts. So when defining a service (re-)design one should not only consider the interaction processes but also the usage and at best also the pre-purchase processes. A proposed approach is illustrated in Figure 21.

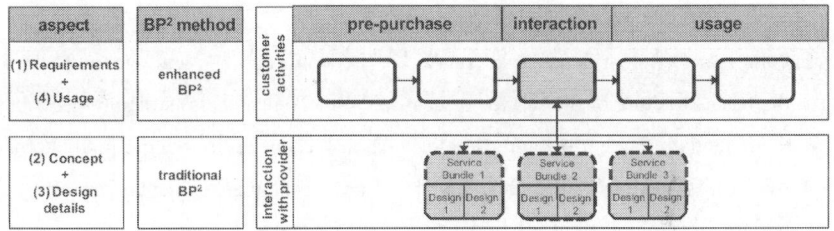

Figure 21. Conceptualization of a customer-oriented service (re-)design definition

For explanatory purposes, the author concentrates on four aspects that a definition of a service (re-)design should unconditionally consider. Other procedure models contain similar aspects but miss out the usage. Therefore this conceptualization seems adaptable to other procedure models. Thus, it should not be seen as a substitution of recent procedure models, but rather as a complement. The four aspects build upon each other and lead from rough process descriptions to precise specification. It can be seen as a multi-level approach to design services such as the one introduced by Patrício et al. (2011). Their approach differentiates between the general "Value Constellation Experience", a more detailed characterization of the "Service Experience" and the very information-rich "Service Encounter Experience", which is suggested to be designed with the Service Blueprinting. Another multi-level approach is to organize markets, customer segments, specific business relationship and single transactions into a hierarchy (Gersch 1998, p. 27; Kleinaltenkamp 2000, p. 232; Plinke 1991, p. 175). Such an aggregation could also be transferred to a Service Engineering procedure model. In reference to these approaches the proposed procedure model contains similar phases. In the following the multi-level stages are explained in more detail:

(1) **Requirements:** The definition starts with idea generation in order to push requirement analysis. At this stage ideas are developed to marketable service offers defining the core benefits that shall satisfy customer needs and fit market conditions. At this stage a factsheet describes the fundamentals of the service offer including the central performance bond of the business system and the specification of the targeted customers.

(2) **Concept:** Different concepts of service delivery are outlined and evaluated. Here the basic structure of the service offer is laid out. The (process) structure describes the essential process flow and its core functions. Then service bundles and alternative process designs can be created to fit different customer segments. For instance, besides accommodation additional services like wellness programs or entertainment can be offered in the hospitality industry in order to address a variety of clientele like managers or families.

(3) **Design details:** Once the core functions are determined, the design details of service bundles can be optimized using the BP^2 in combination with marketing methods such as the conjoint analysis (see chapter 6.2.1 for further details). For these activities the traditional Business Process Blueprinting seems most fitting. The development of a Service Blueprinting is described in further detail in Lovelock and Wirtz (2006, pp. 232–245). Yet, one must additionally consider the specifications and rules of the relative Business Process Modeling notation.

(4) **Usage:** After the market-launch and start of service production and consumption, usage processes emerge. Information about usage processes can be gathered through primary (i.a. interviews, observations and surveys) and/or secondary research (i.a. actively [blogs, forums] or passively [sensors, ICT, user-generated data]). For instance, those processes may become apparent for the provider through a (re-)configuration of infrastructure towards the collection of usage data, which in turn can be structured with the extended BP^2. The gathered information on usage can lead to new findings in customer behavior and therefore to new requirements, resulting in adjusted or complete new service offers. Customer activities that generate data such as user comments may also be a starting point for conceivable future transactions and influence upcoming activities, which could be treated as activities of pre-purchase.

Modeling with the extended version of BP^2 follows the same rules as the traditional one, just with different swimlanes. For the classification of process elements a look at Appendix 10 is beneficial. It points out which process element belongs to which activity level.

Besides an iterative approach, this procedure model can be seen as cyclic with regard to the information gathered in usage which points to new requirements. While the concept and design phases focus on direct interaction with the customer, the usage and requirement phases concentrate on the usage and pre-purchase processes. The integration of detailed customer process analysis supports a customer-centered perspective in Service Engineering and can be seen as a guideline for the modeling of customer processes in BPM. For instance, innovation management is often conducted in cooperation with external service providers that integrate a different view for a holistic perspective on the issue. This way new insight on innovation possibilities might be revealed. Thus, the guideline along with the BP^2 can be very much of use for consultants, who want to focus on the analysis of customer processes in order to discuss and analyze a rather new and neglected issue. Referring to the "exploration of processes", Rosemann (2013b) points to an innovation-driven process management that focuses rather on the identification of opportunities than on the analysis of problems. One part of such an opportunity-driven approach can be the proactive management of customer processes, which means that beside articulated needs, an anticipated understanding of the customer's latent and future needs shall be considered. When offers address needs that haven't been realized yet by the customer, it can be very much appreciated (i.a. Beverland, Farrelly and Woodhatch 2007; Tuli, Kohli and Bharadwaj 2007). For instance, customer generated events that are accessible by companies (e.g. twitter messages) can be a trigger to analyze their content, using data mining in order to re-act adequate (Rosemann 2011a). However, research in the field of proactive customer orientation is still quite limited in marketing (Narver, Slater and MacLachlan 2004, p. 335) as well as in BPM. BP² can be seen as one of the first efforts to close this gap. Because the method raises awareness of yet barely analyzed (customer) processes and points to specific redesign possibilities, it can be seen as one foundation for an opportunity- and innovation-driven process management.

4.3 Revisiting the Requirements: the Artifact against the Background of the Solution Objectives

The solution objectives an artifact has to meet have been extracted from the explanation on current research gaps and the deriving research problem. While with the SDL discussion research efforts in marketing are heading towards new boundaries, BPM still remains caught within the long-established, product-oriented perception of value creation and barely takes the customer's processes into account. Moreover, the realm of marketing does not comprise technically mature concepts of process modeling. A gap can be identified in the formal modeling of customer processes. From this area of conflict the author aggregated four requirements a solution has to address in order to release the stress field between the two disciplines (see chapter 3.3). In what follows, the artifact "Business Process Blueprinting" that has been developed and described throughout chapter 4 will be checked against these four requirements by logical reasoning.

The first two requirements related to the concepts and approaches that have been approved in both disciplines. In order to be able to integrate current knowledge and to find acceptance in the marketing and BPM community a solution should consider already existing methods. This means that an artifact should preferably build upon current modeling languages in BPM and their syntaxes. Further, a method to model customer activities should consider current concepts of marketing and be able to illustrate interaction and usage processes. The specifications of the Business Process Blueprinting satisfy the criteria of both requirements. The developed artifact is very much based on recent modeling notations and takes the popular process approach Service Blueprinting from marketing into account, whose logic is applied to usage processes that take place beyond the direct interaction with the provider. The modeling notation does not need to be changed. Current syntaxes can be integrated without any complications. Thus, instead of a process flow from the top to the bottom of the page, the elements are now ordered from left to right. Also the lines of the Service Blueprinting can be integrated without alteration. With BP^2 one is able to draw interaction and usage activities of the customer processes without altering existing concepts (requirements 1 and 2).

Requirement three and four point to the increased awareness of customer processes that shall derive from the artifact's layout. The developed method uses swimlanes to differentiate between activity levels, which in turn enable the classification of process elements according to aspects of interests. For interaction processes the well-established lines of the Service Blueprinting have been reused. This logic has been extended to the customer's side, so that now usage processes can be modeled as well. Thus, the customer and his or her processes stay in focus (requirement 3).

Each line of traditional Business Process Blueprinting points to a specific design question (requirement 4) and the lines of the enhanced BP^2 address the task to alter the usage design to gain further insight in order to be able to support the customer in his or her processes. Thus, (re-)design options are more apparent when using the method instead of traditional modeling techniques. This has already been shown by the case study of the traditional BP^2. Furthermore, the proposed (multi-level) procedure model not only serves as a guideline for an application of method but also contributes to strengthening the focus on the customer's side.

As all four requirements are considered by the developed artifact, an evaluation of its application in a real context seems reasonable. The next chapter therefore proposes to study the employment of method in practice. Because the literature review revealed that approaches of the traditional BP^2 are already well-established and accepted in both communities, the upcoming evaluation rather focuses on the evaluation of the enhanced BP^2 and the management of usage processes.

5 Evaluation of Business Process Blueprinting: a Case Study on the Application of the Method to the "BIOTRONIK Home Monitoring®" Service

After the design phase has been illustrated and a procedure model proposed in chapter 4, this chapter evaluates the artifact's utility (regarding the problem proposed in chapter 3.3). Before moving on to the case study, the author elucidates the necessity of evaluating this research and explains why a case study fits best to do so.

An evaluation can be described as the "...systematic determination of merit, worth, and significance of something..." (Hevner and Chatterjee 2010, p. 109). In Design Science Research, the focus lies on the examination of how business information is handled by using IT artifacts – either from a technical (e.g. accuracy) or socio-technical (e.g. usefulness for user) perspective. Due to promotional, scholarly and practical reasons an evaluation is a crucial element in DSR. It shows and tests the significance of the developed artifact for problem solving and examines its impact on business activities. Though initial evaluation frameworks have recently emerged (e.g. Cleven, Gubler and Hüner 2009; Pries-Heje, Baskerville and Venable 2008) current DSR literature still provides little guidance for justifying the choice of evaluation strategy and method (Sonnenberg and vom Brocke 2012a, p. 71).

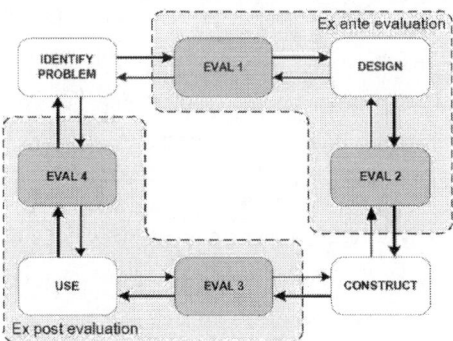

Figure 22. Evaluation activities within a DSR process (Sonnenberg and vom Brocke 2012b, p. 392)

However, Sonnenberg and vom Brocke (2012b) recently introduced an evaluation framework for the DSR process with four evaluation activities to be performed. To ensure further rigor, this framework is described in short and applied to this research. According to the authors there are two points on the timeline of an artifact's development process where an evaluation of the artifact is feasible.

One is an ex-ante evaluation, which refers to the interior mode before the artifact's construction, in which prescriptive knowledge is generated that justifies and informs the artifact design pursued. They identify two evaluation activities that should be conducted at this stage. One concerns the problem statement and necessity of research, which results in a justification of research gap and design objectives. Exemplary evaluation criteria are factors such as "importance" and "novelty" (EVAL 1). This activity has been executed through a detailed description of underlying concepts and the literature review in chapter 3.2.2, which identified a research gap and sustains the importance of research. The other ex-ante evaluation activity considers the choice of the artifact's design specifications using criteria such as feasibility, understandability, clarity or simplicity (EVAL 2). One method to evaluate this activity is, among others, logical reasoning. This has been applied with the detailed description of how the artifact merges two established approaches and how it transfers their basic logic to the customer side. The results of both activities have been put up for discussion and supported in several reviews and scholarly debates at conferences (i.a. Gersch, Hewing and Schöler 2011; Gersch, Schöler and Hewing 2010, 2011; Hewing 2011). The artifact developed is coherent with current research and has found acceptance in both research communities. Thus, these activities seem to fulfill the requirements of an ex-ante evaluation.

After the construction of the artifact, an ex-post evaluation of the artifact's application is proposed that describes the exterior mode of the research process and refers to descriptive knowledge of the real use of the artifact. The first activity in this stage is a demonstration of how the artifact functions (EVAL 3). This activity has been conducted in the description of a practical example (tracking jogging) in which the application and the added value of the method has been demonstrated. The other activity recommended aims to prove the usefulness of the artifact in a naturalistic setting such as a business environment (EVAL 4). Evaluation methods for this activity run the gamut from case studies to field experiments and surveys. As the activities EVAL 1 to 3 have already been approved to a certain degree this chapter concentrates on the fourth evaluation activity.

According to Friedman and Wyatt (2010, pp. 28–29), evaluation studies usually follow a certain structure. Evaluations start with someone, an individual or a group, who wants to know something. After the goals or questions of the evaluation are consolidated with these stakeholders, appropriate investigations are conducted in order to collect data. Finally, the results of the data analysis are reported back to the stakeholders. A common mistake of many evaluation studies is that there is no or only vague verbalization of the evaluation's goals, which in turn most likely do not address the questions of the stakeholders (Jain 1991, p. 14). Therefore, in this chapter the intentions of the evaluation and its design shall be properly explained.

This design research primarily addresses academics interested in BPM and correspondingly requires empirical evidence, defined in Design Science Research as "…a demonstration that the design can be utilized to solve real problems" (Hevner and Chatterjee 2010, p. 200). Practioners of the DSR approach are also interested in proof that this method is advantageous. Therefore, the goal of this evaluation is to survey whether the artifact developed dissolves the problem highlighted in chapter 3.3, and whether it can be regarded as an answer to the question of how customer processes can be modeled beneficially through Business Process Management. Because the method focuses on a relatively young research area, it aims to initiate activities that have not yet been conducted in such detail: the management of customer (usage) activities. To put it in concrete terms, the aim of this evaluation is to show that customer processes can be visualized in Business Process Modeling by using the enhanced Business Process Blueprinting, which in turn points to new design options not previously identified. Accordingly, the question of this evaluation is:

Can customer processes be illustrated and (re-)design options identified by using Business Process Blueprinting?

So far, no methodological standard has been established for the evaluation of artifacts in DSR. But there is a range of methods that are typically applied (Siau and Rossi 2011, pp. 256–260), which all can be assigned to the observational, analytical, experimental, testing or descriptive category (Hevner et al. 2004, p. 86). Among the most common methods are case studies, controlled or field experiments and surveys. Additionally, prototyping is sometimes used in software development as a means of evaluation. But as this research does not focus on the functional evaluation of an individual instance, which in this case would be a template for modeling suites, this method is not suitable. For further reading on the variables and values of artifacts' evaluation in DSR, the review of existing approaches by Cleven, Gubler and Hüner (2009) is recommended.

However, in this instance a case study is most appropriate. According to Hedrick, Bickman and Rog (1993) the preferred method can be preselected by the form of the research question. If the research question is based on the interrogative words "who", "what", "where", "how many" and/or "how much", surveys or archival analysis seem most fitting. Explanatory research questions, which rely on the interrogative pro-adverbs "how" and/or "why", lead to the use of case studies, experiments or historical analysis as the preferred method. As the primary research question of this project is how customer processes are perceived and modeled by using Business Process Blueprinting, an explanatory method seems appropriate. The historical method focuses on a retrospective investigation of documents. Experiments can be conducted in a setting where all the variables that are relevant to the subject can be controlled. Neither method is appropriate here. The evaluation of a newly developed artifact cannot be performed retrospectively. Furthermore, the artifact regards a new approach on how to look at processes and can hardly serve as an independent variable within an experiment.

Accordingly, the most promising method is the case study, which can be described as "an empirical inquiry that investigates a contemporary phenomenon within its real-life context, especially when the boundaries between phenomenon and context are not clearly evident" (Yin 2009, p. 18). The case study method is an in-depth examination of an instance or event including the collection and analysis of data as well as the report of results. The researchers try to get insights on the subject matter through exploratory and descriptive statements. As the evident data is gathered through observation, interviews and the collection of artifacts or documents (Yin 2009, p. 102), case studies offer a chance of capturing the object of research in all its complexity, including various dimensions and relevant variables. In addition, this method has already been used several times for the evaluation of modeling methods (e.g. Fitzgerald 1997; Kawalek and Wastell 2002; Lutherer et al. 1994; Salo and Abrahamsson 2004).

Hevner et al. (2004, p. 86) define a case study in Information Systems as the in-depth study of an artifact in a business environment. Since we want to study the artifact's implementation process in a business environment, our case needs to deal with the actual deployment of the method by an individual within a company. This case study therefore describes the deployment of method in practice. When insight on a specific issue is needed and the case itself takes a supportive role, Stake (1994, p. 237) uses the term "instrumental case study". Though the case is still described and examined in detail, the case itself is less important than the process being studied. It primarily serves to advance understanding. Under specific circumstances, a single-case study is sufficient for evaluation (Yin 2009, p. 47). In critical testing (as in this case), a single case can already confirm whether the objects of the solution are addressed. Thus, critical testing answers the evaluation's question of whether customer processes can be illustrated and (re-)design options identified using Business Process Blueprinting. A single case can also be used when it is representative or typical, meaning that the phenomenon observed in the case could be transferred to other cases (Stake 1994, p. 243). To facilitate understanding, this empirical study is based on a single-case design, representative for the phenomenon of interest. The case study relates to the field of e-health. Due to the accumulation of a huge amount of data, e-health is a prime field for potential insight on customer activities. Therefore it can be seen as characteristical.

Data was collected using the techniques participant observation and focused discussion. In participant observation, the researcher takes an active role in the case study. This technique enables the analysis of the events and content of the case in real time. Because the subject matter is new and complex, it was necessary to apply this technique as it helps to support the progression of the case study. This approach picks up the assumptions of Action Research in which a complex issue is studied by introducing change and observing the effects (Baskerville 2001, pp. 194–195; Hevner and Chatterjee 2010, p. 182). Further information was collected by a focused discussion in which the author and the company's representative discussed the course of events and redesign options. In the following chapters, the case study is explained in detail, giving insight on the choice of unit, the case study setting and the results that reinforce the proof-of-concept.

5.1 Description of the Service "BIOTRONIK Home Monitoring®" for Implantable Electronic Cardiovascular Devices

A case study in the field of e-health illustrates the artifact's utility for the analysis of customer activities. In cooperation with the medical technology company BIOTRONIK SE & Co. KG, which is headquartered in Berlin and provides cardiovascular solutions in the areas of cardiac rhythm management, electrophysiology and vascular intervention to all continents of the world, a project for modeling their monitoring service was initiated. The goal of the project was to visualize their processes from a market-oriented perspective and to identify (based upon this) new design options in order to extend the range of services offer.

As this case study deals with a very complex medical indication that concerns multiple parties, a comprehensive description of setting is required. To understand the design options discovered using the BP², one needs first to know the conditions the monitoring service acts within. First, a brief insight into the therapeutic area focused upon is given in order to identify the general characteristics of the market. Special attention needs to be paid to the incentives of the protagonists, which are indispensable for the realization of service (redesigns). After this, BIOTRONIK's service "Home Monitoring" is explained in more detail, so that the reader fully understands the context and the case study. Finally, the case study is explained after the general description of the service. For the sake of clarity, the following information is summed up with additional information in a short profile that is attached to the appendix (Appendix 11).

5.1.1 Cardiac Rhythm Disorders and their Treatment

BIOTRONIK is one of the biggest manufacturers of implantable cardiac pacemakers and defibrillators worldwide. Furthermore, BIOTRONIK offers comprehensive solutions for the diagnosis and treatment of cardiovascular diseases. These solutions are meant to preserve and extend the lives of patients.

Cardiovascular disease is the major cause of death in the western world and it is predicted to remain so at least over the next decades (WHO 2004, p. 122). The most common cardiovascular diseases include cardiac infarction, arrhythmia and insufficiency (European Society of Cardiology 2011). These are concisely explained in the following.

Myocardial infarction, colloquially known as "heart attack", refers to the death of the heart muscle tissue (myocardium) due to a lack of blood and consequently oxygen supply. It is usually caused by a blood clot (thrombus) formed after the rupture of an arteriosclerotic plaque in a coronary artery, which leads to occlusion of the vessel. As a consequence of myocardial infarction, the myocardium can turn into scar tissue, which can lead to heart failure or be the origin of cardiac arrhythmia.

Cardiac arrhythmia is an irregular heartbeat. Bradycardia is defined as a heart rate of less than 60 beats per minute. Symptoms of a bradycardia are very diverse as they may range from dizziness to blackouts or even a complete cardiac arrest, including cardiac shocks. In contrast, tachycardia denotes a continuous accelerated pulse of over 100 beats per minute. Tachycardia of the heart chamber can result in ventricular flatter or fibrillation, life threatening and sometimes fatal events.

Third, cardiac insufficiency (commonly known as heart failure) is a syndrome that is caused by various cardiac diseases such as coronary artery disease, arrhythmia or myocarditis (inflammation of the heart muscle) and describes the pathological inability of the heart to meet the body's metabolic demands because of a disturbed cardiac pump function. Complaints of chronic left-heart failure can be similar to those of bradycardia. Right-heart failure can lead to swollen arms, legs or lungs due to water deposits.

While vascular diseases are handled primarily through medication and a change of lifestyle, cardiac arrhythmia and heart failure are supplementally treated with pacemakers (PM), implantable cardioverter-defibrillators (ICD) or systems for cardiac re-synchronization therapy (CRT). All three implantable electronic cardiovascular devices are based on the technique of releasing electric impulses to stimulate the heart's muscles. PMs are used, for example, for the treatment of patients with bradycardia. The PM device can sense the induction of the heart and support stimulation by a contraction of the atrium or ventricle. ICDs are designed to terminate fibrillation by giving short intracardiac electric shocks via a pacemaker lead located in the right ventricular. Patients with heart failure who meet certain criteria may be additionally treated with a CRT device, which synchronizes the interactions of the two heart chambers and within the relative heart chambers by means of permanent electrical pulses. For further information on cardiovascular diseases and their treatment, see the Guidelines Compendium of the European Society of Cardiology (2011).

5.1.2 The Market of Implantable Electronic Cardiovascular Devices and its Framework Conditions

At present more than 2000 different implantable electronic cardiovascular devices (IECD) by 26 different companies are available on the market. The global market of IECD is dominated by five companies. Most companies are American, namely Medtronic, St. Jude Medical and Boston Scientific. The biggest manufacturer outside the United States of America is BIOTRONIK. The smallest of these device companies is Sorin that is headquartered in Italy.

Producers primarily fabricate IECDs and related equipment to provide hospitals or outpatient centers with implants that are needed for the surgery of affected patients. This contact can be seen as a B2B relation. The producers do not usually have immediate contact to the final customer, the patient who benefits from the devices' electrical impulses. By delivering the necessary sub-components for surgery and post-operative treatment, they mostly maintain commercial transactions only with hospitals and out-patient centers.

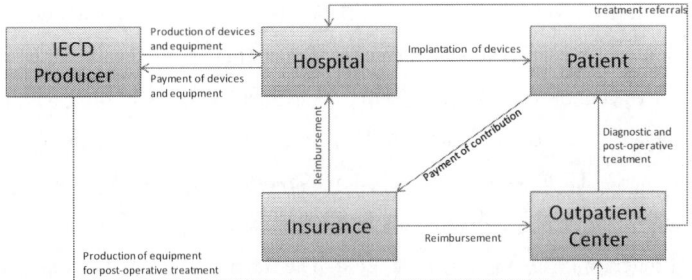

Figure 23. Relations between the protagonists of IECD supply

When a cardiac arrhythmia or heart insufficiency is diagnosed and an implant is oblig-atory, the (registered) doctor advices the patient about the next steps to be taken and may arrange an appointment for the patient with the hospital or outpatient station that can provide surgery. There, the patient is briefed in detail about the surgical procedure. In those two consultations – one with the registered doctor, the other with the hospital staff – the patient also is informed about the current state of implantable electronic cardiovascular devices and additional offers. As the patient is (usually) unfamiliar with this issue, the doctors conducting the conversation can strongly influence the choice of device. For instance, because a company's system is widely used in the region and the processes for post-operative treatment in the doctor's office are geared accordingly, the doctor may direct the patient to hospitals that usually implant devices from this specific company due to benefits in procurement and easier administration. The busi-ness relationship with the medical service providers for the distribution of devices has two important implications. First, the medical technology companies need to know the decision-making processes of the hospital's buying center and all persons involved. Second, they also may woo the medics in order to trigger preferences for their own products, which can lead to a recommendation for their devices.

The horizontal value chain ends in a device maintenance loop. This means that after surgery, the patient needs to attend post-operation treatment at regular intervals at the outpatient centers, in which the doctor checks on device functionality and adjusts the parameters programmed to the course of the disease.

In addition to the indirect contact of IECD producers to the end customers, there are also special features of treatment financing. Depending on the health care system of the respective country (i.a. Wieners 2000), companies operating in the health care sector are subject to a more or less highly regulated environment containing severe restrictions, particularly with regard to administration and financing. In general, the health care sector can be differentiated into a first and second health care market (i.a. Gersch, Lindert and Hewing 2010, pp. 2–3). The main criterion for distinguishing between the two markets is whether or not the funding of the service is covered by statutory health insurance.

The second health care market rests upon the market-based coordination of suppliers and customers, where common mechanisms of the market economy rule. This market consists primarily of privately paid products and services that are related to the field of health (e.g. over the counter, fitness and wellness services).

In contrast, the first health care market, also referred to as public health, consists of the governmentally directed standard provision of medical care financed by the social security system. This includes all medical care that is granted by health insurance companies. Members pay an (income-related) fee to the health insurance companies and in return get the health service coverage that the insurance companies and medical providers have agreed upon. Further explanations and a conceptual model of the public health care system can be found in Santerre and Neun (2012). As monitoring is part of the standard provision, integrated care concepts are currently not of concern. Therefore, companies like BIOTRONIK, which operate almost exclusively in the first health care market, also need to interact with public and private insurance companies in addition to medical service providers. For instance, in the public health care system of Germany, health insurance companies transfer a merit-based amount of money to the hospitals each year for the purchase of implants. The amount depends on the number of IECD surgeries conducted in the previous year and planned for the upcoming period. The exact amount transferred by the health insurances for one IECD surgery is set by the funds available for this domain and the total number of surgeries performed in Germany. Thus, hospitals and outpatient centers able to provide outpatient surgery obtain a fixed amount of money for each device implanted. Accordingly, in the short term they save money and increase their yield when they cut the purchase prices for implants. Because all implants possess a certified standard of quality, many hospitals focus strongly on price and try to beat down prices by comparing offers and thereby pressuring the producers of devices. As this procedure also lowers the amount of money transferred by the insurance companies in the long term, it can cause a downward spiral that puts producers under further pressure. Some producers react to this and try to strengthen their negotiating power by cross-subsiding their implants through a combined sales contract that includes equipment for other domains. Nonetheless, profit is not made easily in this market of tough conditions and fierce competition.

5.1.3 Monitoring Services for Implantable Electronic Cardiovascular Devices

As the market for implantable electronic cardiovascular devices is highly competitive, the players try to differentiate themselves by offering additional services like the remote monitoring systems that have recently begun to gain ground. Currently there is a window of opportunity in the telemedicine sector to set standards, establish (new) structures (including competitive advantages by implementing new or changing old business models) and to actively participate in these transformation processes.

Four of the five IECD producers named above have funded the development of such a monitoring system. Each of their monitoring systems follows the same basic concept, which includes at least four components (Jung et al. 2008). It starts with the recording of events by the (1) implant, which is able to transfer the data collected manually or automatically to a (2) transmission device. This device is connected by a mobile network (GPRS) or landline with a (3) central server for data storage. There the data is edited and prepared for presentation at a (4) front end platform (e.g. internet, e-mail, fax and/or text messages). The medical service provider can now access and analyze the data and initiate all necessary steps, such as contacting the patient to make an appointment for an additional check up.

Figure 24. Home Monitoring - path of data including business partners (modified from BIOTRONIK 2013)

To assure compatibility with pre-existing systems, all monitoring concepts are aligned to the Health Level 7 norm, which is the standard for the exchange of data between the computer systems of organizations in health care. A multitude of information is collected and subsequently transmitted by the implant, ranging from technical parameters like battery voltage and lead impedances to diagnostic conditions such as atrial or ventricular heart rhythm episodes. A reference list of parameters evaluated by implants can be found in Jung et al. (2008, p. 77).

The monitoring service is an additional service for outpatient centers and patients with implantable electronic cardiovascular devices. The central proposition of the remote monitoring of patients with implantable devices is the improvement of treatment documentation through the regular transmission of systemic and diagnostic data (improved patient management). The supplementary information provided by the system promises to lower medical costs and contribute to patient safety as well as quality of life (Saxon et al. 2010). Critical events are now registered on a daily basis and not only at regular follow-ups. This way the medical service provider can intervene in time, preventing an impairment of health. For the sake of completeness it should be mentioned that the monitoring system is classified as a follow-up check-up and not as an emergency service. This means that the treating physician is not in charge in case of emergencies, even though s/he might be able to intervene due to a timely notification by the system. This differentiation is especially important when it comes to legal disputes. The monitoring service is an addition to the traditional treatment and should result in a more closely meshed check-up that potentially enables an earlier detection and intervention.

As already stated earlier, producers of devices offer such services to distinguish themselves from competitors and actively influence the development process to their own benefit. Nonetheless, in order to gain acceptance and sustain usage, it is mandatory to take into account the underlying incentives of every protagonist involved in and affected by the home monitoring service (listed in Figure 23). One needs to understand the subjectively perceived assets and drawbacks from each protagonist's perspective when adopting the system. The processes of hospitals, which are not in charge of after-operation treatment, are almost unaffected by the service, as they "only" implant the devices. Though differentiation may be one incentive, hospitals merely focus on the unit price. The remaining three protagonists (patient, outpatient center and insurance) have a stronger influence on service diffusion. Therefore it is important that they perceive the service as beneficial and are convinced of its advantages.

If the patient does not see the service as an intrusion into privacy, the service is mostly favorable for this person, unless the insurance does not reimburse the extra charges for auxiliary monitoring. Then the one-time costs must be compensated by the subjectively perceived advantages. Through a faster diagnosis, treatment can be initiated more quickly, leading to increased life quality and life expectancy. For instance, the number of inadequate shocks in patients with an ICD can be reduced by quicker responses (Mabo et al. 2012). Surveys report that patients have an increased sense of security, as the monitoring system gives them a high level of assurance that the IECD is working properly (Marzegalli et al. 2008; Schwab et al. 2008). Another major advantage is the omission of unnecessary follow-ups, saving the time patients previously spent to travel to the facility and wait in line (Varma et al. 2011).

The main users of the system are the medical service providers in charge of the post-operative treatment. As they are the essential protagonists for keeping the service running, they have to see this service favorably, and not as an extra work load. The cardiologists in the outpatient centers need to deal daily with the additional front-end information, as currently none of the monitoring services are capable of being integrated into the existing software-systems. For this reason, the new platform radically changes work routines and work flows. It may also require further training of staff and an upgrade of equipment. For instance, some monitoring platforms are only accessible via the web, but several centers do not have an internet connection at every working station for several reasons (e.g. data protection). As the service impacts the established workflow, it is regarded with suspicion. Convincing arguments are therefore required for implementation. The comprehensive database seems to enable a more tightly focused treatment. Using state-of-the-art scientific and technical knowledge to protect and promote the patient's well-being fits the ethical principles of medicine. However, most arguments focus on gains in efficiency and service effectiveness. The consistent and reliable information allows faster decision making (Crossley et al. 2011). Timetables and staff schedules can be planned according to the necessary treatments, which are now calculable in advance. Further, a study shows that monitored patients tend to keep their appointments (Varma et al. 2011). This relates to the perceived quality of the follow-up service, which is rated higher by patients equipped with a home monitoring system. In addition the monitoring service can also be seen as a competitive differentiator. Aside from the additional effort of having a supplemental system, this service does have considerable advantages for the medical service providers – especially for those setting up their infrastructure.

Finally, the insurance companies, which are financing this additional service, also need to benefit from this service. This means basically that the extra costs have to be counterbalanced by savings in post-operative treatments. That is why the providers, in cooperation with doctors, conduct clinical studies that should prove the medical and concurrent financial benefits for insurance companies. A series of current studies and scientific publications attest that costs can be saved. For instance, the coordination of follow-up treatments using the data collected can decrease the cost of total treatment by $650 (Raatikainen et al. 2008). This cost leverage is progressive in relation to the distance of the patient's home to the next care center (Eisner et al. 2006; Fauchier et al. 2005), and therefore especially promising in countries with a widespread rural population like Australia or the Scandinavian countries. Another study points out that the detection of critical events at a very early stage lowers the cost of hospital stays. The study determined an average saving of $1793 for the entire treatment (Mabo et al. 2012). Despite the evident benefits, insurance companies are hesitant to incorporate this service into their list of services covered. This is mostly due to their short refinancing period of usually just one year. Yet, costs savings accumulate over years of treatment. Nevertheless, some insurance already see this service as a means of differentiating themselves from their competitors and appealing to customers.

5.1.4 BIOTRONIK Home Monitoring®

Now that the setting has been described comprehensively, BIOTRONIK's home monitoring service and its special characteristics, which make the service especially worth studying, are explained in detail. BIOTRONIK started to develop its "Home Monitoring" (HM) service in the 1990s. First clinically applied in 2000, it is currently the leading monitoring service for IECD. Not only has the service been on the market the longest, with 3800 clinics in 55 countries it also represents the largest remote monitoring community worldwide.

Although all monitoring concepts share a common structure, the monitoring services differ in important details. One reasons for the competitive advantage of BIOTRONIK's service is its well-arranged concept, which provides patients and medical providers with a smooth operation of the system without any particular problems (Marzegalli et al. 2008; Schoenfeld et al. 2004). Of special concern from the patient's perspective is the effort that is needed for data transmission and the reliability of service, while medical providers benefit from the smooth workflow at the front end.

All other systems need the active cooperation of the patient to initiate data transmission. But a manual trigger can be a problem as most patients are of higher age and not very technophile. They may not know how to use the devices or simply forget to activate transmission. The whole service is based on the analysis of data and is therefore dependent on a fully functional transmission. Thus handling needs to be easy to operate, intuitive and robust. BIOTRONIK's HM service has been designed to user specifications and is the only system that does not require the active participation of the patient. The implant transfers all data automatically (triggered by events) on a preserved radio frequency for implants (403 MHz) to the transmission device. The only limitation is that the patient needs to be within a distance of two meters to the transmitter. Otherwise the data transfer is put on hold until this is the case.

Further, in contrast to the competitors' products, the long range transmission is not only based on landline, but also on 4-band GSM and GPRS mobile technology, which makes the system also work away from the patient's stationary home, even beyond the respective country's borders. At present, the mobile system functions in more than 70 countries. The transmission module, which is called Cardio Messenger, is delivered with a pre-configured SIM card and therefore ready to use immediately. For this data transmission service, BIOTRONIK remits a single payment for each SIM card to the T-Systems GmbH, which in return is in charge of the communication infrastructure. The data processing center is equipped with IBM technology. The additional costs for the data transmission and handling are passed on to the purchasers as they are allocated to the extra charges for the auxiliary monitoring service.

The front end, named Service Center, filters and prioritizes clinical information about the status of the patient according to the user's specifications in order to reduce workload and increase the efficiency of patient care. This includes intuitive and clearly structured menu navigation for smooth operation with only a few mouse clicks. For instance, the Service Center uses a traffic light scheme, which marks event notifications in green, yellow or red, to direct the physician's attention to important cases and provide an easy overview of each patient's status. Another special feature is that physicians can activate a LED on the Cardio Messenger's display to request a call back from the patient.

Due to the special features that enable the operation of the system without complications, the service is very much appreciated by patients and medical service providers. For this reason, the system's diffusion accelerated so fast that it is now the largest remote community worldwide and delivers an extensive database for the analysis of customer's activities. Currently, more than 100.000 implants across the globe are monitored daily by the system. The system's wide dissemination offers the possibility of making a significant impact on patient activities by redesigning processes and is therefore a worthwhile object for a case study.

5.2 Process Mapping and Analysis using Business Process Blueprinting

As the redesign of customer activities seems very promising for this service, a project for modeling the monitoring service was initiated in May 2012 by the Competence Center E-Commerce of the Freie Universität Berlin together with the medical technology company BIOTRONIK, a previous spin off of the Technische Universität Berlin. Analog to design science, the goal of this project contained a practical and a scientific dimension. For the company it was appealing to identify stimulating redesign ideas for further differentiation of their service and to have their processes visualized in a flowchart that also contained the perspective of the customer. From a scientific viewpoint, the project evaluates whether it is possible to model customer activities and identify design options by using the artifact. The project took place in two phases – process mapping (chapter 5.2.2) and process analysis (chapter 5.2.3). The processes were modeled and subsequently discussed in the period between April and June 2012.

The process mapping phase contained activities for understanding the process entities in detail in order to visualize processes. Through the study of literature and the company's information material, first process models were created using Business Architect of IDS Scheer's ARIS suite. Further unwritten information was gathered in two interview sessions with a representative of the company who was in charge of marketing and communication for the HM service at this time. As some of the processes visualized refer to activities in the medical service providers' sphere, a registered doctor and an assistant physician also reviewed the processes and explanations.

After the final revision and approval of process visualizations, options for redesign were discussed with the BIOTRONIK representative in the process analysis phase. In contrast to usual process analyses, the focus was not on the internal activities of the company, but on the interaction of protagonists and the customer's perspective – especially the interpretation of processes beyond the service providers' impact.

Table 8. Overview of meetings with BIOTRONIK representatives

Date	Participant	Focus
2012-04-18	Senior Marketing Manager	Project Initiation
2012-05-16	Communications and Marketing Manager	Process Mapping
2012-05-23	Communications and Marketing Manager	Process Mapping
2012-06-13	Communications and Marketing Manager	Process Analysis

5.2.1 The horizontal Process Chain from the Patient's Point of View

To get an overview of the processes modeled, it is reasonable to first illustrate the core processes that have been reviewed. Usually, internal processes concerning production or marketing would have been modeled when mapping processes. Figure 25 visualizes a prototypical model of such an internal view of the company's processes which does not consider the customer and his activities.

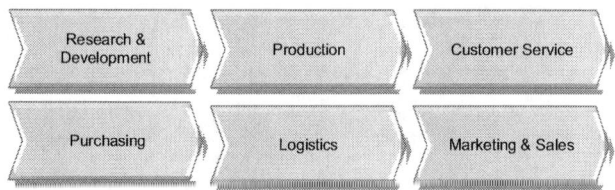

Figure 25. Internal view of company processes

Yet, if one regards the shift of view from an internal to an external perspective as has been discussed in chapter 3.1.2, it is basically the patient who initiates and passes through a process chain. The processes of the company submit themselves to the superior overall process of cardiac rhythm disorder treatment. The chain starts with the detection of the cardiovascular disease and ends in a loop of follow-up treatments. All processes are aligned to support the patient's well-being. It is actually the patient and not the other protagonists who directs the processes. In order to identify effective redesign options, an illustration of the patient's value chain is advisable, because s/he is the ultimate consumer who is affected by these redesign options. That is the reason why this project visualizes the core processes of servicing an implant patient instead of the internal processes of BIOTRONIK's HM service system. In consultation with the in-

terviewees mentioned above, the four main processes mapped in Figure 26 were identified for the treatment of patients with cardiac rhythm disorders.

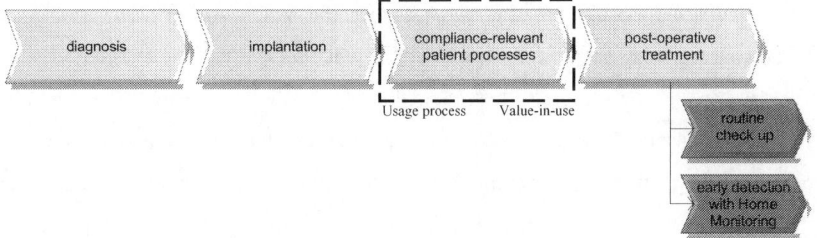

Figure 26. Core processes to service an implant patient

In the following, the process chain will be explained in short. The process chain begins
with the diagnosis of a disorder, which ends – if an implantation is necessary – with a
referral to the hospital. After the operation, the patient needs to attend routine check-
ups at periodic intervals. It is also recommended that the patient adjust his or her conduct in ways that are known to positively influence the course of the disease. The sub-
processes in Figure 26 that are marked in dark grey are the ones that are strongly influenced by the additional HM service. First, a Service Center platform is needed to gain
access to the data of the implant at the routine check-up. The staff needs to interact
with a system that runs parallel to the usual software. Because the effort needed for the
check-up can be calculated in advance, the HM service can also affect the timetable
and resource management. The biggest alteration of workflow however is the additional activity due to the early detection of critical events by the HM service. Doctors
can now pro-actively react to occurrences that threaten patients' cardiovascular systems or decide to change the current treatment strategy (i.a. programming or medication).

After reading chapter 5.1, one may understand why it may be advantageous to visualize this processes from the perspective of the protagonist to whom the process chain is
aligned, in this case the patient. Though process models with an internal perspective
are still important to discover efficiency potentials, they do not cover the special characteristics of the IECD market or promote discussions about improvements in effec-

tiveness. This relates especially to the consideration of incentives and the impact of the other protagonists. For example, consultations with doctors can be seen as part of the system's distribution as they strongly influence the patient in his or her choice of IECD. One feedback from the company's representative was that the external view on processes is the only process illustration that covers the special market conditions, which is very useful for further documents such as presentations or handouts as well as for the familiarization (of new employees) with the topic. Furthermore, the aggregated perspective on the overall process chain is the first step to identify customer processes. For instance, in this case study one of the four core processes relies heavily on the customer's performance. The following chapters examine the application of the BP² for the visualization and analysis of processes.

5.2.2 Visualization of Processes

After an overview of the customer-oriented core processes for the treatment of cardiac rhythm disorders and an explanation of the advantages of such a view, the visualization of the processes will be described. Figure 27 gives an overview of the process models that visualize the core processes. All process models can be seen in further detail in the appendix. Due to the BP² method presented, there are now two ways to illustrate these processes. One is the common process model in which the processes flow from top to bottom. These process models are presented in the second row of the graph. The other possibility is to align the process elements to the specific activity layers of Service Blueprinting. This is the BP² illustration type, which can be seen in the third row of the graph. In the direct comparison of the two visualization styles, one may already recognize the distinct structuring of the BP² model. This is the result of the swimlane concept and provides additional information due to important design aspects. The BP² method also facilitates the illustration of customer processes. It not only raises awareness for these kinds of processes, but also makes it easier to initiate a process model. Due to the dividing lines, processes with a higher abstraction level, which for instance contain elements that are not connected to each other (for example the empowerment processes in this case study), also appear more structured when using the swimlanes rather than a loose collocation without any activity levels. This is because the swimlanes assign process elements to a managerial context and thus provide a stronger focus on customer-oriented process design.

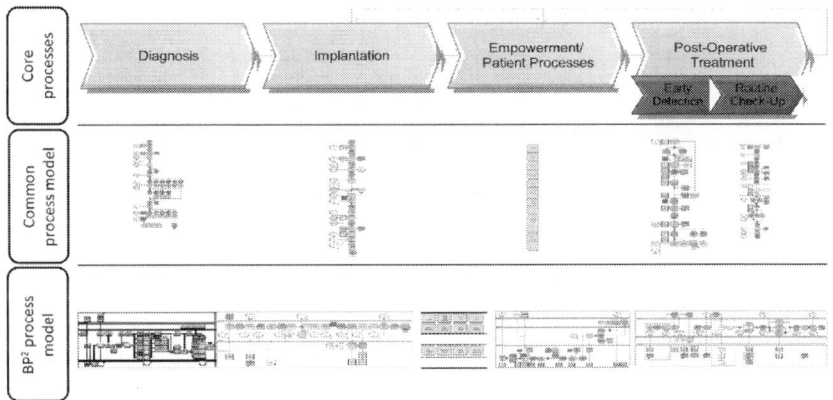

Figure 27. Overview of the process models

The models were created by the author using ARIS Business Architect 7.2, which is includes the modeling notations of IDS Scheer's eEPC. The process structure and the processes elements included are based on discussions with the company's Communications and Marketing Manager on May 16 and 23, 2012, the company's information material and relevant publications such as clinical and patient guidelines (i.a. Barold, Stroobandt and Sinnaeve 2003; European Society of Cardiology 2011). Further inquiries were clarified via telephone or e-mail. Additionally, two cardiologists looked over the processes and made small suggestion for improvement, in particular as regards medical terms.

The activities and events that represent the main drive of the process were illustrated first. Additional process elements such as organization units, documents and application systems were subsequently added. In order to get an insight on how well common process models can be changed into BP²-based models, the processes were first visualized in a common process layout. Afterwards, swimlanes were inserted and process elements reallocated to the correct activity level. Swimlanes were added by simple drawing lines and labeling them. The transformation of these processes to a BP² model was easy to conduct as only little time was necessary and no complications occurred.

Because the activity levels were unambiguous as defined by clear criteria (see Appendix 10), there was no uncertainty in the assignment of the process elements.

As the customer-induced process elements are of primary interest, it should be stated that the secondary activities, such as support, preparation and facility, have been consolidated in one activity level. Because the focus is on customer activities and direct interaction (primary provider activities) rather than on internal processes, the level of abstraction is set to operational process flows (Scheer and Bräbander 2010, pp. 255–257), which results in a reduced number of support and preparation activities. Thus these activities have been consolidated with facility elements such as the IT infrastructure. Accordingly, there is no further differentiation of elements below the "Line of internal interaction". However, as customer activities are the subject of analysis in this case study, this can be disregarded.

5.2.2.1   Visualization of Processes with Direct Interaction

Processes with direct interaction are described first. These represent the first layer of the BP². The activities visualized for the interactive core processes "Diagnosis", "Implantation" and "Post-Operative Treatment" can be seen in the illustrations in Appendix 12 to Appendix 19. As the focus of the evaluation is on autonomous customer processes, interaction processes were merely visualized. Although the illustrations are discussed, processes are not studied with the aim of identifying potentials as regards efficiency or effectiveness. However, because they give further credence to the previously evaluated advantages of the BP² method for the management of service processes with direct interaction, they are mentioned here in short.

As in the illustration of the traditional BP², the process illustration omits trivial events to support an easy understanding of the process flow and avoid redundancies. This concerns in particular events that naturally follow the preceding function, but do not themselves carry additional information. It should also be noted that due to consistent scales the captions of some of the models' elements are not presented in their entirety.

Because they are still comprehensible in this context and can be seen in full in the data files attached to this document, this matter is of little importance.[3]

The first four models in the appendix illustrate the processes using the traditional syntax (Appendix 12 to Appendix 15). Though they are very structured, they do not consider the activity levels of the BP². These are followed by the BP² version of these models (Appendix 16 to Appendix 19). In the direct comparison of both visualizations one may notice the additional information within the swimlanes of the BP². These involve yet another focus of the analysis which may not have been considered using the usual syntax. It can be seen that the BP² creates a space to highlight matters for further considerations. The contrasting juxtaposition of graphs affirms the advantages of the BP². The customer gets at one glance the information about when and how the patient integrates him- or herself in the service process and which processes the patient perceives. This information is not present in the common visualization of processes. Also (technical) elements such as the supporting system become more prominent.

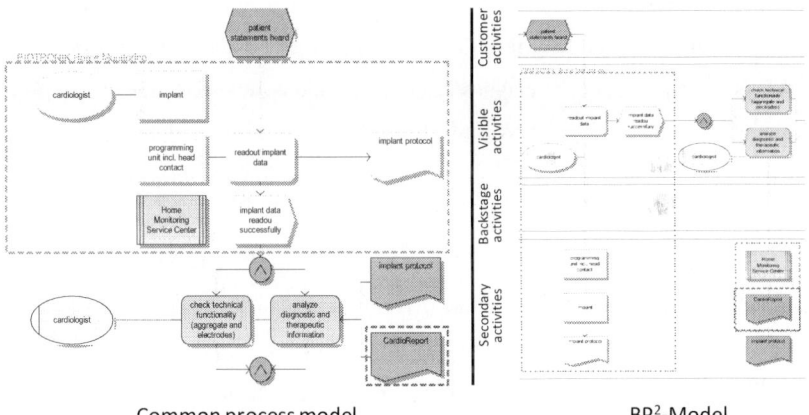

Common process model   BP²-Model

Figure 28. Comparison of the common and BP² process models using an excerpt of the routine check-up process (complete process in Appendix 14 and Appendix 18)

---

[3] In case of interest please contact the author for complete data files and further information.

A demonstrative example can be seen in Figure 28. In the traditional routine check-up of implant patients, the data, which has been collected by the implant since the last consultation, is read out via a programming unit that contains a contact head. Afterwards, the data that contains therapeutic information needs to be analyzed. With BIOTRONIK's Home Monitoring service, the physical attendance of the patient is obsolete for the collection of data (white process elements in the graph). This means that the time of technical procedures can be shortened in favor of longer consultations. This change can have an impact on effectiveness and efficiency. This issue is vividly visualized by the BP² model, through which one can clearly see that a whole segment of "onstage" activities are no longer necessary. This illustration can be used to communicate the benefits of monitoring system to stakeholders. In contrast, in the common visualization this issue is not directly displayed. It merely shows that some elements are now dispensable. Another conceivable scenario is that the physician analyses the data collected in advance, which may drive the performance of the consultation even more. In the process model, this would mean that the activity of diagnostic analysis would be shifted one activity level lower to backstage activities. The scenario can be developed even further. The diagnostic analysis could also be performed by a specialized physician, whose single task is to analyze the data for expert reports. This way the activity would be shifted to support activities below the "Line of internal interaction".

Another example of the advantage of the BP² chart can be seen in the early detection process based on the HM system and visualized in Figure 29. With a monitoring system the patient usually needs to initiate data transfer manually by applying a wand that interrogates the device and/or entering further information into the transmitter (Jung et al. 2008, p. 75). The advantage and one of the unique selling points of the BIOTRONIK HM is that all products are wireless and transmit data automatically via the mobile communications network without any patient assistance. This issue is very obviously illustrated by the BP² visualization style. The graph points out that the service operates autonomously most of the time, without anyone's assistance. As opposed to the common process model, the BP²-model emphasizes this issue with three empty activity levels that reflect the small number of human-human and human-computer interactions. As this part of the process does not contain any front-office activities, all process elements, including the software workflow, are beneath the "Line of internal interaction". The graph clarifies that in contrast to competing systems, the patient is not actively involved in the instigation data transfer. It can thus be used by the company to promote the unique stability of their system.

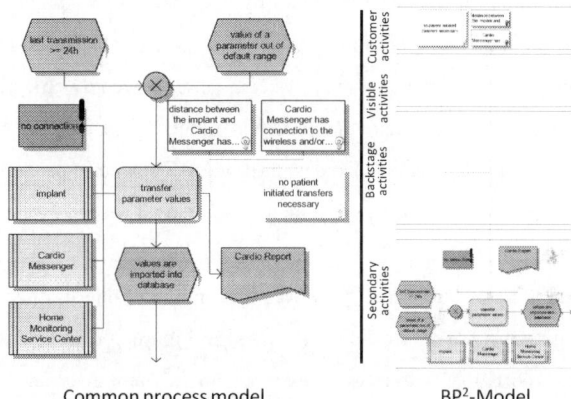

Common process model   BP²-Model

Figure 29. Comparison of the common and BP² process models using an excerpt of the routine check-up process (complete process in Appendix 15 and Appendix 19)

The examples given above affirm the advantages of the BP² method for the illustration of processes. In this case it can be used for the presentation of unique selling propositions. Processes elements that are very important for the system's diffusion are now visualized very clearly and can be used by the company for quick references. Nonetheless, one should remember that these process models are also particularly useful for the redesign of processes. This issue has already been exemplified by an example when the method was introduced (see chapter 4.1.1.3).

5.2.2.2   Visualization of Usage Processes

Now that process visualizations of direct interactions have been shown to be useful, we turn to the application of the enhanced BP². It is important to understand that this upcoming discussion is on the activities of patients only, though it also reflects the effect of redesign options on other protagonists.

The list of core processes to service an implant patient (see Figure 26) contains four interactive processes and only one process that is performed autonomously by the patient. In order to analyze options of supporting the patient in his or her autonomous processes, it is advisable to first get an idea of the tasks the patient should conduct to promote the treatment of his or her cardiac rhythm disorder. By studying information material about the medical condition (i.a. European Society of Cardiology 2011) and considering the comments made by the physicians interviewed, twelve generic salutary sub-processes were identified that should be performed by the patient. As the focus of analysis lies on the identification of redesign options for generic processes, these empowerment processes have been visualized in a main process model (Scheer and Bräbander 2010, p. 256) that reflects its elementary activities. At this aggregation level, activities are not interconnected; they are independent of one another and should be conducted continuously. The activities illustrated in Figure 30 can be seen as a collection of twelve important activities as regards the patient's empowerment.

Figure 30. List of activities the patient should conduct to promote the treatment of his or her cardiac rhythm disorder

It should be noted that these activities are of significant value for the overall outcome of treatment. The success of the therapy is to a great extent related to the empowerment, the cooperative behavior, of the patient. An inadequate consideration of medical advice on the part of the patient can cause a worse quality of life. So if the patient does not follow the doctor's recommendation, the treatment is very likely to fail. Problems may arise especially for patients that are newly diagnosed with the disease and have to adapt and change their lifestyle.

The recommended tasks may vary by indication. For instance, the activities "Measure weight daily" and "Restrict daily liquid intake" is mostly applicable to patients with heart insufficiency, because these activities are meant to detect pleural effusions. This term denotes fluids accumulated in the area that surrounds the lungs, often caused by a weak heart. Another example is the activity "Measure blood pressure", applicable mostly to people with tachycardia. In contrast, other activities such as "Observe symptoms" or "Keep check-up appointments" apply to all indications. It should be further stated that the activities are not ordered regarding their relevance.

After the visualization of all processes has explained in further detail, an analysis is made of the empowerment activities illustrated in this chapter. Because the enhanced BP² model is part of the process analysis, it will be explained in the next chapter.

5.2.3 Analyzing Usage Processes – Empowering the Patient

This chapter outlines possibilities to further support patients in their process activities. Empowerment activities were discussed on June 13, 2012, with the Communications and Marketing Manager of BIOTRONIK. Though the representative was already introduced to the concepts of SDL, value-in-use and usage processes during the meetings on process mapping on May 16 and 23, 2012, a comprehensive presentation was given on the topic to create a basis for the identification of redesign options concerning empowerment activities.

In order to gain insight on the usefulness of the artifact developed, an examination was conducted inspired by experimental procedure, providing information on the relationship of causes and effects by manipulating a specific factor (i.a. Hinkelmann and Kempthorne 2008). As already mentioned once, this approach considers assumptions of Action Research in which the issue of interest is studied by introducing change and observing its effects (Hevner and Chatterjee 2010, p. 182). In this case, the factor that was altered was visualization of the process. The following setting and tasks were written down and given to the test person, i.e. the company's representative.

The setting:

Patients with a diagnosed heart rhythm disorder can influence their long-term treatment outcomes and contribute to their own well-being through the following empowerment activities:

With the BIOTRONIK Home Monitoring service and its automatic data transfer, new possibilities arise of gaining insight into the empowerment activities of the patient. Further, on the basis of the information collected, one might even be able to redesign the service in order to (pro-actively) support the patient in his or her activities.

The tasks:

- *Consider redesign options for the Home Monitoring service that provide further insights on the patient's empowerment activities.*
- *Consider redesign options of the Home Monitoring service that may support the patient in his empowerment activities.*

Now, after the conceptual background of usage processes were thoroughly explained to the company representative and after the instructions were clearly set, her task was to reflect aloud on possible redesign options. Because the subject matter was still new and complex, the author took the role of a participating observer, who explained the test person's questions as they arose. Thereby the author was an influencing element. This is why the procedure should not be seen as an explanatory experiment, which gives details on cognitive processing. This examination rather affirms the usefulness of the method developed and fortifies the proof-of-concept. It should be treated as a detailed report of one step towards answering the evaluation's research question of whether customer processes can be illustrated and (re-)design option identified using Business Process Blueprinting.

As can be seen in the instructions, the twelve activities were first illustrated without any swimlanes. Because the modeling of customer processes was new to her, one could see that the task remained rather abstract for the test person. No managerial context was given to aid the test person's orientation. The result was that no redesign option was articulated.

Next, the representative was given the structured swimlane layout of the BP^2 and was asked to allocate each empowerment activity to one of the activity levels. In collaboration with the author, who moved each empowerment activity to the relative activity level in ARIS Business Architect 7.2, the test person reflected on the actual insights and influence of the Home Monitoring system. Then she was asked to repeat the task of identifying redesign options. Due to the layout of the enhanced BP^2, the task was easily understood. Now there was a context within which activities were aligned. It even facilitated playing around and thinking about how activities might be shifted to a lower activity level by redesigning processes. After the examination, the test person was asked to reflect on the BP^2 layout. The manager stated that by applying the method, it was easier to understand the issue of managing customer processes and the concept of redesigning process elements to get insight into or influence the patient. This observation thus shows that the issue became more tangible, which in turn fostered understanding.

Before we move on to the redesign options identified, we give a short statement on the transformation already completed as a result of the HM service. This serves further understanding of the project's focus and the method's application.

5.2.3.1 Reflecting the Change of Insight due to the Monitoring Service

On the basis of the extended BP^2, the representative of BIOTRONIK reflected with the author on the changing insight into the usually not examinable empowerment activities of the patient. An initial point was the illustration of insight without any monitoring system. In such a situation no insight is given into the patient activities for any protagonists. Therapy relevant parameters are analyzed at regular appointments only. Physicians merely access the data every time the patient attends the physical check-ups.

Thus, the data is assessed at large intervals. Empowerment activities cannot be tracked and are to be aligned above the "Line of insight".

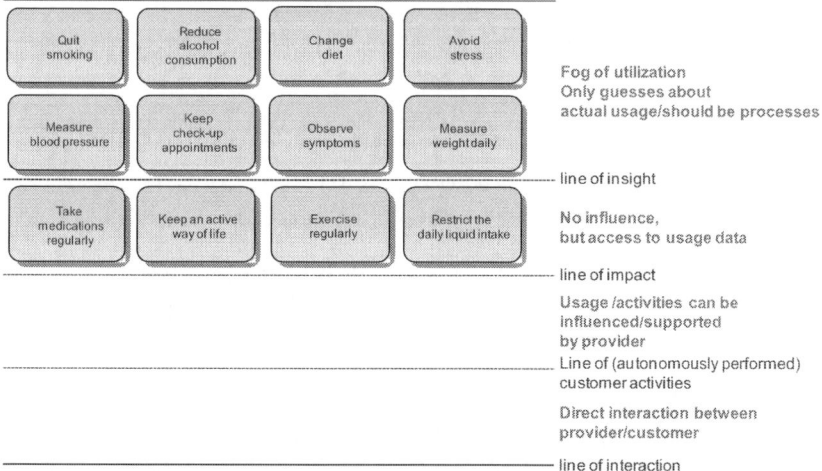

Figure 31. Insight on the empowerment activities with the HM visualized with the extended BP²

With the launch of the HM service and the daily transmission of system-related and diagnostic data, several empowerment activities shifted from the upper layer of invisible activities to the area of not influenceable activities, which is located between the "Line of visibility" and "Line of impact" (see Figure 31). This means that through the redesign of core processes to supply an implant patient, in concrete terms by introducing a home monitoring service, those activities can now be tracked by the service provider and physicians. For instance, with the impedance the restriction of the daily liquid intake can be observed. A change of impedance inside the thorax points to fluid accumulation. This tends to occur when patients affected by heart insufficiency do not restrict their liquid intake. Another example of further insight on the customer processes is the ability to monitor whether a patient exercises regularly and follows the recommendation to stay active with an active lifestyle. Through the combination of heart rate and the motion detection of the accelerometer, which is integrated in the IECD, a movement profile can be generated. Furthermore, by merging several parameters that are transmitted to the Service Center conclusions can be drawn with regard to whether medication has been taken as advised.

However, the processing of patient's data, which is performed by the medics in order to intervene at critical events, is of little assistance for the patient to sustain his or her empowerment activities. The current status of service does not contain considerations with regard to analyzing the patient's behavior and does not seize opportunities to support the patient in his or her task of contributing to the treatment of his or her disease.

5.2.3.2 Identifying Redesign Options to support Empowerment Activities

On the basis of current insight into patient activity, the representative of BIOTRONIK reflected in dialogue with the author redesign options to effectively influence and support the empowerment activities. This means that design options need to be identified, which lower activities that are visualized in the extended BP² to a subjacent activity level. Accordingly the company's representative was asked to consider arrangements that change the current classification of the twelve recommended activities to a lower layer. This implies that those activities will be either traceable or can be influenced by the provider. The already enabled insight into the activities mentioned above is one example of such a drift. The evolved ideas of this discussion were subsequently summed up with the author into four prospects for further redesigning options that support the patient in his or her usage processes. The corresponding drifts from one activity level to another are visualized in Figure 31 and in further detail in the Appendix 20 to Appendix 24.

The slide of activities is highlighted by bold lines. The sequence of graphs goes from left to right and illustrates the continuous slide of activities from insight over the impact layer to the lowest activity level, i.e. the interaction. The numbers in the lower lefthand corner of the graphs point to the relative redesigns that are listed below and explain the shift of activities in further detail.

Figure 32. Activity drifts from an activity level to lower one on the basis of the identified redesign options

The first graph reflects the current situations as it already has been discussed in chapter 5.2.3.1. In the second graph four activities slide below the "Line of insight", when one would implement the first redesign option. If one realizes redesign options two and three, eight activities move below the "Line of impact". As described in redesign option four, these activities can even be located at the lowest activity layer. Subsequently, the identified design options are described comprehensively:

(1) **Integration of additional components:** The first consideration was to integrate further components. Competing services like "Latitude" of Boston Scientific, for example, have the ability to connect other components like blood pressure cuffs and weight scales. The added information collected through these components can

have multiple influences. Regarding the usual monitoring service a more tightly focused therapy can be obtained.

Moreover, the externalization of activities to the patient like weight measuring, which are usually performed in interaction with the doctor at the examination, also leads to time saving, which in turn can be used for a longer consultation. As the tracing of activities is closely meshed, the identified design options two and four would also benefit from such additional data. Because further data is gathered about the patient activities, the relative elements have to be aligned between the "Line of insight" and "Line of impact" where the provider gains new insights.

Due to the early stage of the system's diffusion, the integration of additional components may yet seem unfavorable. Extras might overburden the patient and contradict the simplicity of BIOTRONIK's Home Monitoring service. Nevertheless, at a time when such a monitoring system is common, this design option seems essential.

(2) **Automated reporting system:** As already mentioned in the description of service, the monitoring service in its current form does not impact or address the patients. They merely have to passively enable the data transfer to the Cardio Messenger and receive in the case of a critical event a notification to contact the physician in charge. But especially patients who have been diagnosed recently and have been ordered to change their lifestyle may find it difficult to keep all the recommended activities in mind.

An automated reporting system that analyses the collected data regarding the empowerment activities may help to remind the patient of his or her duty. For instance, a weekly feedback via e-mail showing whether or how a person behaved according to his or her objectives could help train awareness of the problem and help those involved reconsider and consequently rearrange the performance. With a little bit of effort, such a reporting system is technically realizable. The report would help avoid or counter the often mentioned forgetfulness factor and could increase the patient's subjective perception of progress in his or her therapy. This design idea can be thought of as an extended version of the feedback that patients otherwise get in abbreviated form at the few follow-up appointments they receive. More thorough assistance would support those patients who need extra help meeting their objectives or are overwhelmed when left to their own devices. However, before implementing this design option the legal liability of such an automated reporting system would need to be established. On the BP² illustration activities would shift down from the layer of insight to the level of influencing the patient, which is between the "Line of impact" and "Line of (autonomously performed) customer activities".

(3) **Data insight for the patient:** Another idea that is quite easy to implement, is the inclusion of the patient as a user of the Service Center. Currently only the service providers have access to the metered vital parameters, which are only checked in case they are critical. In the meantime the gathered data lies idle and is unused though it may be of interest for the patient to view this data and thereby follow the progress of parameters. This way not only the assurance of operational reliability is given to the patient, but also a stronger commitment to therapy can be achieved. Furthermore, the collected data could be also utilized for other purposes than the treatment where such parameters are of relevance. For example, vital parameters are very useful for sports and could enable an enriching analysis of training. It can also be of interest for participants of current society platforms like Quantified Self, who share an interest in exploring and gathering knowledge about themselves by self-tracking and measuring their lives. They would thus take control of their health data and exchange information and advices about their own projects. As the topic has been picked up in the media recently the movement is growing (Quantified Self 2013). It is a prime example of how providers can hardly anticipate the customers' usage processes and the utilization of services or products. With the BP² the option of giving the patient insight into his or her own data has been identified. By subjective incentives the patient may feel more empowered. Accordingly the respective activities can be aligned to the layer of taking influence.

(4) **Mentoring by a (third-party) service provider:** This design option can be seen as an extended version of the second one as it relocates the concerned activities from the influenceable layer to the lowest. It was already mentioned that the medics can gain insight into relevant data for the post-operative treatment. Yet, due to time restrictions they often only view data that is relevant to observe the course of disease. Empowerment activities are only considered at larger intervals. This is where an additional service provider might be of use, one that observes and supervises the empowerment activities of the customer in particular. In this scenario the patient behavior is supported and/or controlled by the provider with the aim of achieving a higher level of empowerment and thus improve performance of the (total) treatment with extended health benefits. The interaction between patient and provider would be much more intensified. This supplementary service might be especially of advantage for patients having problems to adjust their lifestyle according to the medical advice. It absolves them further from their responsibility. The drift from the follow-up to comprehensive care might also influence the sense of well-being and security of the patient and lead to a better overall perception of service.

This additional service may be appreciated by medical professionals who are already overstrained by their daily workload. Unless the costs of this service were to be compensated by savings in the short term, it is unlikely the health insurances would cover the service. It would therefore most probably have to be funded through private payments by patients. In terms of privacy protection it seems reasonable to assume that the patient ought to be able to determine which provider supports and can view which activities. In the BP² graph the relative activities slide one level lower between the "Line of (autonomously performed) customer activities" and "Line of interaction" to the level of direct interaction.

The four summarized options can be clustered into two categories. Redesign option two and four support the empowerment of the patient from the service provider side, while options one and three cast a more active role for the patient by offering further possibilities of using the service for his or her empowerment.

The BP² served as a basis for discussion as it visualized all activities according to the insight and influence of the service provider and helped (with its task to lower activities from the levels above) to focus on the main issue of analysis. Due to the circumstance that the analysis of usage processes is a relatively new research area, one may lose track of the specific issue or miss the point. BP² with its concrete task supports one in recapturing the essential focus of analysis. Thus, this case study answers in the affirmative the initially raised question of whether one can illustrate customer processes and identify redesign options on the basis of the BP².

The possibility as well feasibility of the design options that have been identified by the company's representative and the author are currently under review of the company. The next chapter gives a short outlook on how the business system may develop in the future.

5.2.4 Future Prospects and further Developments in the Light of typical Stages in Industries' E-transformation

The development of e-health and the business system of BIOTRONIK can be anticipated by looking at typical stages of e-transformations. By comparing several industries Deise et al. (2000, p. 2) discovered four stages in the diffusion of e-business – each with its own characteristics (Figure 33). The first development is "channel enhancement", which implies operative improvements in the production and/or delivery of goods and services. One example would be the simplification of internal and external communication throughout e-mails, intra- or extranets to reduce the effort of protagonists. In the next stage, which is called "value chain integration", enterprises use technology to optimize the interaction and data transfer between all players involved. This stage also contains concepts like supply chain management or efficient consumer-response and often requires specific investments in a smooth data exchange between the application systems. The stage "industry transformation" characterizes radical changes of an industry, which are often driven by companies outside the particular industry. The usual value chain is replaced by newly established structures that address the altered customer needs through innovative bundles of services. The final stage describes the "convergence" of before separated industries that merged together over time and form henceforth a new market. Almost every industry affected by e-business can be classified into one of the four stages. Factors of the industry development are numerous and differ depending on factors like the importance of information, complexity of value chain, behavior of important players or the acceptability and willingness to pay on the customers' side (Gersch and Goeke 2007, p. 286).

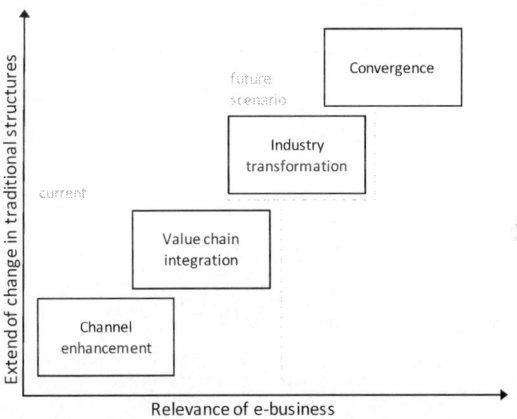

Figure 33. Four stages in the diffusion of e-business (modified from Deise, Wright and Nowikow 2000, p. 2)

Presently evolving topics like e-health, telemedicine and Ambient Assisted Living already indicate the change in the health care sector. With the growing diffusion and acceptance of e-health services future scenarios concerning the next stages can be considered. The HM service in its current form moves the IECD market to the stage of value chain integration. In its current form it is an isolated application that serves exclusively the indication of cardiac rhythm disorders. However, in the long-term an expansion of service for other scenarios seems reasonable.

Due to its solid operation and subsequent customer acceptance the system could serve as a fundament for additional services regarding other indications or even unrelated industries. An exemplary area of application would be the growing multi-morbidity of patients. Currently there is the window of opportunity to create standards and become a relevant and indispensable player beyond the IECD market. Anticipating the stages of industry transformation and convergence the company might be able to push its current system through cooperation with other enterprises and a growing network to become a central element for most e-health services in the long run. Besides the value that results from the direct use of the system, positive economies of scale and scope through the dissemination of the application might arise causing further (snowball-like) effects. Such diffusion could also lead to self-energizing effects like demand-pulls by the customers. In contrast to the usual distribution of devices through physicians, who can be seen as intermediaries, the customer pro-actively looks into the subject and due to its benefits demands this specific monitoring system. In marketing such an occurrence is called demand-pull. Figure 34 is a modified version of the graph in chapter 5.1.2 and illustrates such a shift in demand.

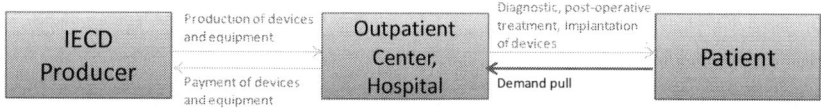

Figure 34. Demand-pull instead of push due to demanders' wants

This short excursion shows that the analysis of usage processes and possible design options as well as the reflection of the status quo can lead one to take a look ahead and anticipate with one's eyes open the opportunity to actively and knowingly change the current structures in order to position oneself advantageously for future competition. However, there are entrepreneurial risks to bear for acquiring such an opportunity.

5.3 Summary of the Artifact's Evaluation

In order to classify the relevance of what has been described before and regain an overview, this chapter sums up the evaluation. First the main findings of the case study are described. Afterwards the quality of this evaluation will be tested and further evaluation options elucidated.

5.3.1 Findings and Suggestions taken from the Case Study

The aim of the evaluation was to certify that customer processes, especially the usage processes, can be visualized and analyzed by applying the developed Business Process Blueprinting method. This section showed with the illustration of the interaction processes, usage processes and future scenarios that even complex contexts can be displayed when using this artifact. The case study portrays the artifact's utility for the analysis of customer activities. Because customer processes have been beneficially managed in Business Process Modeling, the problem emphasized in chapter 3.3 has been solved by the artifact. In this case study the following findings have been made:

- By starting with the illustrations of the customer process chain a totally different view is given on the overall process. The remarks on the importance of gaining the customer's perspective are pointed out with emphasis. Without such a perspective the special characteristics and unique selling propositions, which are of highest relevance for the system's distribution, would not have been visualized and consequently not considered in process management. With the change of perspective from internal to external these processes are now included for the analysis of processes.

- The visualization of processes with direct interaction based on the layer of the Service Blueprinting gives the operator additional information s/he might not be aware of otherwise. As already stated the customer processes and the customer's insight on processes as well as the technical elements can be seen at one glance. Furthermore, it gives the company the advantage to visually address the special circumstance the company interacts in. That the artifact eases the handling of usage processes has been approved by the company representative, who stated that the issue of customer processes management is more tangible when using the method.

- By using the BP² layers, usage processes have been successfully visualized in the common modeling language eEPC. In discussion with the company's representative the change of insight due to the monitoring service has been visually illustrated and possibilities for further support of empowerment activities have been considered. By doing so four new design options have been identified that would enrich the service offer of the company. The design options "Automated reporting system" and "Mentoring by a (third-party) service provider" address the patient's problems in carrying out his or her activities. The other two design options "Data insight for the patient" and "Integration of additional components" expand the service offer by giving the patient further possibilities of collecting information while performing his or her empowerment activities. As explained in chapter 5.2.4 these two options might be relevant for future developments in the health care market. Thus, it would be considerable to develop a business system that provides medical care providers with the telemetry infrastructure to establish integrated care concepts.

It must be stated that the analysis of usage processes involves sensitive data, which has to be handled with care. As a matter of course the analysis must comply with formalities like consumer and privacy protection. The design options in this case study, for example, should not serve the interests of insurance companies. They must remain excluded from the insights gained through this monitoring service and identified redesign options.

However, the case study not only revealed management options, but also provided insight into the artifact's application in general. The implementation of method and its procedure revealed how to use the artifact. While it was not necessary to revise the artifact, novel information on how to apply the method evolved. In total three important issues have been detected:

- As the literature about Service Blueprinting does not go into detail with regard to how to classify process elements to one of the activity levels, novices using the method might face problems structuring processes appropriately. The experiences regarding typical classification problems have been gathered by the author while visualizing the processes in order to distinguish each activity level with unmistakable comments on what kind of elements they contain. Appendix 10 gives a short but straightforward classification of process elements for future users of this method.

- The visualization of processes with direct interaction (traditional BP²) also offered insight into when usage processes can be perceived by the provider through technology. It is noticed that automated data and therefore insight is most likely given when the organizational element of the patient or an activity in the swimlane "customer activity" is connected to a technical element in the areas of the provider, especially below the preparation layer. In the very beginning of the "early detection with Home Monitoring" process this is the case. Here data is collected automatically, giving insight into the patient's behavior and his or her empowerment activities. For this reason the concept of swimlanes fits very well to identify opportunities where customer activities can be perceived. A direct relation between elements in the highest and lowest elements of the traditional BP² point to such possibilities. This aspect can be seen as the bridging element of the traditional and enhanced BP².

- Last, the analysis of usage processes of the case study in the field of health care showed that there are at least two approaches to look on usage processes. One is to analyze the activities the customer actually performs by using the provider's service. This approach can be seen as an exploratory one. The other approach is to structure usage processes to support the intended purpose of the provider's service. For instance, in this case study the analysis focused on further support of the empowerment activities the physicians recommended the patient to perform.

In conclusion, the evaluation has shown that customer processes can be managed beneficially when applying the BP² method. Beside the evaluation of artifact, suggestions have been taken for the method's application.

5.3.2 Scientific Quality of the Evaluation and the Benefit of further Studies

Finally, the evaluation results have to be checked against common criteria for judging the quality of research. Regarding case studies, Yin (2009, pp. 40–45) refers in particular to four logical tests that are commonly used. In the following paragraphs the tests are first explained and subsequently applied to the case study:

(1) Construct validity indicates if the research concept being studied is operationalized with the correct measures. It questions the extent to which the study examines the subject matter. The subject of investigation in this case study was to show that usage processes are manageable when one applies Business Process Blueprinting. Accordingly the measures were "applicability of artifact" and "identification of redesign options", which have both been fulfilled.

(2) Internal validity checks whether a causal relationship exists between the measures and findings, meaning that there is no other factor than the investigated variable that caused the results. This test is of special importance for experiment research but can also be applied to explanatory case studies. As the measures of the case study contains Boolean operators with the question "Can customer processes be illustrated and (re-)design option identified by using the Business Process Blueprinting?", a direct causal relationship is established.

(3) External validity defines the extent to which findings can be generalized. The question is if the study's findings can be transferred beyond the immediate case study. Critics may remark that especially single case studies hardly contain generalizable statements. Yet, contrary to survey research, case studies rely on analytical generalization, meaning that findings of case studies cannot be transferred to the main unit, but they contribute to the phenomenon being studied (Yin 2009, pp. 43–44). No case study can be generalized to all settings. However, the investigation focused on critical testing and the case itself primarily served to advance the understanding. The single case already proves that the artifact addresses the objects of solution. Furthermore the field of e-health, which the case study is based on, is typical for the phenomenon of interest.

(4) Reliability describes the reproducibility of a study. This test aims to uncover biases and mistakes in the study. Reliability is given when other investigators could also have achieved comparable results when conducting this study. As the proceeding of the case study has been elucidated in detail and the reader has been presented the exact course of events, the study can be considered reliable. The procedure model on how to apply the method would seem to contribute to this issue as well.

Accordingly the case study complies with the minimum standard on research and fulfills all requirements of the logical tests. Though the case study matches the tests, further extensions seem appropriate, especially regarding the external validity factor. The application of artifact in further case studies, particularly in other industries, seems essential for at least two reasons. First, a further confirmation of findings would substantiate the universal validity and strengthen the results against critics of single case studies. The other reason is that another application can reveal new insight on the implementation process of method. In order to smoothen operability, special attention should be given to novices dealing with this subject.

The author would like to conclude this chapter by referring to DSR evaluation and its current shortcomings. Though initial approaches are proposed for the evaluation of artifacts, no methodological standard or guideline has been established and there is still no consensus on a common direction. Current publications on this topic often try to give an overview by reviewing well-accepted papers. Also frameworks and guidelines on how to evaluate artifacts are discussed occasionally. However, there is still a general lack of detailed outlines that zoom in on a specific evaluation method or technique and relates it to DSR evaluation. Hard as it is to provide and explain a reliable guideline, it is indispensable for the sake of the IS profession that one go into further detail. In order to appeal to a wider public and gain further acceptance, a set of standards for evaluation must be established. This is achieved by means of intense discussions and engagements within the profession as well as dialogues with method experts within and outside the subject area. Being a sample of case study evaluation this thesis may contribute to this subject matter.

6 Limitations and Development Perspectives

Though the DSRM does not explicitly lists limitations and future prospects, these two aspects can be seen as part of the communication activity. It is important that limitations are noted. Only then can the addressees know the boundaries of the research and respond accordingly. Development perspectives and an outlook can evolve from these limitations and point to current research gaps that may be covered by future research efforts in the community. First, this chapter reflects the limitations of this research in the first sub-chapter. Afterwards, development perspectives for the BP² are proposed. Last, an outlook is given, which aggregates the point of view from very concrete concepts to global aspects of IS and embeds this research into the "big picture".

6.1 Limitations of Research

Reflecting the basic idea of combining approaches from BPM and marketing, Business Process Blueprinting is still at an early stage of development and requires substantial empirical fortification. As there are certain conceptual limitations, BP² cannot analyze all aspects of customer-oriented process design. For instance, beside the control flow, ARIS contains further views, such as the organization, functions and data view, which also need to adapt usage processes. Further discussion about the symbiotic relationship between customer orientation and Business Process Management is necessary. This thesis mostly discussed interaction and usage processes of the customer, although pre-purchase and lateral processes that are not directly associated with the provider's offers may also be insight- and influenceable and therefore illustratable with the enhanced BP².

A limitation of the traditional BP² method is that it provides a benefit to integrative processes only. There is no added value when transferred, for example, to pure physical goods which are produced autonomously by the manufacturer without any customer integration. At the same time one implication of the service-dominant logic is that all kinds of goods and services contain integrative activities that need to be considered in process modeling, at the latest during sales processes. Because usage processes arise from every marketing offer, it is at least beneficial to apply the enhanced BP^2 in order to illustrate value-in-use.

Another limitation of the traditional BP^2 is that services do not always follow a conditional branched procedure. Kingman-Brundage (1989, p. 31) was already concerned that service operations do not necessarily follow the strict path of flowcharts when she stated that "Service blueprints follow the service path, an operations route, which is neither black or white nor entirely consistent in terms of flowchart logic". The issue she addressed in this sentence is the limited ability to standardize service processes (Gersch 1995; Jacob and Kleinaltenkamp 2004). However, most often a certain script is commonly known that covers at least the most important activities. For the level of detail is scalable in Business Process Blueprinting, the specification of the process structure is up to the user and should be rather seen as a freedom of choice.

Shortcomings can also be recognized for the enhanced version of BP^2. While interaction processes at least follow a rough script, usage processes can differ very much from person to person. This circumstance has several implications. In the worst case, one may not be able to draw a generic usage process. One may identify recurrent process elements, but not necessarily need to connect them in a flowchart (as is the case in the evaluation study). Nevertheless, there certainly is a common utilization of marketing offers. Thus, business analytics can be used to discover more information on the customer processes and their structure.

The lines of the enhanced BP^2 very much concentrate on the provider's perspective on the customer and therefore focus on design options that merely concern the supplier. The (re-)design options may influence the customer, but serve primarily the provider. Therefore the proposed lines should be seen as an initial and rather complementary input to the question of how usage processes can be managed. Certainly, further considerations on different separating lines that implicate other (re-)design options seem appropriate.

Also the preferred approach to collect data on usage processes via ICT to enable data mining can be seen as complicated and conditional. First, the customer privacy has to be preserved. Second, insight via ICT is mostly given by a communication device on physical products. How does one collect information on the usage processes of an immaterial service such as the knowledge transfer at university? Further research on the methodical gathering of usage information such as the mobile-phone text messaging to capture experiences in real time (Macdonald, Wilson and Konus 2012) is necessary. Conceivable for further insight on the customer processes is the development of a survey with central questions regarding usage.

Next, BP^2 is currently set to map only bilateral processes between one provider and one customer. Other providers or customers are not considered. Services produced by several providers are not taken into account, although that may affect the perceived quality from the customer's point of view. As there is, for example, a rising demand for individual production and fulfillments distributed by just one source (Montreuil and Poulin 2005), it seems important to show which provider has direct customer contact and which brand appears to him or her. Brady and Cronin (2001b) suggest that the type, behavior and amount of other customers may have an influence on the perceived quality (e.g. in the case of unpleasant people). Therefore, it would be helpful to know and see what kind of activities relating to one person may affect another person's perception. For instance, a discount received by another customer can have an impact on the purchase satisfaction and fairness of another client (Darke and Dahl 2003). A picture of the interdependencies between B2B, Business-to-Consumer (B2C) and Consumer-to-Consumer (C2C) would therefore be advantageous. This also concerns usage processes. Considering the SDL-proposition that value is embedded in networks of resource integrators, the method's bi-lateral view ought to be extended to all resource integrators in the long-term.

The method also needs further evaluation. For additional empirical validation of benefits a field study in a very service-intensive industry should be initiated, applying the proposed reference model for a customer-oriented Service Engineering. The explanations on the BP^2 are very much focused on B2C markets and neglect the field of B2B. Insights on an application to B2B areas would be beneficial.

Concerning practical aspects another issue can be seen in the instance of missing software. In order to gain attention in the community and increase practical relevance the method should be integrated in a software template. In a first step this can be done with open source modeling tools such as "ProcessMaker Open Source", "Questetra BPM Suite" or "Visual Paradigm for UML".

Lastly, the method alone is of little value. It has to be aligned with other concepts, methods or tools. The idea of combining the method with concepts, methods and tools of diverse disciplines is described in more detail in the next chapter.

6.2 Development Perspectives: Illustrating the Method as a Toolkit

The goal of BP² is to structure processes appropriately to highlight customer activities, i.e. to reveal type, extent and progress throughout the process. It raises awareness for customer processes and can be a great advantage for an explorative BPM, which un-covers aspects that have not been considered before.

Yet, the BP² method alone is not sufficient to solve the question of how to design effi-cient and effective processes that are economically viable. The method alone promotes an awareness to pay attention to both perspectives. But further integration of tools is needed in order to gain useful information. Additional concepts and methods are nec-essary. In this regard BP² can be seen as the core of a toolkit which provides an inter-face for additional methods or as a starting point for deeper analysis with additional concepts, methods and tools. Although the method has been refined over the years and applied in practice, its full potential has not yet been reached. The toolkit needs to be elaborated and extended in the future. Figure 35 shows a simplified illustration of this approach. It describes methods that can either be supported by or easily combined with BP². Through a mix of methods new insights might be gathered that can be used for a redesign of service processes and/or products. BP² in combination with further meth-ods from various disciplines, such as marketing or IS, is very suitable for the develop-ment of new or the restructure of already established services. This is why BP² can serve in particular as a toolbox in Service Engineering, which combines the concepts of IS and marketing. It should be stated that the illustration does not claim to be com-plete as it only lists a few concepts. The dots point out that further research areas, methods and insights can and should be integrated. Currently the graph merely outlines the basic idea of the BP²-toolkit.

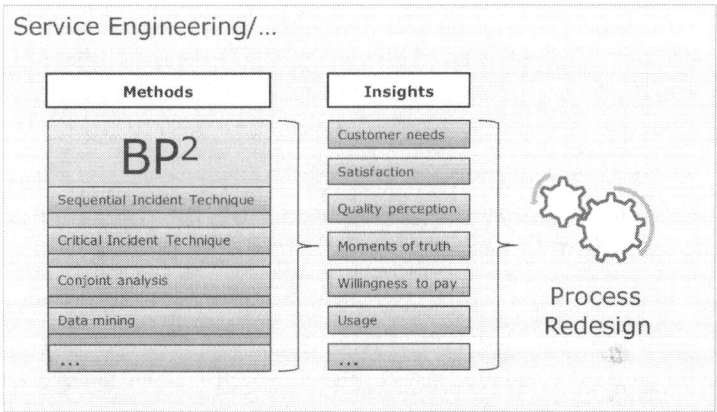

Figure 35. BP² as a toolkit - exemplary extensions

One example for the application of further method can be seen in the case study that has been mentioned in the explanation of traditional BP². Through the integration of BP² the points of interaction and the activities that are perceivable by the customer have been quickly identified. Now, the individual stations can be subject of a deeper analysis (Fließ 2006, p. 150). Event-driven approaches, such as the Sequential Incident Technique (Stauss and Weinlich 1997) and the Critical Incident Technique (Flanagan 1954) can be connected. In the first method the customer is asked open-ended questions pertaining to the individual phases of the service operation in the form of personal interviews. The Critical Incident Technique subdivides the experiences into positive and negative events. Through open questions particularly satisfactory or unsatisfactory incidents are to be explained in greater detail, which leads to a comprehensive insight into process perception from the perspective of the customer. The detailed BP²-illustration helps to promote a detailed playback of the experiences, so important points can be identified.

Accordingly, based on the improved awareness of the customer's point of view, well-established controlling and marketing methods (e.g. the analysis of willingness to pay, customer satisfaction and/or customer segmentation and differentiation) are now applicable. The future toolkit can provide those additional instruments to address a variety of (research as well as practical) questions. Thus the accurate development of a service needs appropriate methodological support to design, control and enhance customer integrated value creation processes. The future toolkit can provide those additional instruments to address a variety of issues and specific questions. In the following two promising themes for an expansion of toolset are exemplarily highlighted.

6.2.1 Enhancing Existing Cost Management Tools Towards an Integrated Process Revenue and Cost Management

One research gap is the pending problem of aligning revenues to processes. In addition calculating production costs, it is necessary to estimate the expected revenues in order to rate the processes' cost-effectiveness. Yet, in the course of the re-engineering approach, many process evaluations merely focus on cost and cost-reductions as decision variables. In order to decide whether a process design is economically beneficial, revenues as well as costs need to be taken into account. Widening current cost-oriented methods with these revenue-based elements would provide real added value for the design of economically attractive processes. It could be seen as an important step towards an integrated performance management (Gersch, Hewing and Schöler 2011, pp. 742–744; Gersch 2006, p. 14) that takes both the supply side (costs) and demand side (revenue) into account, balancing between the aims of the provider (e.g. earnings, flexibility) and customer (e.g. personal value, saving in time).

One approach to gathering information on revenues is the evaluation of the customers' willingness to pay. According to Brady and Cronin (2001b), contact with employees and certain properties of the premises contribute to influencing the customers' quality assessment and their willingness to pay for services. As BP² illustrates, these contact points and interaction between company and customer, it can serve as a basis to align revenues to processes. Combined with cost management, which is already addressed in depth by existing BPM tools and thereby connected to the method of BP², a calculation of total contribution margins for complete process designs would become possible. Only favorable process designs – i.e. designs with a positive total contribution margin

– would be implemented. This chapter reflects on how BP² enables the evaluation of process revenues by concentrating on the customers' willingness to pay.

So far the central question has concerned the costs that arise as a result of customized products or services. Now, however, the main question becomes how high total contribution margins are for various process designs. This requires an analysis of revenue. Enhancing current cost-oriented methods with these revenue-oriented elements would provide added value for designing economically advantageous processes. The aim is to evaluate the revenues and costs for different service designs.

As promoted by the enhanced BP², variations of usage processes concern in particular a shift from customer activities without any provider support to ICT coordinated ones or an intensified interaction of previously autonomously performed activities. The four design options that have been identified in the "BIOTRONIK Home Monitoring" case study, for instance, are different layouts to support the patient in his empowerment activities. The company can determine the costs that arise when realizing each one of these options. However, they still need information on the patients' willingness to pay for each layout. The point of interest is how much the patient is likely to value a personal mentoring of empowerment activities in contrast to an automated reporting system or even no support at all.

From a scientific point of view the significant question is whether a variation of process elements influences a person's willingness to pay. To respond to this question and to enable a revenue/cost-based process management, the procedure model proposed in Figure 36 is helpful.

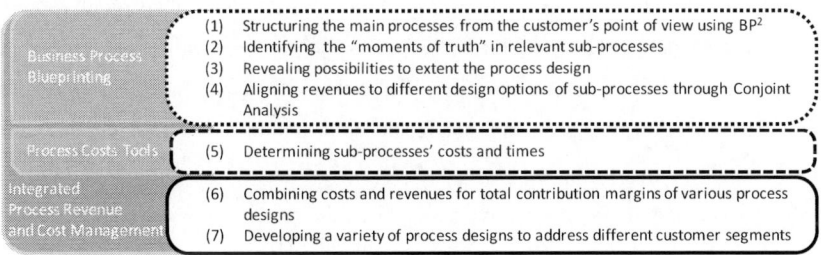

Figure 36. Procedure model for an integrated process revenue and cost management

First, the whole process should be structured from the customer's point of view. In fact, BP² provides methodological support for categorizing processes and their elements. Sub-processes located in activity layers above the "Line of visibility" including usage processes can be assumed to be of higher importance for the effectiveness-oriented perspective, because it is here that customer perception and interaction takes place. Sub-processes below the "Line of visibility" are not directly perceived by the customer.

Based upon this visualization, the important sub-processes and contact points, so called "moments of truth" (Grönroos 1990; Martini 2008), need to be identified along the whole service process. In other words, (re-)designing a new value creation process should start with the identification of such "moments of truth" that are part of the actual value creation process, i.e. by modeling the interaction process between customer and provider and the autonomously performed usage processes as perceived by the customer. This step can be enhanced by the previously mentioned incident techniques that facilitate a detailed opinion survey.

Once these "moments of truth" have emerged, possibilities to extend the processes by redesigning these moments can be identified. This involves identifying opportunities for improvement and innovation. Techniques and concepts from innovation management such as creative thinking and lead user integration can be stimulating at this point (i.a. Roos and Anemo 2011). When a particular amount of design options have been identified, the most promising ones are to be selected by discussion.

After the "moments of truth" have been unveiled and design options have been picked, customers' willingness to pay for these design options needs to be surveyed by empirical studies. A direct inquiry on the willingness to pay for a specific design option is rather easy to conduct, but tends to be of less reliability due to an artificial decision situation. Several factors can falsify the result (i.a. Cummings, Harrison and Rutström 1995; Johannesson, Liljas and O'Conor 1997). For instance, the question regarding the willingness to pay might put too much weight on the price. Moreover, some respondents might not consciously be aware of their willingness to pay when no price range is given. In order to avoid such influencing factors the price is often asked indirectly. A common method of doing so is conjoint analysis, which is a statistical technique to determine people's preferred attributes in decision making (i.a. Orme 2009). The design options that have been previously identified have to be described as an attribute of a corresponding product or service. Next, the respondents are asked to rate sets of these attributes. The aim of such an analysis is to identify the attributes that most influence the respondents' decisions. The respondents' preferences are analyzed statistically, resulting in values for each attribute. Because the price can be one of these attributes, one is able to evaluate the partial willingness to pay for all the others attributes. This approach is very much applicable to different process designs with various elements. At the end of this step insight can be reliably attained with regard to the degree to which each attributed process element affects a person's willingness to pay.

Before implementing the most favorable design option one needs to consider aspects of efficiency such as process cost (i.a. Fließ 2006, pp. 182–202; Salman 2004; Schweikart 1997) and time (i.a. Gadatsch 2010, pp. 294–296). For innovative services this concerns every process element, while in a redesign of service only the process elements that are affected by the revision need to be incorporated. When the revenues and costs have been evaluated, the margins of various process decisions can be evaluated. As a result there can be a variety of process designs with diverging margins that are tailored specifically for different individuals/customer groups. It should be stated that the yield is not the only measurement for decisions on process designs. There might also be other variables that need to be considered (e.g. organizational aspects such as the working conditions of employees who are involved in the process).

This procedure for an integrated process revenue management has already been successfully applied in an empirical study developed in the context of master thesis in which the process variations of a copy shop service were analyzed, resulting in a first validation of the propositions that the variation of process elements can affect customers' willingness to pay (Mitreva 2012).

The development of a process result management tool is one of two examples of how to enrich BP² with additional methods and techniques. Next, an example of deployment on unstructured processes is given.

6.2.2 Adaptive Case Management for the Analysis of Usage Processes

Recent publications have discussed the problem of unstructured processes (Swenson 2010). Often processes do not follow a precise sequence that can be determined from the outset. This is especially the case for services that, depending on external factors, may involve several heterogeneous process flows to obtain a specific outcome. For instance, the selection of examination and therapy depends very much on the results of the diagnosis and medical history of a patient. Though there are certain rules that must be complied by and some sub-processes are very well defined within the entire treatment, the physician must decide the further steps for each treatment. In such processes the path can only be defined to some extent a priori. Because every activity has to be specified in detail, traditional BPM systems are not well suited to handling processes that recombine activities or contain new and unforeseen activities. Current approaches mostly illustrate routine processes, which are always conducted in the same variant (Swenson 2010, p. 24). Although ad-hoc exceptions are already integrated, the modeling of unstructured processes becomes more inefficient with an increasing number of variables and design options. However, the spectrum of process structure reaches from "routine processes" or "structured processes with ad-hoc exception" to "unstructured processes with pre-defined fragments" or even "completely unstructured processes" (Kemsley 2011).

So while routine processes may be becoming increasingly automated, there is a trend in BPM to include complex and knowledge-based processes within the focus of analysis. This issue is picked up under the terms "Dynamic Case Management" and "Adaptive Case Management" (ACM). The anthology of Swenson (2010) gives a comprehensive overview of the various approaches. The central theme of this discipline is to support barely structured business processes via technology and IS. In contrast to BPM, where information runs through a predetermined process, the central focus of analysis lies on the data originated in performed cases. Based on this data, a process or a variety of designs can be generated for a process (Reichert and Weber 2012). In other words, processes are aligned to data rather than the other way around (Kemsley 2011). The data contains important information about the course of events and their results. So depending on the scope of analysis, the study of unstructured processes can be complex and may need references to disciplines like Business Intelligence, Business Analytics and Document Management in order to detect unperceived clusters, association and/or relations. While a decent Document Management will facilitate the smooth pre-processing of data, Business Intelligence and Analytics is needed for querying the data with statistical, quantitative, explanatory and predictive analysis in order to detect process patterns. This kind of procedure is also often labeled process mining (i.a. van der Aalst 2011).

As one can see from the titles of publications (i.a. Kemsley 2011; Swenson et al. 2012) the ACM discussion is mostly focused on knowledge workers who do not follow a given workflow but rather autonomously work out a process for themselves. Again, the focus is on the provider's internal (working) processes. Customer processes are not yet considered, though there are close similarities in the features of customer and knowledge worker activities. Both can contain unique and anarchic structures without any recurring arrangements. This is especially true for usage processes, which the customer performs almost autonomously with little support (if at all) from the supplier. With reference to the activity logs of knowledge workers, companies may gain insight into the actual behavior and activities of the customer by exploratory analysis of transmitted data. This means that the data that is collected from the customer side can be analyzed. This way insight can be gained into the real usage of marketing offers. The usage of a service or product can proceed in a similar way across every individual, but there might also be dynamic variations.

With the BIOTRONIK HM service, data is collected by the IECD and send to the provider via CardioMessenger. The evaluated data could be processed with data mining methods in order to identify patterns of activities. This information could be used by the provider to further support the patient in his empowerment activities and health-related behavior. Contrary to the suggested design options, which actually apply rules on the collected data to achieve a specific processes flow, this approach searches in an explorative manner for unseen patterns by analyzing data. Potential processes or process fragments may be detected and become illustratable. BP² with its swimlanes is helpful for this approach. Figure 37 portrays the BP² based procedure for the analysis of usage processes.

First, BP² can be used to find activities in the interaction processes where the customer originates and transfers data to the provider's systems. The graphs highlight customer processes that can be perceived by the provider through technology. Elements on the customer side that are connected to technical elements in the areas of the provider, especially the preparation layer, point to such a situation. As already mentioned, this is, for example, the case in the very beginning of the "early detection with Home Monitoring" process. The detection of data access can be seen as the first step towards an explorative analysis of usage. In a second step, data mining techniques (i.a. Berry and Linoff 2004) should be applied (i.a. Li, Reichert and Wombacher 2011). This method can be applied for the identification of usage processes. In cases where data analysis detects process fragments, these can be illustrated afterwards on the gridlines of the BP². This way, process elements are already aligned to the relative activity layer giving the management a helpful structure for further considerations.

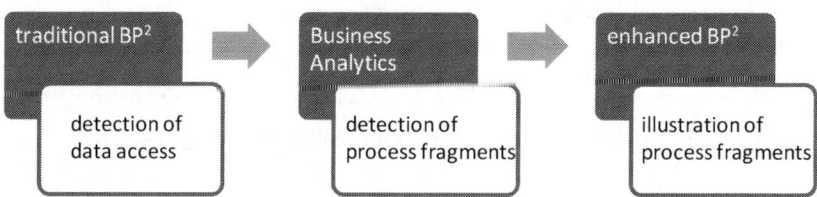

Figure 37. Procedure to analyze usage processes based on BP²

Thus, BP² can be an auxiliary method to support the detection, analysis and illustration of unstructured processes. As the method focuses on the unnoted customer perspective, a further integration into the field of ACM seems beneficial.

6.3 Outlook

With BP², a first step has been achieved towards widening the focus from provider's internal processes to the customer side. The artifact does not only consider interaction but also autonomously performed usage processes of service offers that derive after the common service production process. Nevertheless, this research and the artifact that has been developed amount to but a small contribution compared with what is still ahead. Not only do the artifact's limitations have yet to be resolved. Further considerations on the management of customer processes are necessary. Although with its adaptability to further methods and tools, the basic concept of BP^2 provides a comprehensive foundation, it may not be suitable for every kind of problem or issue. The development of further conceptualizations that approach the subject from a different angle would be beneficial. Further research on pre-purchase and latent processes should be considered.

This research has proven that there still is a huge gap between areas of research. This relates internally to different fields of research in the same discipline such as BPM and Service Engineering but also to the external collaboration with disciplines outside the subject area (e.g. IS and marketing). It is essential that researchers communicate with externals in order to keep up to date on recent research and avoid having to establish knowledge that already exists. For instance, the origin of BPM lies in three different research streams of which some often do not regard the advances of BPM. However, as most fields of management have recently picked-up a process-based perspective, it seems that BPM can serve as a "lingua franca" between the different research areas and disciplines.

This thesis presents a plea for the importance of customer processes and recommends to appropriately orienting one's business activities to these processes. An opportunity-driven approach should be considered by analyzing the customer's "birth-to-death value chain" (Rosemann 2011b). This means that one searches for opportunities to support personal processes concerning a specific area of life, such as health, finance, education, work, administration, or social life (Knackstedt and Dahlke 2004, p. 48). As processes in these areas can be rather complex or even new to an individual once their life situation changes, a guideline of how to perform these processes can be very much appreciated. However, "corporations have not yet explored the commercialization of such personal processes" (Rosemann 2011b). One may even think ahead and imagine an IS that centralizes the coordination of such activities and provider offers (Rosemann 2013a). Caesar et al. (2005), for instance, refer to internet platforms that help the user to coordinate his or her processes for a specific aspect of life. Kagermann, Österle and Jordan (2010, pp. 38–43) even propose aspects that the user expects from such a process support. The concept of customer life areas and the idea of centralizing such offers lead to another aspect for future areas of research.

Research on customer activities (whether it is on pre-purchase, interaction, usage or latent processes) needs to be embedded to the next higher context – the "overarching whole". One forthcoming issue may be the convergence of process landscapes. The approach to understanding business as a complex system of processes has already gained widespread acceptance. Process-oriented thinking is very much established for the management of organizations. Yet, process landscapes are becoming increasingly complex, particularly with regard to the interoperability between the organizing institutions and the arising importance of the customers' value chain, which is rapidly becoming digitized and interconnected. Controversial topics such as outsourcing and cloud-services, IT-Management increasingly deal with the integration of systems and its security in the B2B sector. Future discussions in the B2C sector concern process landscapes that slowly grow together on the customer's side (i.a. life systems mentioned above). The evolution of convergence currently bundles entertainment and communication services in fields like 1-to-1 interaction, music, photography, television, social platforms and is beginning to further expand under labels such as "Ambient Assisted Living", "e-health", "e-/Smart-Mobility" or "Smart Grid" to health care, mobility and energy related applications. Besides the reflection of traditional product and service bundles, innovative business models seek for new or at least changing value propositions. Nevertheless, it is challenging to capture, analyze, understand and design these complex and interwoven process structures to provide adequate value propositions. In order to support and coordinate complex process landscapes from the customers' and suppliers' perspectives, a combined analysis of all relevant processes is necessary. Figure 38 illustrates the issue of barely converged process landscapes. The interfaces between the protagonists do not fit accurately. The connection is far apart, not on the same level and needs therefore further adjustment. This is also true for processes outside the specific value chain such as other fields of (competing) applications (illustrated in the background). Thus, research for a holistic view on process landscapes is inevitable.

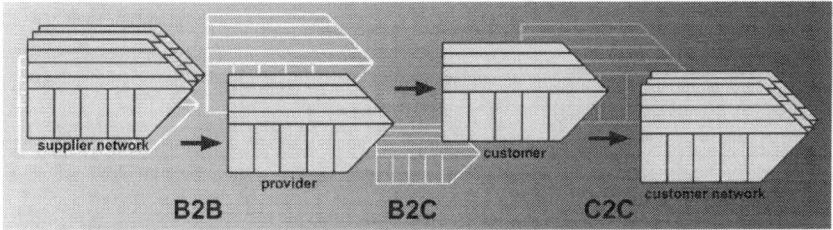

Figure 38. Converging process landscapes

As mentioned above, BPM can be considered as the denominator between all resorts of Information Systems and as an established unifying and vehicular language between scientific disciplines. BPM is suited to be a common ground for research on complex process landscapes, but emphasizes with its traditional focus a rather inside-out perspective that reflects the processes from the providers' point of view. In order to map the whole process landscape from everyone's perspective it is therefore necessary that one open the view to the overall process and integrate the process chains of cooperating partners (B2B) and end-customers (B2C, C2C) as well as their networks and different perspectives on the converging process landscapes. BP² can be considered as a first progression towards strengthening process-based research on the relation between the provider and customer.

7 Conclusion

This research is assigned to Information Systems and based on Design Science Research (*chapter 2*). Its focus of discussion is the customer orientation in Business Process Management. Customer orientation can be seen as the driving force of marketing. It is essential to orient one's business to customer needs and create appropriate value. Only when the customer feel confident with one's performances and his or her needs are satisfied according to his or her expectations, is a long lasting economic success viable. However, customer orientation requires in-depth understanding of the entire value chain of (potential) buyers. In order to do so, a process-based approach is necessary to illustrate every single step a customer goes through to achieve the demanded value. Recent developments such as the service-dominant logic have opened up new perspectives on value creation processes and highlight the need to integrate usage processes that are usually performed by the customer beyond the perception of the provider. Though customer concepts have existed for some time, little research has been done on a process-based approach to manage customer processes.

In total, the question of matter is how customer processes can be captured, documented, analyzed and designed continuously. In order to respond to this question a study of current approaches has been conducted that shows the current status of research on process-oriented customer concepts. A literature review in the disciplines that are most related to this topic, i.e. marketing and BPM, is described in *chapter 3* and reveals that customer processes are hardly considered in BPM. There are almost no methodical approaches that regard the modeling of customer processes.

With regard to Design Science Research, this thesis has aimed to close this gap of research by developing an artifact that fulfills the requirements of such an approach. *Chapter 4* showed how current modeling languages can be combined with marketing methods in order to include the customer's point of view. The artifact that has been developed throughout the research is labeled "Business Process Blueprinting" (BP²) and sets the focus on customer processes. With the possibility to identify and capture customers' activities along their entire process chain, the concept facilitates evaluating customer-orientated aspects in processes. Based on the enhanced version of the method, further insight into customers' usage and their value-in-use can be provided for a pro-active customer management.

The evaluation, which has been elucidated *in chapter 5,* proves the applicability of the method and the benefits that derive from it. A comprehensive case study on the health care service "BIOTRONIK Home Monitoring" affirmed that customer processes can be captured, illustrated and subsequently analyzed by using BP². Throughout the analysis, redesign options have been identified that advance the service offer. Thus, the developed BP²-method can be seen as a first answer to the question of how customer processes can be managed.

Nevertheless, as with most concepts, BP² includes certain limitations and is not suitable to analyze all aspects on its own. The most promising approach is to take the method as a process-oriented foundation to which further concepts can be adapted. *Chapter 6* considers the restrictions that are assigned to the method in its current state and gives an outlook on how the method can serve as a toolbox that adapts further methods and tools. Finally, this research is contextually embedded to a potential future research agenda in IS and a topic that is most likely to be picked out as a central theme for the next few years. A summarizing overview of advancements throughout this research project can be seen in Table 1.

Appendix

Appendix 1. DSRM process model (Peffers et al. 2007, p. 54)

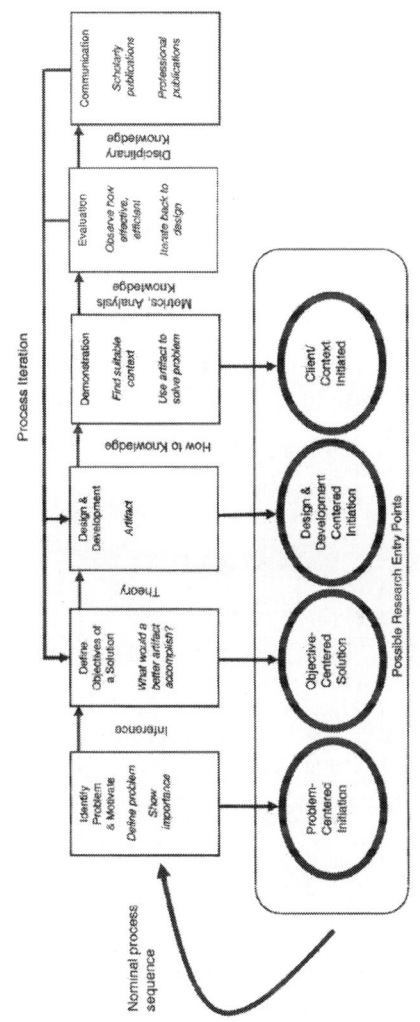

Appendix 2. Overview of preliminary work and its advancement throughout this research project

No	Chapter	Focus*	Preliminary work (chronically)	State of the art*	Advancement throughout this research project*
1	3.1	Linkage of value creation and customer orientation to a process-based perspective	amongst others: Engelhardt (1996) Engelhardt/Kleinaltenkamp/Reckenfelderbäumer (1993) Gersch (2006) Vargo/Lusch (2004a)	Concepts that open up the view on value creation to the customer side	Plead for the importance of a process-based view on customer orientation by a review of the transformation from a product-over-service to an experience-oriented focus on value creation
2	3.2	Insufficient considerations of customer (modeling) concepts in BPM	Gersch (2006) Batista/Smart/Maull (2008)	First insights by conceptual discussions and an explorative analysis	Comprehensive literature review with quantitive and qualitative analysis affirms the proposition with a high level of realibility and validity
3	4.1.1	Artifact Development I: Combination of the Service Blueprinting with Business Process Modeling notations	Knackstedt/Dahlke (2004) Becker/Klose/Knackstedt (2005) Gersch/Goeke/Lux (2006) Meis/Menschner/Leimeister (2010) Coenen/Felten/Schmid (2011) Milton/Johnson (2012)	Initial combination of methods and technical explanations	Journal and conference publications with conceptual embedding, further evaluation and discussion of advantages/limitations (Gersch, Hewing 2010; Gersch, Hewing, Schöler 2011; Hewing 2011)
4	4.1.2 4.2 5 6	Artifact Development II: Modeling of customer processes that take place beyond the direct interaction with the provider	Green/Simister (1999) Fließ (2001) Alt/Puschmann (2005) Frauendorf (2006) Eichentopf/Kleinaltenkamp/van Stiphout (2011) Heckl/Moormann (2007)	Intial reflections on and mapping of customer processes	Development of an approved method to model customer processes that has been critical reflected, considers current Business Process Modeling notations, the logic of the Service Blueprinting, evolving concepts on customer processes (in particular insight/influence) and to which further methods are applicable (Gersch, Schöler, Hewing 2011)

* detailed explanations can be seen in the relative chapters

Appendix 3. Informal description of important term

Term	Description
Concept	Concepts can be defined as an abstract object or a mental image, which refers to a specific entity
Customer orientation	Customer orientation is the organization-wide generation of market intelligence pertaining to current and future customer needs.
Customer process	Customer processes describe the entire procedure customers pass through to meet a desire or to solve a problem. They refer to all activities that are conducted by the customer such as pre-purchase, interaction, usage and latent processes.
Customer satisfaction	Customer satisfaction is the outcome of a subjective comparison between the expected and actual perceived performance (over time).
Effectiveness	The effectiveness describes the degree to which the customer's expectations have been met.
Efficiency	Efficiency describes an input-output ratio. Economically efficient means achieving the most favorable ratio of inputs and benefits.
Enhanced BP	The enhanced Business Process Blueprinting focuses on usage processes.
Method	Methods determine a sequence of activities that need to be conducted to reach a particular result
Model	A model illustrates via declared languages the reality in a subjective manner for the benefit of the addressee.
Performance	Performance can be defined as the action of performing a task.
Quality	The customer-oriented quality concept reflects how the customer perceives a marketing offer. In contrary, the production-oriented approach defines quality by physical criteria that have to be fulfilled.
Traditional BP	The traditional Business Process Blueprinting focuses on the interaction between customer and provider.
Usage process	Usage processes are autonomously coordinated customer activities that usually emerge after the interaction with the provider. Usage is therefore traditionally outside the provider's perception.
Value	Customer value describes the expected and subjective perceived net benefits that remain after the subtraction of costs from benefits.
Value-in-exchange	Value is determined by the nominal price of exchange.
Value-in-use	Value merely derives when benefits arise for the customer in his or her usage processes.

Appendix 4. Framework of literature reviewing (modified from vom Brocke et al.
2009, pp. 8-9)

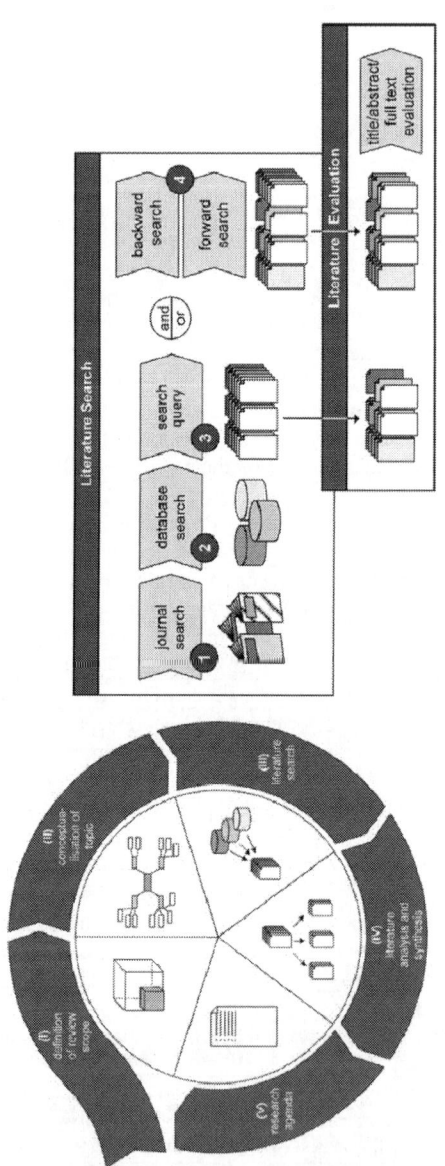

Appendix 5. Settings of the search query for the databases including hit results

Database	Hits	Algorithm	Search mode	Limiters/Expanders
BPM	7	(customer, service dominant logic, usage process, sdl, integrative value creation, co-creation, co-producing, value-in-use) in titles and abstracts of the digital conference proceedings	-	-
Emerald	195	("business process*" OR "BPM" OR "process modelling" OR "process modeling" in All except full text) AND ("customer*" OR "service dominant logic" OR "usage process*" OR "integrative value creation" OR "SDL" "co-creation" OR "co-producing" in All except full text)	Any/Any	All content; incl. Backfiles
EBSCO BSP	424	(AB "business process" OR SU "business process" OR KW "business process" OR AB bpm OR TI bpm OR SU bpm OR KW bpm OR AB "process modelling" OR KW "process modelling" OR TI "process modelling" OR SU "process modeling" OR KW "process modeling" OR AB "process modeling" OR KW "process modeling" OR TI "process modeling") AND (AB customer* OR TI customer* OR SU customer* OR KW customer* OR AB "usage process" OR SU "usage process" OR KW "usage process" OR AB "service dominant logic" OR SU "service dominant logic" OR KW "service dominant logic" OR AB sdl OR SU sdl OR KW sdl OR AB "integrative value creation" OR KW "integrative value creation" OR TI "integrative value creation" OR SU "integrative value creation" OR KW "co-creation" OR AB "co-creation" OR TI "co-creation" OR SU "co-creation" OR KW "co-producing" OR SU "co-producing" OR TI "co-producing" OR SU "co-producing" OR KW "co-producing" OR AB "value-in-use" OR TI "value-in-use" OR SU "value-in-use" OR KW "value-in-use")	Boolean/Phrase	Document Type: Article, Books; Apply related words
AISeL	15	(abstract:("business process*" OR "BPM" OR "process modeling" OR "process modelling") OR title:("business process*" OR "BPM" OR "process modeling" OR "process modelling") AND (abstract:("customer*" OR "usage process*" OR "service dominant value creation" OR "sdl" OR "integrative value creation" OR "co-creation" OR "value-in-use") OR subject:("customer*" OR "service dominant logic" OR "co-creation" OR "co-producing" OR "value-in-use") OR (title:("customer*" OR "usage process*" OR "service dominant logic" OR "sdl" OR "integrative value creation" OR "co-creation" OR "co-producing" OR "value-in-use"))	-	All Repositories
Web of Knowledge	80	Topic:("business process management" OR "bpm" OR "process modelling" OR "process modeling") AND Topic:("customer*" OR "usage process*" OR "service dominant logic" OR "sdl" OR "integrative value creation" OR "co-creation" OR "co-producing" OR "value-in-use")	-	Lemmatization=On, All databases, Timespan = All Years
Duplicates	62			
Total	**659**			Date of query: 2012-11-15

Appendix 6. List of identified articles that relate to the field of interest

Nr.	Author	Year	Title	Publication
1	Alt/Puschmann	2005	Developing customer process orientation: the case of Pharma Corp.	Business Process Management Journal
2	Barua et al.	2004	An Empirical Investigation of Net-Enabled Business Value	MIS Quarterly
3	Batista/Smart/Maull	2008	The systemic perspective of service processes	Production Planning & Control
4	Behara/Fontenot/Gresham	2002	Customer process approach to building loyalty	Total Quality Management
5	Bolton	2004	Customer centric business processing	International Journal of Productivity and Performance Management
6	Borgianni/Cascini/Rotini	2010	Process value analysis for business process re-engineering	Journal of Engineering Manufacture
7	Coenen/von Felten/Schmid	2011	Managing effectiveness and efficiency through FM blueprinting	Facilities
8	Gersch/Hewing/Schöler	2011	Business Process Blueprinting - an enhanced view on process performance	Business Process Management Journal
9	Gersch/Schöler/Hewing	2010	Service Dominant Logic and Business Process Blueprinting	Americas Conference on Information Systems
10	Gossain	2002	Cracking the Collaboration Code	Journal of Business Strategy
11	Green/Simister	1999	Modelling client business processes as an aid to strategic briefing	Construction Management & Economics
12	Heckl/Moormann	2007	Matching Customer Processes with Business Processes of Banks	BPM Conference
13	Huang/Zhu/Wu	2012	Customer-Centered Careflow Modeling Based an Guidelines	Journal of medical systems
14	Kim	1995	Process Modeling For BPR: Event-Process Chain Approach	ICIS 1995
15	Milton/Johnson	2012	Service blueprinting and BPMN: a comparison	Managing Service Quality
16	Rajala/Savolainen	1996	A framework for customer oriented business process modelling	Computer Integrated Manufacturing Systems
17	Tseng/Qinhai/Chuan-Jun	1999	Mapping customers' service experience for operations improvement	Business Process Management Journal

Appendix 7. Case study with a traditional process model in health care

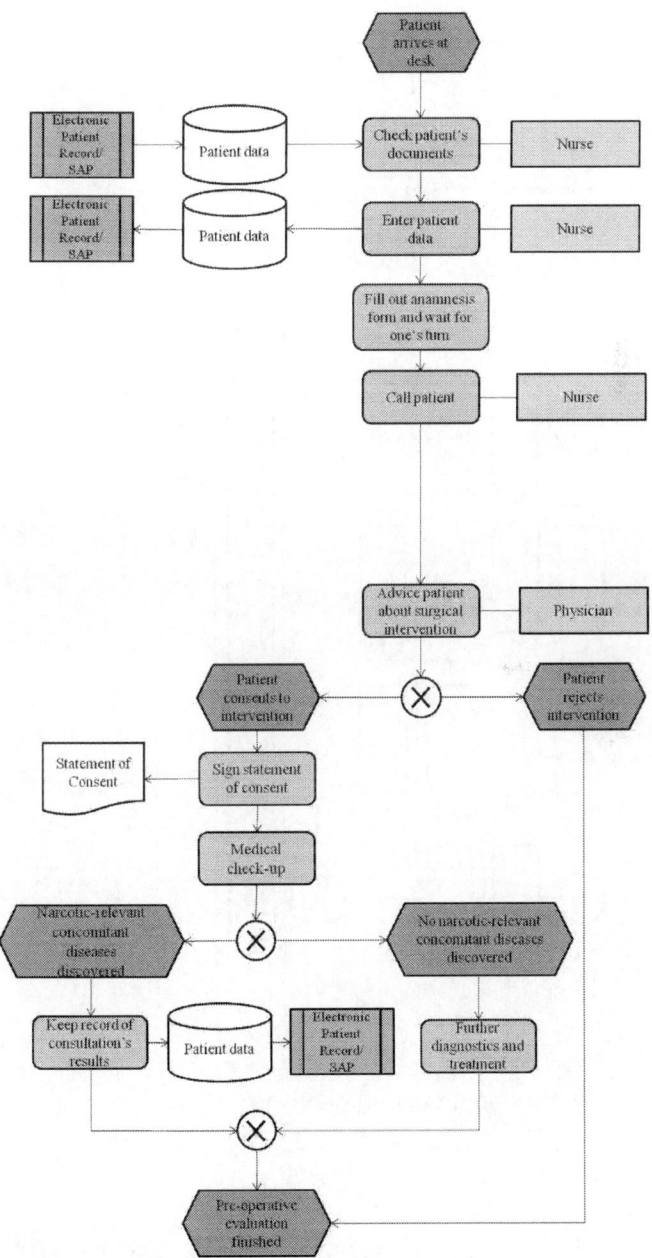

Appendix 8. Business Process Blueprinting Framework

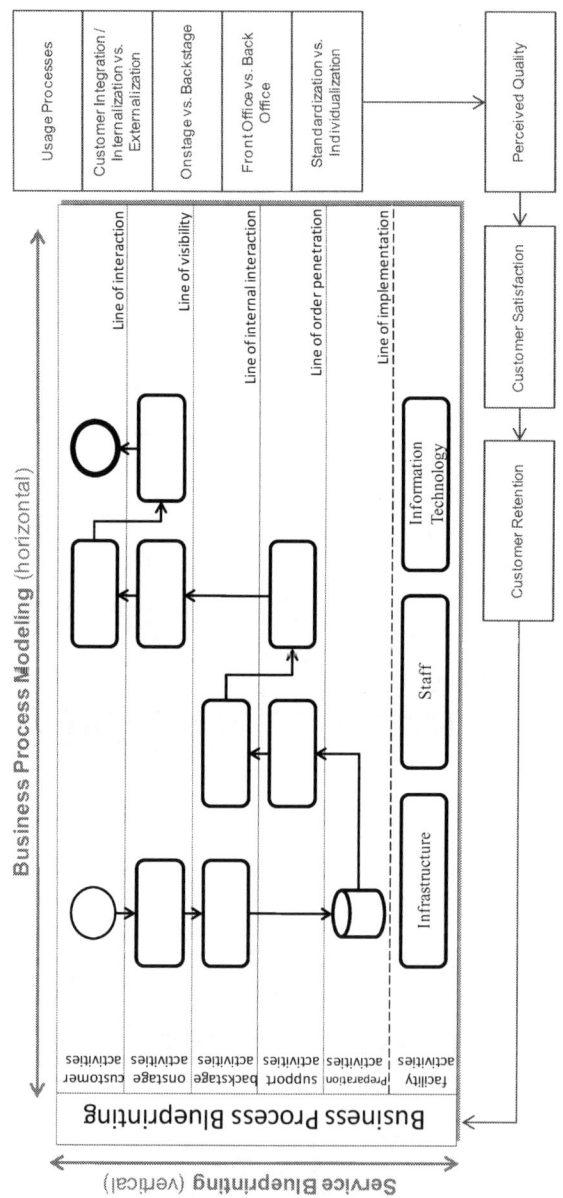

Appendix 9. Case Study of a BP² in health care

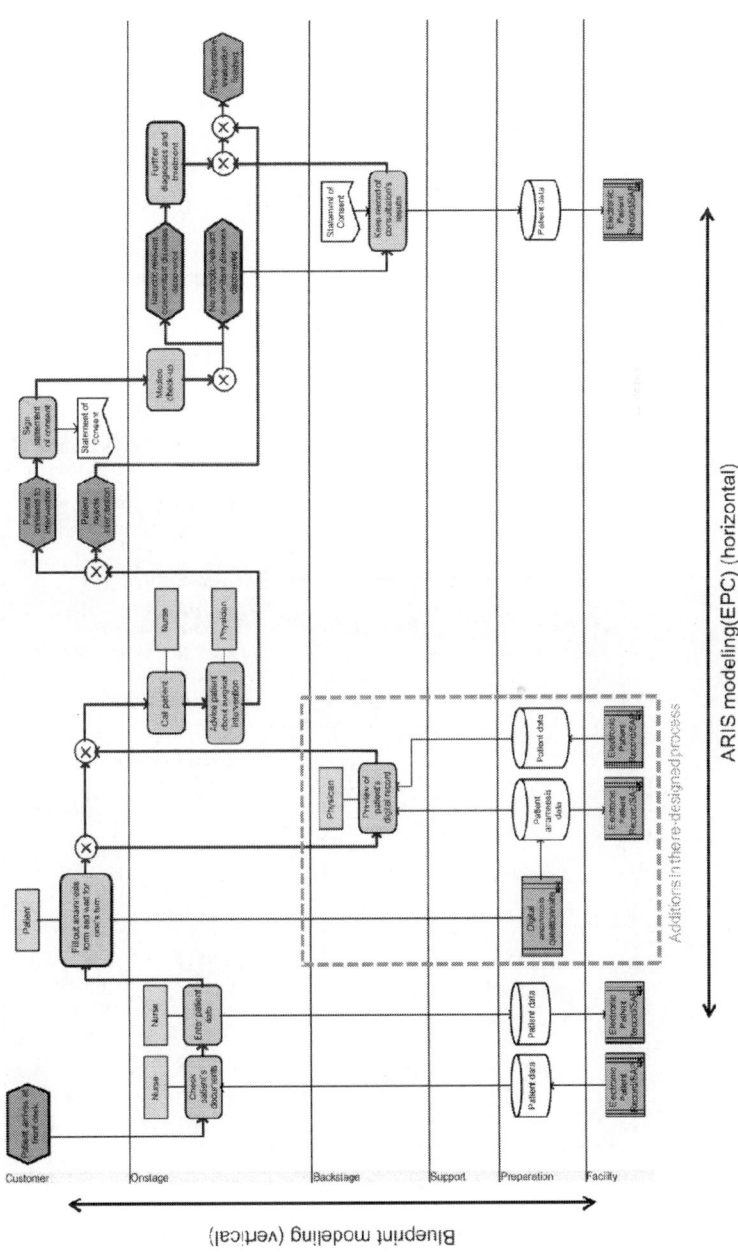

Appendix 10. Template of an extended Business Process Blueprinting

customer activities

Activities the provider
can not perceive

------- line of insight

Activities that are visible
to the provider, but not
influnceable

------- line of impact

Activities that can be
influenced/supported
by the provider

------- line of (autonomously
performed) customer activities

Customer activities
of the direct interaction

------- line of interaction

Provider activities
of the direct interaction

------- line of visibility

provider activities

Activities that are
performed by the front
office

------- line of internal interaction

Activities that are
performed by the back
office

------- line of order penetration

Activities that are not
customer induced (do not
depend on customer orders)

------- line of implementation

Activities that are needed
to enable the entire
provider process

Appendix 11. Profile of BIOTRONIK Home Monitoring

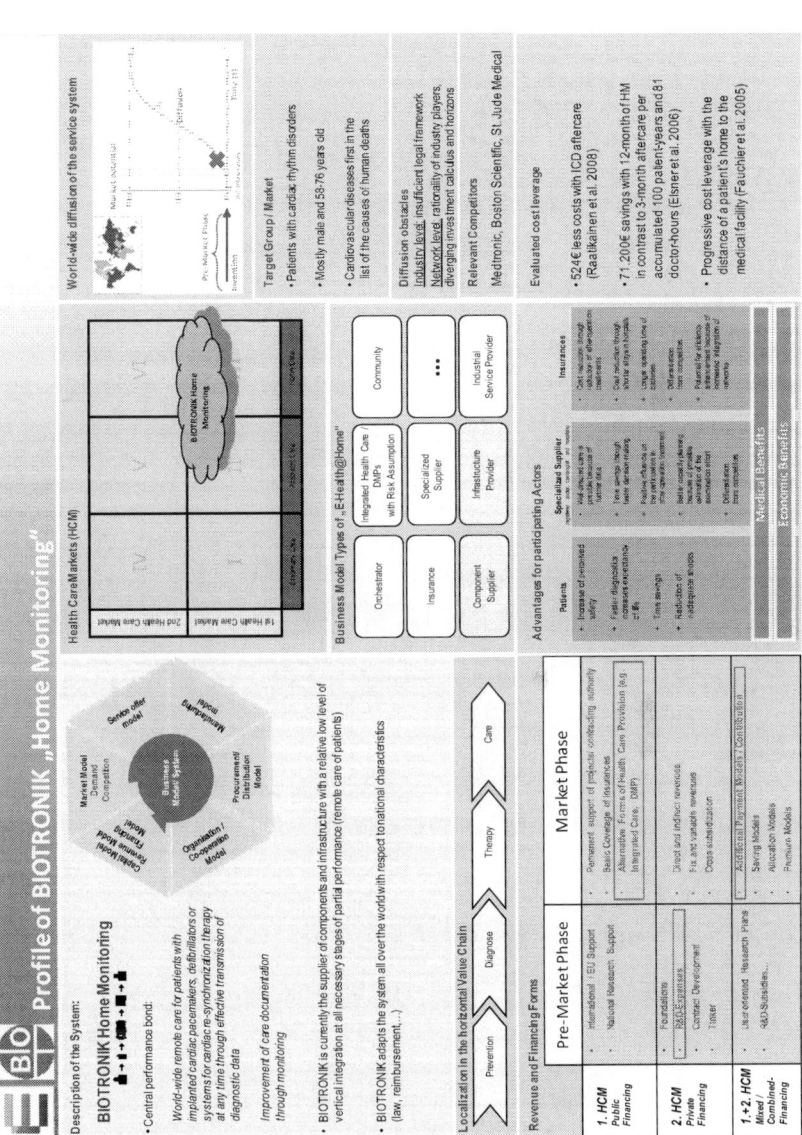

Appendix 12. Diagnosis process in the traditional modeling format

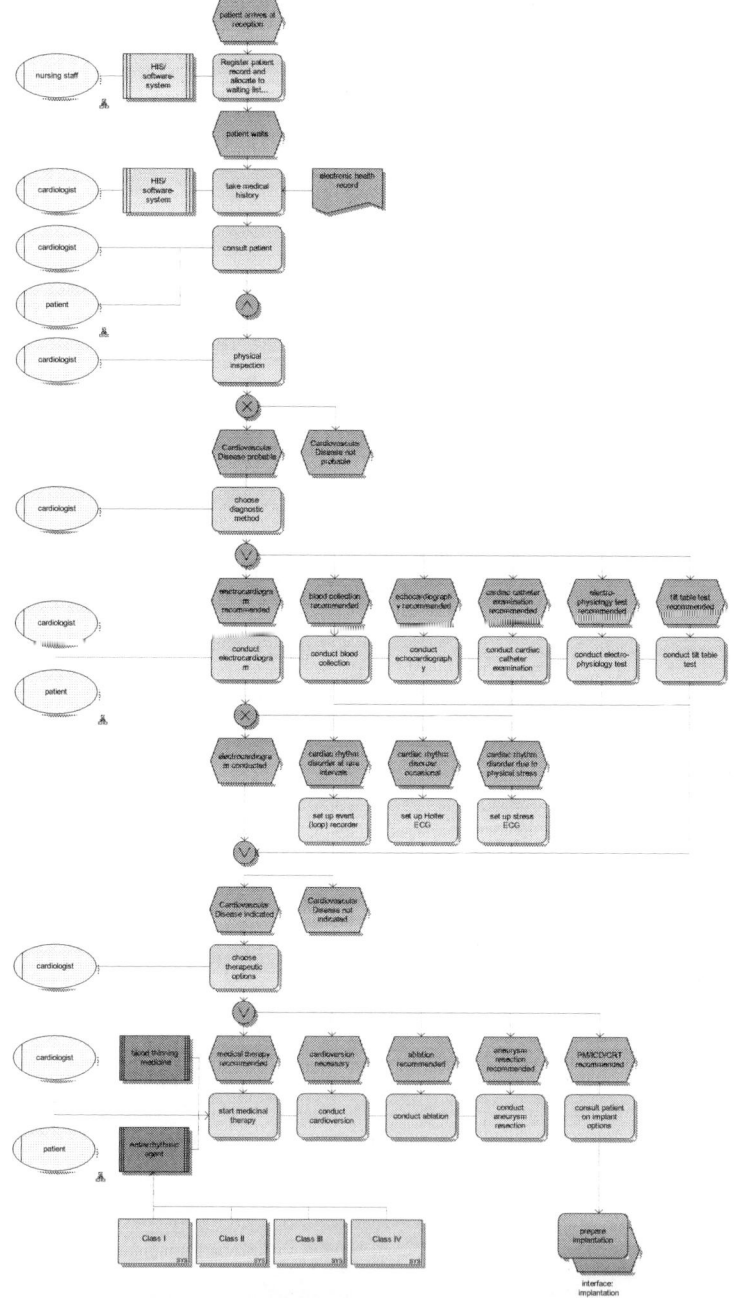

Appendix 13. Implantation process in the traditional modeling format

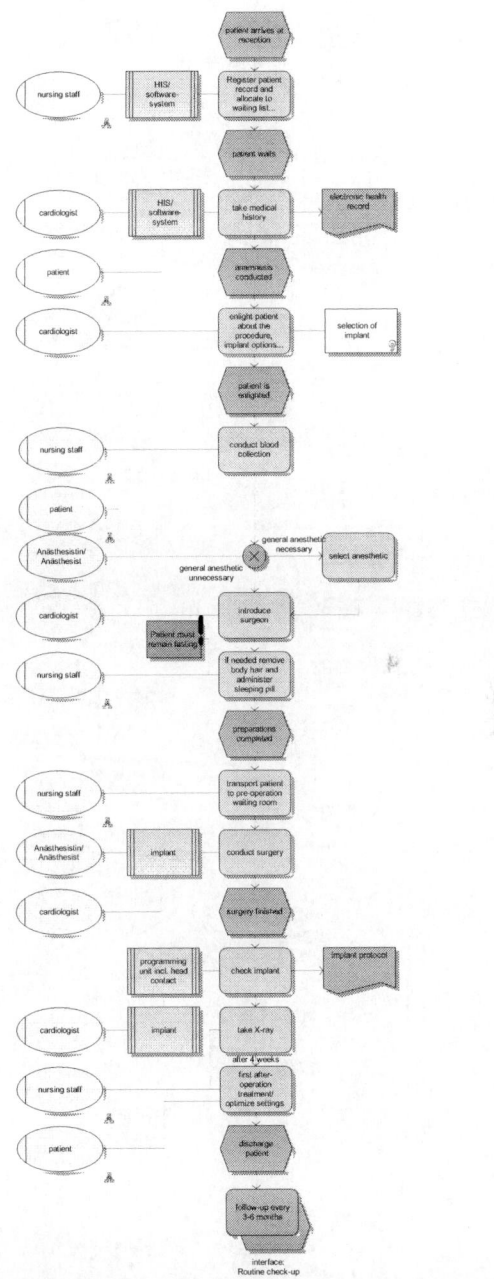

Appendix 14. Routine check-up process in the traditional modeling format

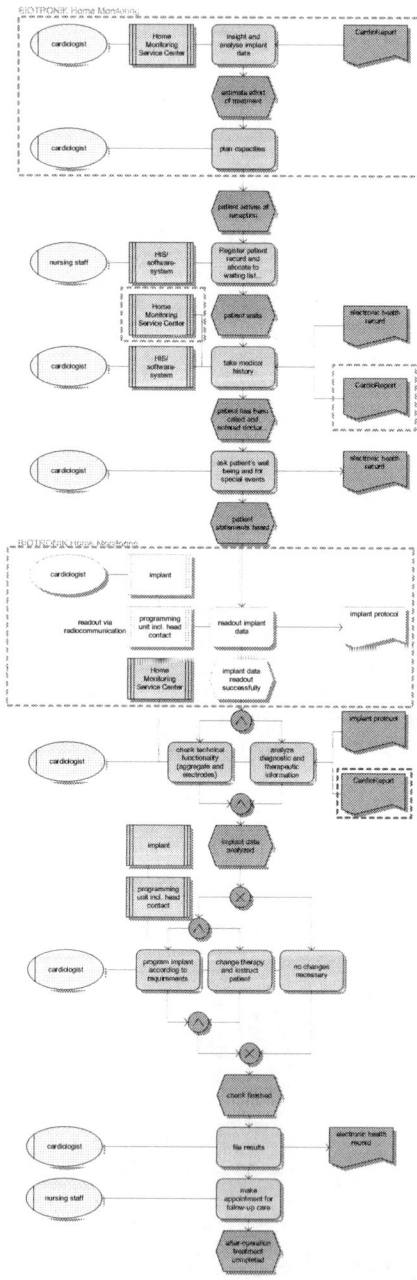

Appendix 15. Early Detection process in the traditional modeling format

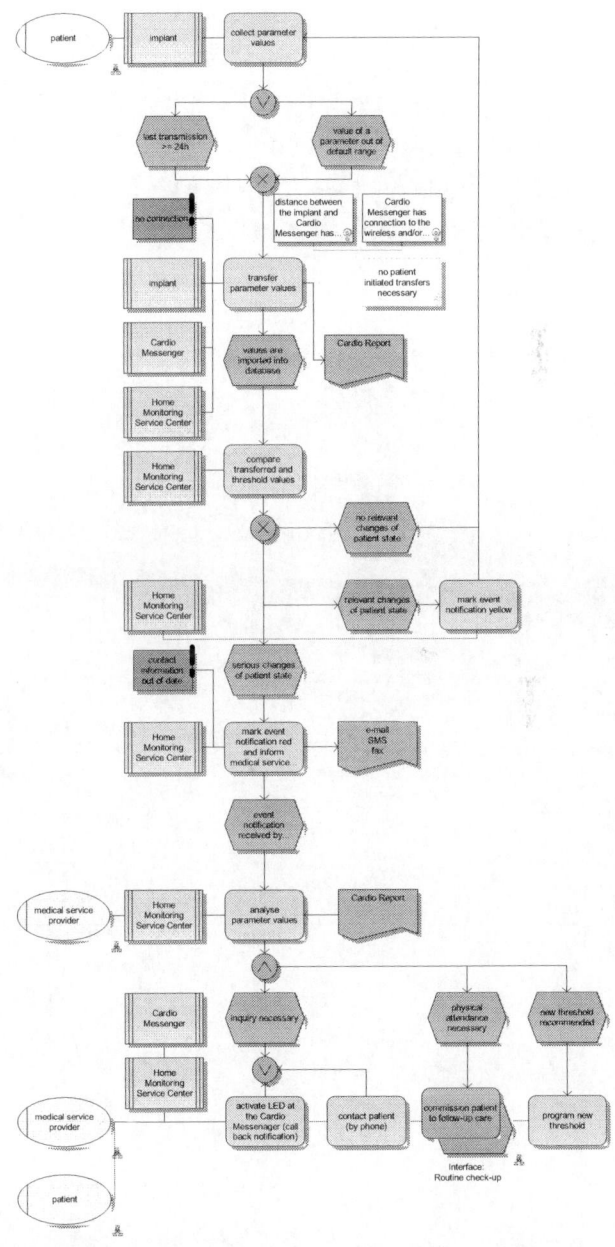

Appendix 16. Diagnosis process in the Business Process Blueprinting layout

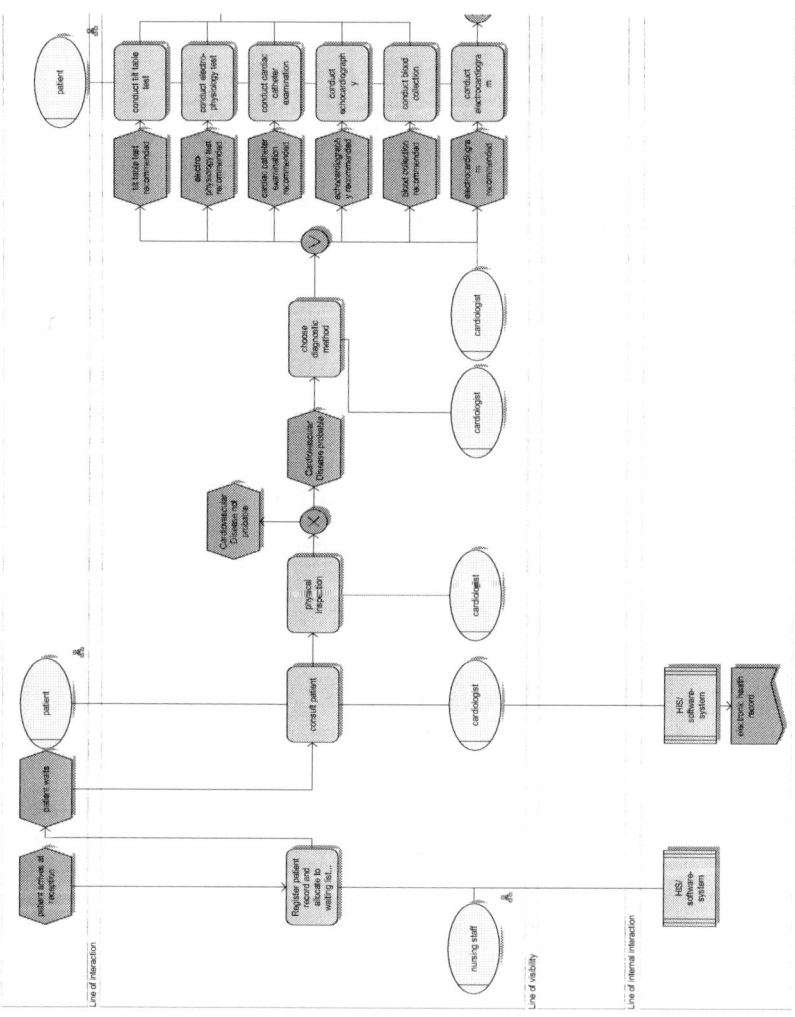

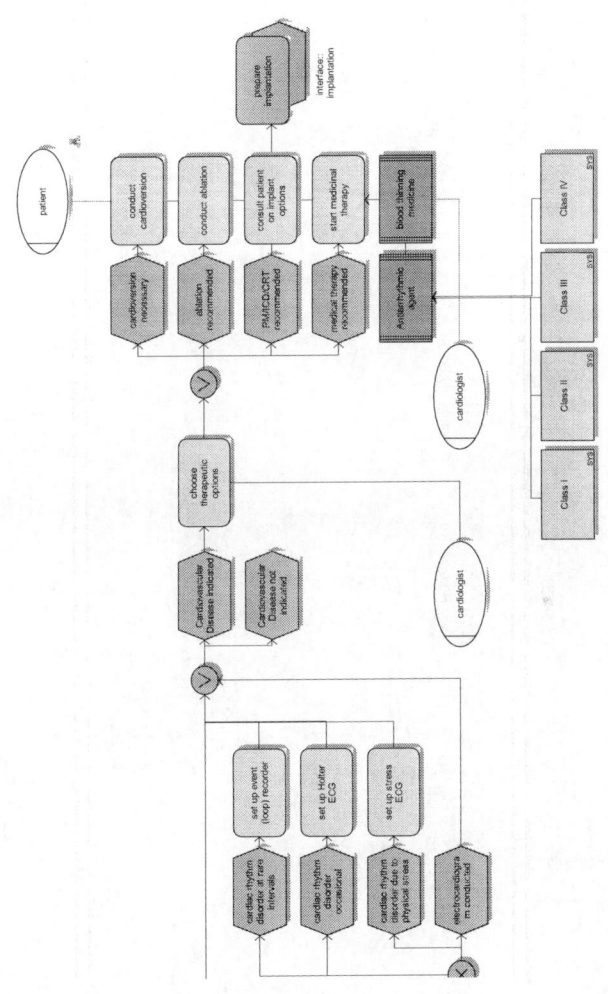

Appendix 17. Implantation process in the Business Process Blueprinting layout

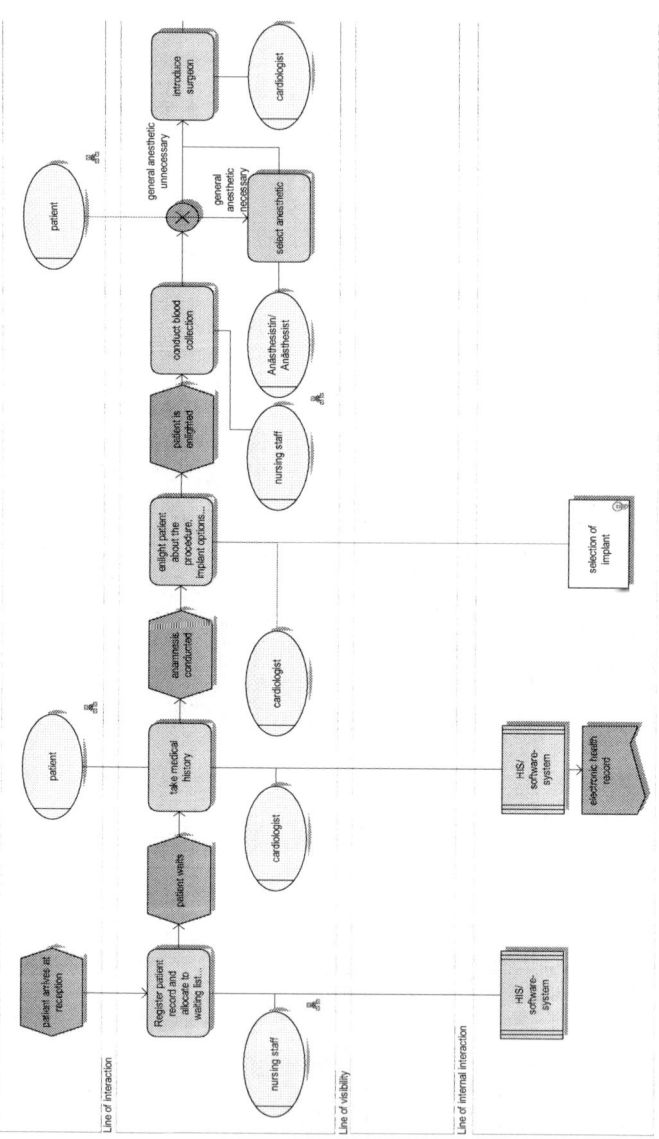

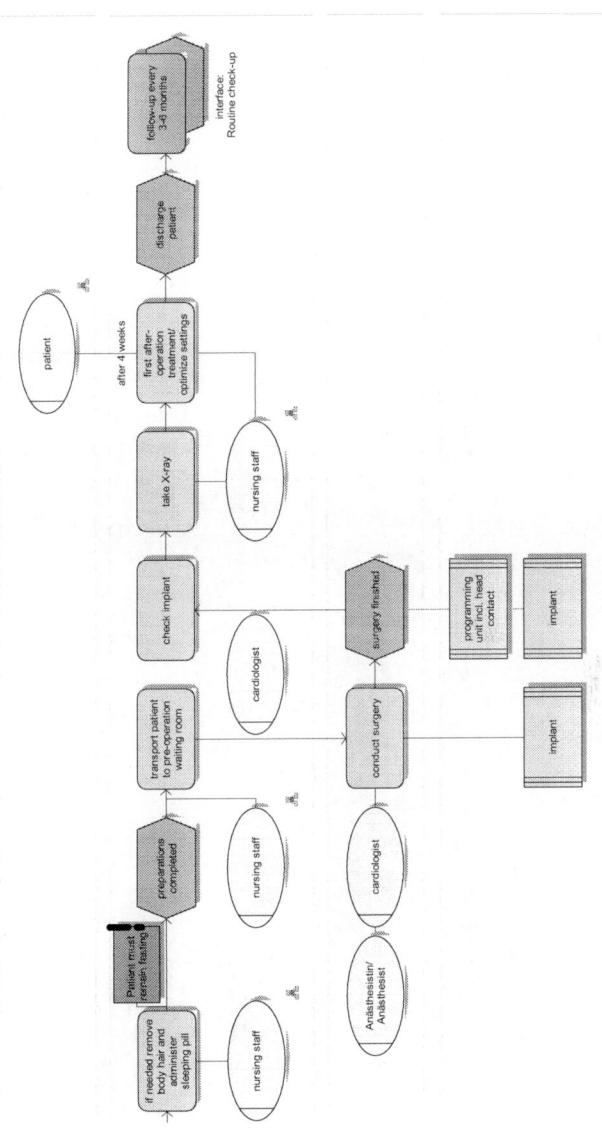

Appendix 18. Routine check-up process in the Business Process Blueprinting layout

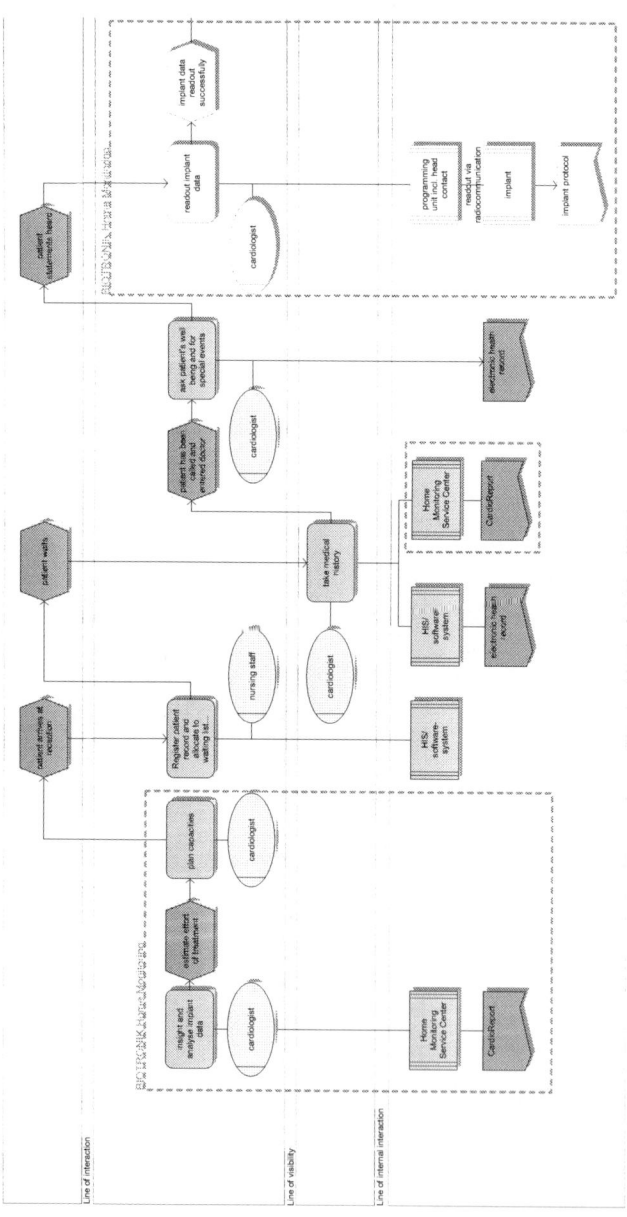

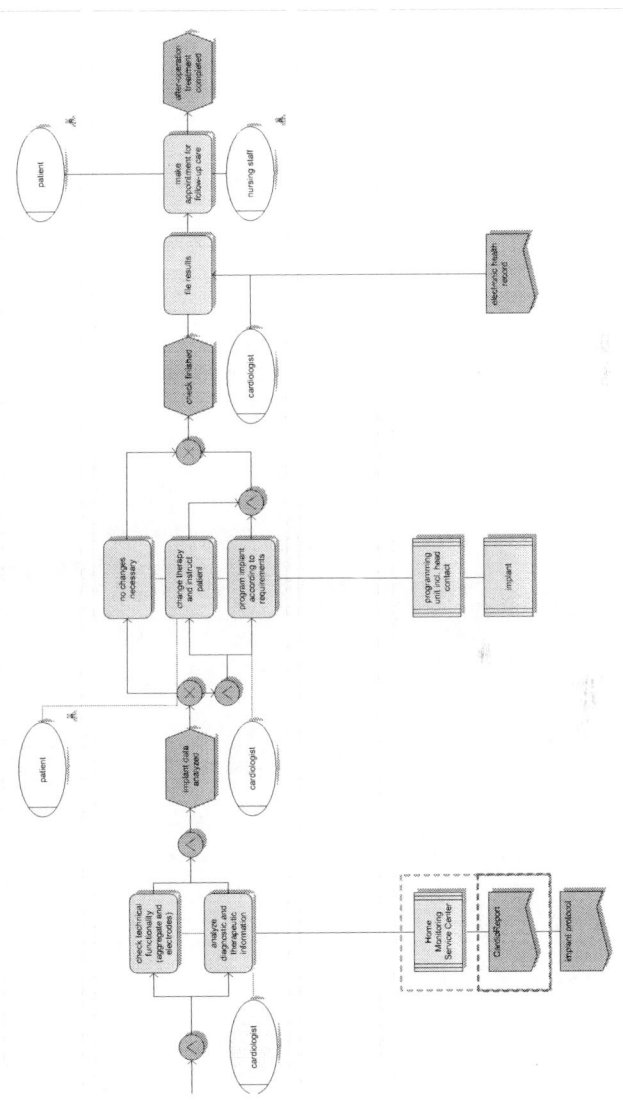

Appendix 19. Early Detection process in the Business Process Blueprinting layout

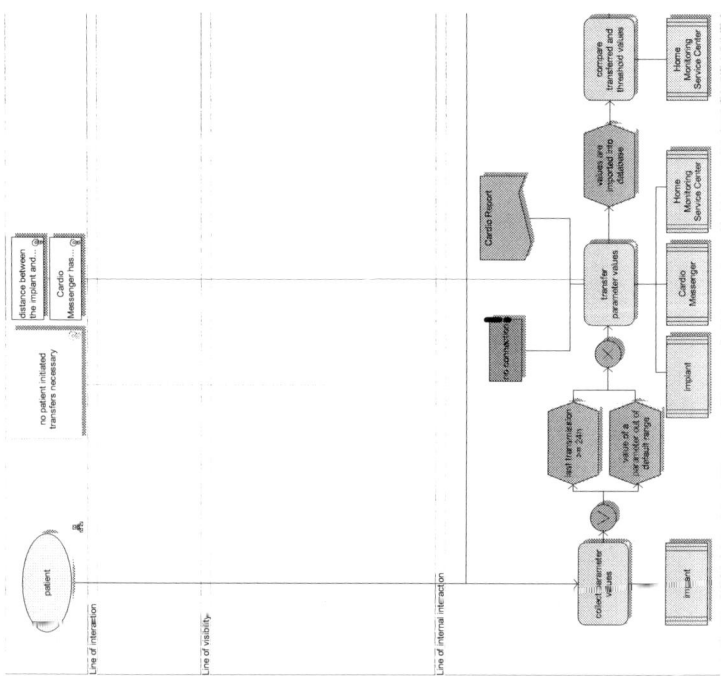

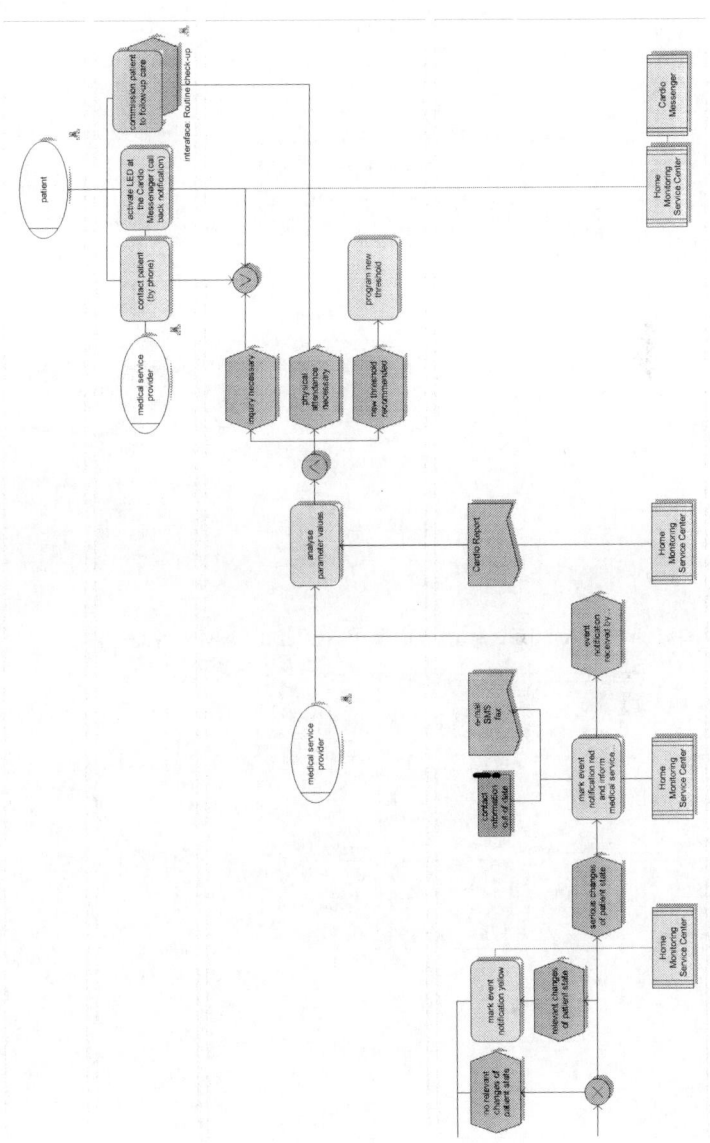

Appendix 20. Insight on the customer activities before the HM service

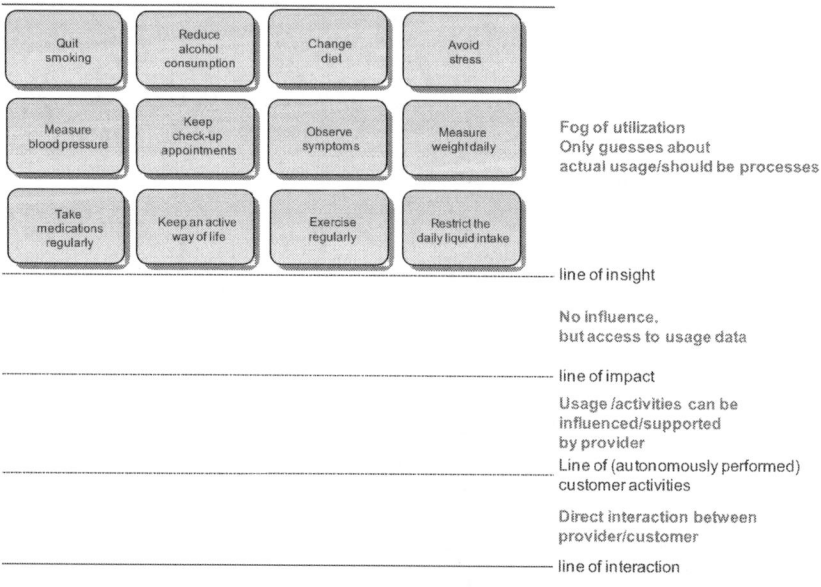

Appendix 21. Insight on the customer activities after the HM service

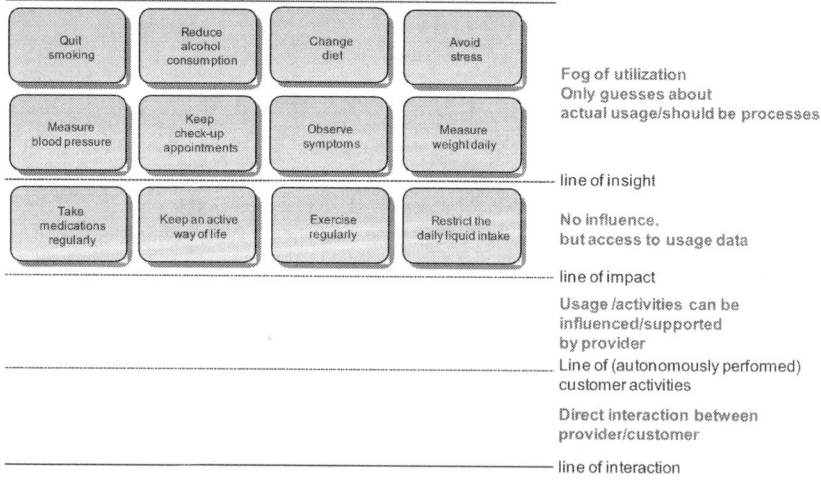

Appendix 22. Insight on the customer activities when adding further devices

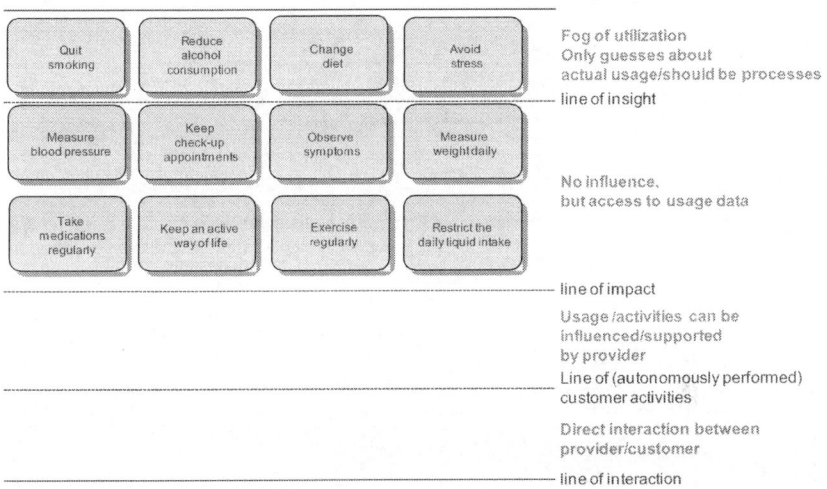

Appendix 23. Influence on the customer activities when redesigning the service offer

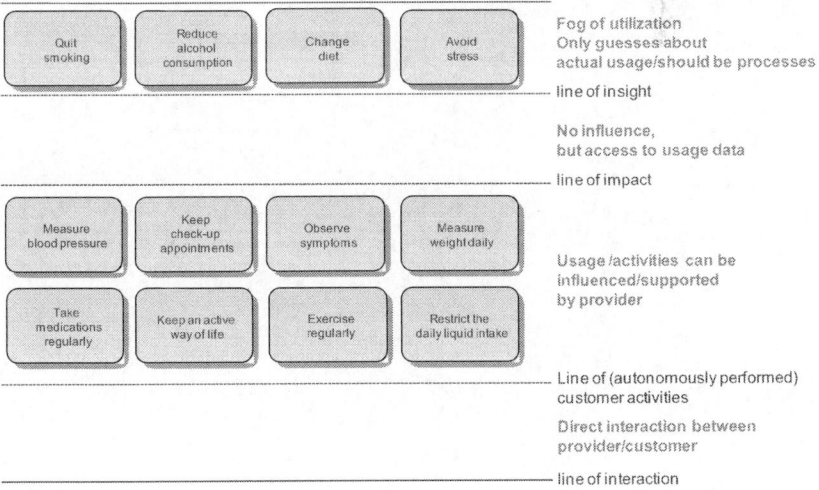

Appendix 24. Influence on the customer activities after a radically redesign of the service offer

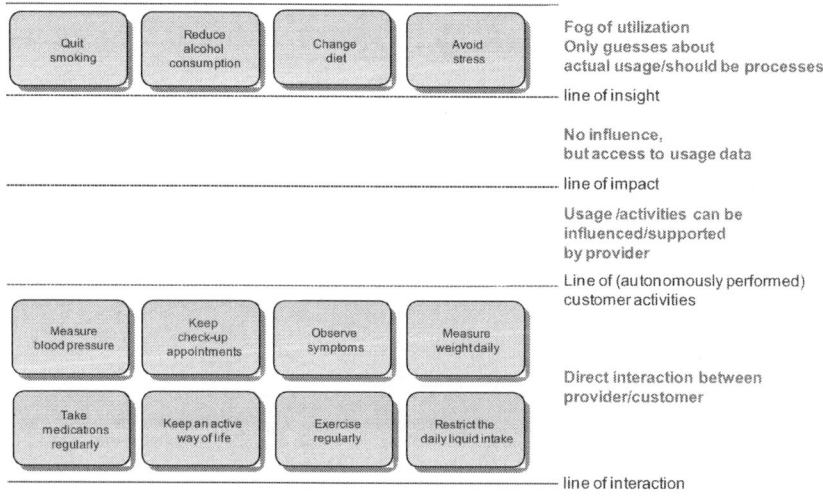

References

van der Aalst, W.M.P. (2011): *Process Mining: Discovery, Conformance and Enhancement of Business Processes*, Heidelberg: Springer.

Aguilar-Saven, R.S. (2004): Business process modelling: Review and framework, *International Journal of production economics*, Vol. 90, No. 2, pp. 129–149.

van Aken, J.E. (2004): Management Research Based on the Paradigm of the Design Sciences: The Quest for Field-Tested and Grounded Technological Rules, *Journal of Management Studies*, Vol. 41, No. 2, pp. 219–246.

Alt, R. and Puschmann, T. (2005): Developing customer process orientation: the case of Pharma Corp., *Business Process Management Journal*, Vol. 11, No. 4, pp. 297–315.

American Marketing Association. (2007): Definition of Marketing. Retrieved November 7, 2012, from http://www.marketingpower.com/AboutAMA/Pages/DefinitionofMarketing. aspx

Anderson, E.W., Fornell, C. and Lehmann, D.R. (1994): Customer Satisfaction, Market Share, and Profitability: Findings from Sweden, *Journal of Marketing*, Vol. 58, No. 3, pp. 53–66.

Appiah-Adu, K. and Singh, S. (1998): Customer orientation and performance: a study of SMEs, *Management Decision*, Vol. 36, No. 6, pp. 385–394.

Arm & Hammer. (2013): Solutions. Retrieved March 20, 2013, from http://armandhammerbakingsoda.ca/solutions

Arnould, E.J., Price, L. and Zinkhan, G.M. (2003): *Consumers*, New York: McGraw-Hill.

Atkinson, R. (1999): Project management: cost time and quality two best guesses and a phenomenon, it's time to accept other success criteria, *International Journal of Project Management*, Vol. 17, No. 6, pp. 337–342.

Atzori, L., Iera, A. and Morabito, G. (2010): The Internet of Things: A survey, *Computer Networks*, Vol. 54, No. 15, pp. 2787–2805.

Babu, A.J.G. and Suresh, N. (1996): Project management with time, cost, and quality considerations, *European Journal of Operational Research*, Vol. 88, No. 2, pp. 320–327.

Baines, P., Macdonald, E.K., Wilson, H. and Blades, F. (2011): Measuring communication channel experiences and their influence on voting in the 2010 British General Election, *Journal of Marketing Management*, Vol. 27, No. 7-8, pp. 691–717.

Baker, M.J. (2000): Writing a Literature Review, *The Marketing Review*, Vol. 1, No. 2, pp. 219–247.

Barold, S.S., Stroobandt, R.X. and Sinnaeve, A.F. (2003): *Cardiac Pacemakers Step by Step: An Illustrated Guide*, Malden: Wiley-Blackwell.

Barua, A., Konana, P., Whinston, A.B. and Yin, F. (2004): An empirical investigation of net-enabled business value, *MIS Quarterly*, Vol. 28, No. 4, pp. 585–620.

Baskerville, R. (2001): Conducting action research: high risk and high reward in theory and practice, in Trauth, E.M. (Ed.): *Qualitative research in IS: issues and trends*, Hershey: Idea Group, pp. 192–217.

Baskerville, R. (2012): Reviving the IT in the IS, *European Journal of Information Systems*, Vol. 21, No. 6, pp. 587–591.

Bastiat, F. (1995): *Selected Essays on Political Economy*, Irvington-on-Hudson: The Foundation for Economic Education.

Batista, L., Smart, A. and Maull, R. (2008): The systemic perspective of service processes; underlying theory, architecture and approach, *Production Planning and Control*, Vol. 19, No. 5, pp. 535–544.

Becker, J., Beverungen, D.F. and Knackstedt, R. (2009): The challenge of conceptual modeling for product–service systems: status-quo and perspectives for reference models and modeling languages, *Information Systems and eBusiness Management*, Vol. 8, No. 1, pp. 33–66.

Becker, J., Delfmann, P. and Knackstedt, R. (2007): Adaptive Reference Modeling: Integrating Configurative and Generic Adaptation Techniques for Information Models, in Becker, J. and Delfmann, P. (Eds.): *Reference Modeling*, Heidelberg: Physica, pp. 27–58.

Behara, R.S., Fontenot, G.F. and Gresham, A.B. (2002): Customer process approach to building loyalty, *Total Quality Management*, Vol. 13, No. 5, pp. 603–611.

Bell, D. (1973): *The Coming of Post-Industrial Society, New York*, New York: Basic Books.

Berry, M.J.A. and Linoff, G.S. (2004): *Data Mining Techniques: For Marketing, Sales, and Customer Relationship Management*, Indianapolis: Wiley.

Beverland, M., Farrelly, F. and Woodhatch, Z. (2007): Exploring the Dimensions of Proactivity Within Advertising Agency-Client Relationships, *Journal of Advertising*, Vol. 36, No. 4, pp. 49–60.

Beyer, H. and Holtzblatt, K. (1997): *Contextual Design: Defining Customer-Centered Systems*, San Francisco: Morgan Kaufmann.

BIOTRONIK. (2013): Home Monitoring - Path of data. Retrieved January 21, 2013, from
http://www.biotronik.de/wps/wcm/connect/de_de_web/biotronik/Presse/media_re
sources/Image_gallery2/img_lib_logos_illustrations

Bitner, M.J. (1992): Servicescapes: Impact of on Physical Surroundings Customers and Employees, *Journal of Marketing*, Vol. 56, No. 2, pp. 57–71.

Blackwell, R., Miniard, P. and Engel, J. (2005): *Consumer behavior*, Mason: Thomson.

Blechar, M.J. (2010): Magic quadrant for business process analysis tools, *Gartner RAS Core Research Note G00148777*, Stamford: Garnter.

Bolton, M. (2004): Customer centric business processing, *International Journal of Productivity and Performance Management*, Vol. 53, No. 1, pp. 44–51.

Booms, B.H. and Bitner, M.J. (1981): Marketing strategies and organization structures for service firms, in Donnelly, J.H. and George, W.R. (Eds.): *Marketing of Services*, Chicago: American Marketing Association, pp. 47–51.

Borden, N.H. (1964): The concept of the marketing mix, *Journal of Advertising Research*, Vol. 4, No. 2, pp. 2–7.

Borgianni, Y., Cascini, G. and Rotini, F. (2010): Process value analysis for business process re-engineering, *Journal of Engineering Manufacture*, Vol. 224, No. 2, pp. 305–327.

Botsman, R. and Rogers, R. (2010): *What's Mine Is Yours: The Rise of Collaborative Consumption*, London: HarperBusiness.

Brady, M. and Cronin, J.J. (2001a): Customer Orientation: Effects on Customer Service Perceptions and Outcome Behaviors, *Journal of Service Research*, Vol. 3, No. 3, pp. 241–251.

Brady, M. and Cronin, J.J. (2001b): Some New Thoughts on Conceptualizing Perceived Service Quality: A Hierarchical Approach, *Journal of Marketing*, Vol. 65, No. 3, pp. 34–49.

Brady, M., Saren, M. and Tzokas, N. (2002): Integrating Information Technology into Marketing Practice - The IT Reality of Contemporary Marketing Practice, *Journal of Marketing Management*, Vol. 18, No. 5-6, pp. 555–577.

Breithaupt, H.-F. (2005): *Dienstleistungen im Internet und ihre Qualität aus Kundensicht*, Wiesbaden: DUV.

vom Brocke, J., Simons, A., Niehaves, B., Riemer, K., Plattfaut, R. and Cleven, A. (2009): Reconstructing the Giant: On the Importance of Rigour in Documenting the Literature Search Process, *17th European Conference on Information Systems (ECIS)*, 8.-10. June, Verona.

vom Brocke, J. and Sinnl, T. (2011): Culture in business process management: a literature review, *Business Process Management Journal*, Vol. 17, No. 2, pp. 357–378.

Brockman, B.K., Jones, M.A. and Becherer, R.C. (2012): Customer Orientation and Performance in Small Firms: Examining the Moderating Influence of Risk-Taking, Innovativeness, and Opportunity Focus, *Journal of Small Business Management*, Vol. 50, No. 3, pp. 429–446.

Brown, R.J. (1987): Marketing - a function and a philosophy, *The Quarterly Review of Marketing*, Vol. 3, No. 12, pp. 25–30.

Bruhn, M. (2009): Das Konzept der kundenorientierten Unternehmensführung, in Hinterhuber, H. and Matzler, K. (Eds.): *Kundenorientierte Unternehmensführung*, Wiesbaden: Gabler, pp. 33–68.

Bruhn, M. (2011): *Kundenorientierung. Bausteine für ein exzellentes Customer Relationship Management (CRM)*, Munich: DTV-Beck.

Bullinger, H.-J., Fähnrich, K.-P. and Meiren, T. (2003): Service engineering - methodical development of new service products, *International Journal of Production Economics*, Vol. 85, No. 3, pp. 275–287.

Bush, A.J., Smart, D. and Nichols, E.L. (2002): Pursuing the concept of marketing productivity: introduction to the JBR Special Issue on Marketing Productivity, *Journal of Business Research*, Vol. 55, No. 5, pp. 343–347.

Caesar, M., Österle, H., Legner, C. and Capt, J.G. (2005): Kundenprozessorientierung durch Service-Portale: Das Beispiel W@M von Endress+Hauser, *Information Management and Consulting*, Vol. 1, No. 20, pp. 77–82.

De Chernatony, L. and Segal-Horn, S. (2003): The criteria for successful services brands, *European Journal of Marketing*, Vol. 37, No. 7/8, pp. 1095–1118.

Churchill, G.A. and Surprenant, C. (1982): An Investigation into the Determinants of Customer Satisfaction, *Journal of Marketing Research*, Vol. 19, No. 4, pp. 491–504.

Cleven, A., Gubler, P. and Hüner, K.M. (2009): Design alternatives for the evaluation of design science research artifacts, *Proceedings of the 4th International Conference on Design Science Research in Information Systems and Technology (DESRIST)*, 7.-8. May, Philadelphia, pp. 1–8.

Coase, R.H. (1937): The nature of the firm, *Economica*, Vol. 4, No. 16, pp. 386–405.

Coenen, C., Felten, D. von and Schmid, M. (2011): Managing effectiveness and efficiency through FM blueprinting, *Facilities*, Vol. 29, No. 9/10, pp. 422–436.

Cooper, H.M. (1988): Organizing knowledge syntheses: A taxonomy of literature reviews, *Knowledge in Society*, Vol. 1, No. 1, pp. 104–126.

Crossley, G.H., Boyle, A., Vitense, H., Chang, Y. and Mead, R.H. (2011): The CONNECT trial: the value of wireless remote monitoring with automatic clinician alerts, *Journal of the American College of Cardiology*, Vol. 57, No. 10, pp. 1181–1189.

Cummings, R.G., Harrison, G.W. and Rutström, E.E. (1995): Homegrown values and hypothetical surveys: Is the dichotomous choice approach incentive-compatible?, *The American Economic Review*, Vol. 85, No. 1, pp. 260–266.

Dabholkar, P.A., Thorpe, D.I. and Rentz, J.O. (1996): A Measure of Service Quality for Retail Stores: Scale Development and Validation, *Journal of the Academy of Marketing Science*, Vol. 24, No. 1, pp. 3–16.

Darke, P.R. and Dahl, D.W. (2003): Fairness and discounts: the subjective value of a bargain, *Journal of Consumer Psychology*, Vol. 13, No. 3, pp. 328–338.

Datta, Y. (1996): Market segmentation: an integrated framework, *Long Range Planning*, Vol. 29, No. 6, pp. 797–811.

Davenport, T.H. (1993): *Process Innovation: Reengineering Work Through Information Technology*, Boston: Harvard Business School Press.

Davenport, T.H. and Short, J.E. (1990): The New Industrial Engineering: Information Technology and Business Process Redesign, *Sloan Management Review*, Vol. 31, No. 4, pp. 11–27.

Deise, M. V., Wright, A. and Nowikow, C. (2000): *Executive's Guide to E-Business: From Tactics to Strategy*, New York: Wiley.

Deshpandé, R., Farley, J.U. and Webster, F.E. (1993): Corporate Culture, Customer Orientation, and Innovativeness in Japanese Firms: A Quadrad Analysis, *Journal of Marketing*, Vol. 57, No. 1, pp. 23–37.

Dev, B.C.S. and Schultz, D.E. (2005): Simply SIVA, *Marketing Management*, Vol. 14, No. 2, pp. 36–41.

Donnelly, J.H. (1976): Marketing intermediaries in channels of distribution for services, *The Journal of Marketing*, Vol. 40, No. 1, pp. 55–57.

Drucker, P.F. (1954): *The Practice of Management*, New York: Harper.

Drucker, P.F. (1974): *Management: tasks, responsibilities, practices*, London: Heinemann.

Dubberly, H., Evenson, S. and Robinson, R. (2008): The analysis-systhesis bridge model, *Interactions*, Vol. 15, No. 2, pp. 57–61.

EBSCO Publishing. (2013): Business Source Premier. Retrieved January 21, 2013, from http://www.ebscohost.com/academic/business-source-premier

Edvardsson, B. (1997): Quality in new service development: Key concepts and a frame of reference, *International Journal of Production Economics*, Vol. 52, No. 1-2, pp. 31–46.

Edvardsson, B. and Olsson, J. (1996): Key concepts for new service development, *Service Industries Journal*, Vol. 16, No. 2, pp. 140–164.

Eekels, J. and Roozenburg, N.F.M. (1991): A methodological comparison of the structures of scientific research and engineering design: their similarities and differences, *Design Studies*, Vol. 12, No. 4, pp. 197–203.

Eichentopf, T., Kleinaltenkamp, M. and van Stiphout, J. (2011): Modelling customer process activities in interactive value creation, *Journal of Service Management*, Vol. 22, No. 5, pp. 650–663.

Eisner, C.H., Sommer, P., Piorkowski, C., Taborsky, M., Neuser, H., Bytesnik, J., Geller, J.C., Kottkamp, H., Wiesmeth, H. and Hindricks, G. (2006): A prospective multicenter comparison trial of home monitoring against regular follow-up in MADIT II patients: additional visits and cost impact, *Computers in Cardiology*, September 17-20, Valencia, pp. 241–244.

Emerald Group Publishing Limited. (2013): About Emerald. Retrieved January 21, 2013, from http://www.emeraldinsight.com/about/index.htm

Endres, A. and Radke, V. (2012): The Economic Approach, *Economics for Environmental Studies*, Berlin: Springer, pp. 17–29.

Engelhardt, W.H. (1966): Grundprobleme der Leistungslehre dargestellt am Beispiel der Warenhandelsbetriebe, *Zeitschrift für betriebswirtschaftliche Forschung*, Vol. 18, No. 2, pp. 158–179.

Engelhardt, W.H. (1989): Dienstleistungsorientiertes Marketing - Antwort auf die Herausforderung durch neue Technologien, in Adam, D., Backhaus, K., Meffert, H. and Wagner, H. (Eds.): *Integration und Flexibilität - Eine Herausforderung für die Allgemeine Betriebswirtschaftslehre*, Wiesbaden: Gabler, pp. 269–288.

Engelhardt, W.H. (1995): Potentiale - Prozesse - Leistungsbündel: Diskussionsbeiträge zur Leistungstheorie, *Schriften zum Marketing Nr. 32*, Bochum: Ruhr-Universität.

Engelhardt, W.H. and Freiling, J. (1995): Die integrative Gestaltung von Leistungspotentialen, *Zeitschrift für betriebswirtschaftliche Forschung*, Vol. 47, No. 10, pp. 899–918.

Engelhardt, W.H., Kleinaltenkamp, M. and Reckenfelderbäumer, M. (1992): *Dienstleistungen als Absatzobjekte*, Working Paper No. 52, Bochum: Institute of Management.

Engelhardt, W.H., Kleinaltenkamp, M. and Reckenfelderbäumer, M. (1993): Leistungsbündel als Absatzobjekte, *Zeitschrift für betriebswirtschaftliche Forschung*, Vol. 45, No. 5, pp. 395–426.

European Society of Cardiology. (2011): *Guidelines compendium*, London: Springer.

Fauchier, L., Sadoul, N., Kouakam, C., Briand, F., Chauvin, M., Babuty, D. and Clementy, J. (2005): Potential cost savings by telemedicine-assisted long-term care of implantable cardioverter defibrillator recipients, *Pacing and clinical electrophysiology*, Vol. 28, No. 1 (supplement 1), pp. 255–259.

Fink, C., Gabriel, R., Gersch, M., Lehr, C. and Weber, P. (2011): Lernservice Engineering - eine ökonomische Perspektive auf technologiegestütztes Lernen, in Ebner, M. and Schön, S. (Eds.): *Lehrbuch für Lernen und Lehren mit Technologien*, Berlin: epubli, pp. 331–338.

Finn, D. and Lamb, C. (1991): An Evaluation of the SERVQUAL Scales in a Retailing Setting, in Holman, R. and Solomon, M. (Eds.): *Advances in Consumer Research*, Association for Consumer Research, pp. 483–490.

Fitzgerald, B. (1997): The use of systems development methodologies in practice: a field study, *Information Systems Journal*, Vol. 7, No. 3, pp. 201–212.

Flanagan, J.C. (1954): The critical incident technique, *Psychological bulletin*, Vol. 51, No. 4, pp. 327–358.

Fließ, S. (2001): *Die Steuerung von Kundenintegrationsprozessen: Effizienz in Dienstleistungsunternehmen*, Wiesbaden: DUV.

Fließ, S. (2006): *Prozessorganisation in Dienstleistungsunternehmen*, Stuttgart: Kohlhammer.

Fließ, S. (2008): *Dienstleistungsmanagement: Kundenintegration gestalten und steuern*, Wiesbaden: Gabler.

Fließ, S. (2009): Health Care - Die Sicht des Kunden, in Nickl-Weller, C., Rämmler, B. and Fernández de Santos, V. (Eds.): *Health Care der Zukunft 2: Auf dem Weg zur Risikokultur*, Berlin: MWV, pp. 61–70.

Fließ, S., Jacob, F. and Fandel, G. (2011): Von der Kundenintegration 1.0 zur Kundenintegration 2.0 - Implikationen für Praxis und Forschung, *Journal of Business Economics*, No. 5 (special issue), pp. 5–20.

Fließ, S. and Kleinaltenkamp, M. (2004): Blueprinting the service company, *Journal of Business Research*, Vol. 57, No. 4, pp. 392–404.

Fließ, S. and Völker-Albert, J.-H. (2002): Going Virtual - Blueprinting als Basis des Prozessmanagements von E-Service-Anbietern, in Stauss, B. and Bruhn, M. (Eds.): *Jahrbuch für Dienstleistungsmanagement 2002 - Electronic Services*, Wiesbaden: Gabler, pp. 263 – 291.

Frank, U, (2006)· *Towards a Pluralistic Conception of Research Methods in Information Systems Research*, ICB-Research Report No. 7, Universität Duisburg-Essen.

Frauendorf, J. (2006): *Customer Processes in Business-to-Business Service Transactions*, Heidelberg: Gabler.

Fried, H.O., Lovell, C.A.K. and Schmidt, S.S. (2008): Efficiency and productivity, *The measurement of productive efficiency and productivity growth*, Oxford University Press New York, pp. 3–91.

Friedman, C.P. and Wyatt, J. (2010): *Evaluation Methods in Biomedical Informatics*, New York: Springer.

Gabriel, R., Gersch, M. and Weber, P. (2008): Blueprinting and Education Service Engineering - Preperations for a Learning-process-oriented Measurement of Satisfaction in Blended Learning Settings, *Proceedings of E-Learn 2008*, November 17-21, Las Vegas.

Gabriel, R., Gersch, M. and Weber, P. (2009): Leistungstiefenentscheidung und IT-Sourcing   -   Veränderte   Herausforderungen   des   Strategischen

Informationsmanagements, in Keuper, F., Wagner, B. and Wysuwa, H. (Eds.): *Managed Services: IT-Sourcing der nächsten Generation*, Wiesbaden: Gabler.

Gadatsch, A. (2010): *Grundkurs Geschäftsprozessmanagement*, Wiesbaden: Vieweg.

Garvin, D.A. (1988): *Managing Quality: The Strategic and Competitive Edge*, New York: Free Press.

Gatignon, H. and Xuereb, J.-M. (1997): Strategic Orientation of the Firm and New Product Performance, *Journal of Marketing Research*, Vol. 34, No. 1, pp. 77–90.

Georgakopoulos, D., Hornick, M. and Sheth, A. (1995): An overview of workflow management: From process modeling to workflow automation infrastructure, *Distributed and Parallel Databases*, Vol. 3, No. 2, pp. 119–153.

Gerpott, T.J. and Berg, S. (2011): Determinants of the Willingness to Use Mobile Location-Based Services, *Business and Information Systems Engineering*, Vol. 3, No. 5, pp. 279–287.

Gersch, M. (1995): *Die Standardisierung integrativ erstellter Leistungen*, Working Paper No. 57, Bochum: Institute of Management.

Gersch, M. (1998): *Vernetzte Geschäftsbeziehungen: die Nutzung von EDI als Instrument des Geschäftsbeziehungsmanagement*, Wiesbaden: Gabler.

Gersch, M. (2006): Kundenorientiertes Blueprinting von Geschäftsprozessen - Ein Vorschlag zur Überwindung identifizierbarer Fachgrenzen zwischen Marketing und Wirtschaftsinformatik, *Habilitation colloquium*, 14. February, Ruhr-Universität Bochum, pp. 1–19.

Gersch, M. and Goeke, C. (2007): Typical stages in industries' e-transformation - hints for forecasting future entrepreneurial challenges in revenue management, *International Journal of Revenue Management*, Vol. 1, No. 3, pp. 276–292.

Gersch, M., Goeke, C. and Lux, T. (2006): *Geschäftsprozess-Blueprinting: Kundenorientierte Prozessgestaltung am Beispiel von E-Services*, Working Paper No. 63, Bochum: Institute of Management.

Gersch, M. and Hewing, M. (2012): AAL-Geschäftsmodelle im Gesundheitswesen - Eine empirisch gestützte Typologie relevanter Grundtypen ökonomischer Aktivitäten zur Nutzung von Ambient Assisted Living in sich verändernden Wertschöpfungsketten, in Gersch, M. and Liesenfeld, J. (Eds.): *E-Health- und AAL-Geschäftsmodelle - Technologie und Dienstleistungen im demografischen Wandel und in sich verändernden Wertschöpfungsarchitekturen*, Wiesbaden: Gabler, pp. 3–26.

Gersch, M., Hewing, M. and Schöler, B. (2011): Business Process Blueprinting - an enhanced view on process performance, *Business Process Management Journal*, Vol. 17, No. 5, pp. 732–747.

Gersch, M., Lindert, R. and Hewing, M. (2010): AAL-business models: Different Prospects for the Successful Implementation of Innovative Services in the Primary and Secondary Healthcare Market, *ALLIANCE*, 11.-12. March, Malaga.

Gersch, M., Schöler, B. and Hewing, M. (2010): Service Dominant Logic and Business Process Blueprinting: Enhancing the View on Performance by Integrating the Customer Perspective, *Proceedings of the 16th Americas Conference on Information Systems (AMCIS)*, 12.-15. August, Lima.

Gersch, M., Schöler, B. and Hewing, M. (2011): Business Process Blueprinting: Analysing and Evaluating Usage Processes, *Special Interest Group 10 of the 40th Annual Conference of the European Marketing Academy (EMAC)*, 24.-27. May, Ljubljana.

Giaglis, G.M. (2001): A taxonomy of business process modeling and information systems modeling techniques, *International Journal of Flexible Manufacturing Systems*, Vol. 13, No. 2, pp. 209–228.

Gossain, S. (2002): Cracking the collaboration code, *Journal of Business Strategy*, Vol. 23, No. 6, pp. 20–25.

Green, S,D, and Simister, S.J. (1999): Modelling client business processes as an aid to strategic briefing, *Construction Management and Economics*, Vol. 17, No. 1, pp. 63–76.

Grewal, D., Levy, M. and Kumar, V. (2009): Customer Experience Management in Retailing: An Organizing Framework, *Journal of Retailing*, Vol. 85, No. 1, pp. 1–14.

Grönroos, C. (1984): A Service Quality Model and its Marketing Implications, *European Journal of Marketing*, Vol. 18, No. 4, pp. 36–44.

Grönroos, C. (1990): *Service management and marketing: managing the moments of truth in service competition*, Lexington: Lexington Books.

Grönroos, C. (2008): Service logic revisited: who creates value? And who co-creates?, *European Business Review*, Vol. 20, No. 4, pp. 298–314.

Grönroos, C. (2011): A service perspective on business relationships: The value creation, interaction and marketing interface, *Industrial Marketing Management*, Vol. 40, No. 2, pp. 240–247.

Grönroos, C. and Voima, P. (2012): Critical service logic: making sense of value creation and co-creation, *Journal of the Academy of Marketing Science*, Vol. 42, No. 2, pp. 1–18.

Hammer, M. (1990): Reengineering Work: Don't Automate, Obliterate, *Harvard Business Review*, Vol. 68, No. 4, pp. 104–112.

Hammer, M. (2010): What is Business Process Management?, in vom Brocke, J. and Rosemann, M. (Eds.): *Handbook on Business Process Management 1*, Heidelberg: Springer, pp. 3–16.

Hammer, M. and Champy, J. (1994): *Reengineering the Corporation: A Manifesto for Business Revolution*, New York: HarperBusiness.

Harmon, P. (2010): The Scope and Evolution of Business Process Management, in Rosemann, M. and vom Brocke, J. (Eds.): *Handbook on Business Process Management 1*, Heidelberg: Springer, pp. 37–81.

Hart, C. (1998): *Doing a Literature Review: Releasing the Social Science Research Imagination, Management*, Sage.

Heckl, D. and Moormann, J. (2007): Matching Customer Processes with Business Processes of Banks: The Example of Small and Medium-Sized Enterprises as Bank Customers., *Proceedings of the 5th International Conference on Business Process Management (BPM)*, 24.-28.September, Brisbane, pp. 112 – 124.

Hedrick, T.E., Bickman, L. and Rog, D. (1993): *Applied Research Design: A Practical Guide*, Newbury Park: Sage.

Herder-Dorneich, P. (1978): Social Control in Health Economics, *Review of Social Economy*, Vol. 36, No. 1, pp. 1–18.

Heskett, J.L., Sasser, W.E. and Schlesinger, L.A. (1997): *The Service Profit Chain*, New York: Free Press.

Hevner, A.R. and Chatterjee, S. (2010): *Design Research in Information Systems: Theory and Practice*, New York: Springer.

Hevner, A.R., March, S.T., Park, J. and Ram, S. (2004): Design Science in Information Systems Research, *MIS Quarterly*, Vol. 28, No. 1, pp. 75–105.

Hewing, M. (2011): In the eye of the beholder: Customer-orientated Process Management through Blueprinting, *PhD Symposium of the 9th International Conference on Business Process Management (BPM)*, 28. August-02. September, Clermont-Ferrand.

Hinkelmann, K. and Kempthorne, O. (2008): *Design and Analysis of Experiments - Volume 1: Introduction to Experimental Design*, Hoboken: Wiley.

van Hoek, R.I. (2001): The rediscovery of postponement a literature review and directions for research, *Journal of Operations Management*, Vol. 19, No. 2, pp. 161–184.

Huang, B., Zhu, P. and Wu, C. (2012): Customer-centered careflow modeling based on guidelines, *Journal of medical systems*, Vol. 36, No. 5, pp. 3307–3319.

ISO (2005): Quality management systems - Fundamentals and vocabulary, *International Organization for Standardization (ISO) 9000:2005*. Retrieved November 20, 2012, from https://www.iso.org/obp/ui/#iso:std:iso:9000:ed-3:v1:en

Jacob, F. and Kleinaltenkamp, M. (2004): Leistungsindividualisierung und - standardisierung, in Backhaus, K. and Voeth, M. (Eds.): *Handbuch Industriegütermarketing*, Wiesbaden: Gabler, pp. 602–623.

Jain, R.K. (1991): *The Art of Computer Systems Performance Analysis: Techniques for Experimental Design, Measurement, Simulation, and Modeling*, New York: Wiley.

Jaworski, B.J. and Kohli, A.K. (1993): Market Orientation: Antecedents and Consequences, *Journal of Marketing*, Vol. 57, No. 3, p. 53.

Jayachandran, S., Hewett, K. and Kaufman, P. (2004): Customer Response Capability in a Sense-and-Respond Era: The Role of Customer Knowledge Process, *Journal of the Academy of Marketing Science*, Vol. 32, No. 3, pp. 219–233.

Johannesson, M., Liljas, B. and O'Conor, R.M. (1997): Hypothetical versus real willingness to pay: some experimental results, *Applied Economics Letters*, Vol. 4, No. 3, pp. 149–151.

Johnson, M.D. (1997): *Customer Orientation and Market Action*, Upper Saddle River: Prentice Hall.

Judd, R.C. (1964): The Case for Redefining Services, *Journal of Marketing*, Vol. 28, No. 1, p. 58.

Jung, W., Rillig, A., Birkemeyer, R., Miljak, T. and Meyerfeldt, U. (2008): Advances in remote monitoring of implantable pacemakers, cardioverter defibrillators and cardiac resynchronization therapy systems, *Journal of interventional cardiac electrophysiology an international journal of arrhythmias and pacing*, Vol. 23, No. 1, pp. 73–85.

Kagermann, H., Österle, H. and Jordan, J.M. (2010): *IT-Driven Business Models*, Hoboken: Wiley.

Kaplan, R.S. and Norton, D.P. (1996): *The Balanced Scorecard: Translating Strategy into Action*, Boston: Harvard Business School Press.

Kawalek, P. and Wastell, D. (2002): A case study evaluation of the use of the viable system model in information systems development, in van Grembergen, W. (Ed.): *Information Systems Evaluation Management*, Hershey: IGI Global, pp. 17–34.

Keh, H.T., Chu, S. and Xu, J. (2006): Efficiency, effectiveness and productivity of marketing in services, *European Journal of Operational Research*, Vol. 170, No. 1, pp. 265–276.

Kemsley, S. (2011): The Changing Nature of Work: From Structured to Unstructured, from Controlled to Social, *Keynote of the 9th International Conference on Business Process Management (BPM)*, 28. August-02. September, Clermont-Ferrand.

Kennedy, K.N., Goolsby, J.R. and Arnould, E.J. (2003): Implementing a Customer Orientation: Extension of Theory and Application, *Journal of Marketing*, Vol. 67, No. 4, pp. 67–81.

Khang, D.B. and Myint, Y.M. (1999): Time, cost and quality trade-off in project management: a case study, *International Journal of Project Management*, Vol. 17, No. 4, pp. 249–256.

Kim, Y.-G. (1995): Process Modeling For BPR: Event-Process Chain Approach, *Proceedings of the 16th International Conference on Information Systems (ECIS)*, 10.-13. December, Amsterdam, pp. 109–121.

Kingman-Brundage, J. (1989): The ABC's of service system blueprinting, in Bitner, L. and Cosby, L. (Eds.): *Designing a winning service strategy*, Chicago: American Marketing Association, pp. 30–33.

Kingman-Brundage, J. (1993): Service mapping: gaining a concrete perspective on service system design, in Eberhard, E. and Christopher, W. (Eds.): *The service quality handbook*, New York: Amacon, pp. 148–163.

Kingman-Brundage, J. (1995): Service Mapping: Back to Basics, in Glynn, W.J. and Barnes, J.G. (Eds.): *Understanding Services Management*, Chichester: Wiley, pp. 119–142.

Kingman-Brundage, J., George, W. and Bowen, D. (1995): Service logic: achieving system integration, *International Journal of Service Industry Management*, Vol. 6, No. 4, pp. 20–39.

Kingman-Brundage, J. and Shostack, G.L. (1991): How to design a service, in Congram, C.A. and Friedman, M.L. (Eds.): *The American Marketing Association Handbook of Marketing for the Service Industries*, New York: Amacom, pp. 243–261.

Kissel, E. and Vigneau, E. (2009): *Architectural Photoreproductions: A Manual for Identification and Care*, New Castle: Oak Knoll Press.

Kleinaltenkamp, M. (1997): Integrativität als Kern einer umfassenden Leistungslehre, in Backhaus, K., Günter, B., Plinke, W. and Raffée, H. (Eds.): *Marktleistung und Wettbewerb*, Wiesbaden: Gabler, pp. 83–114.

Kleinaltenkamp, M. (1999): Service-Blueprinting. Ein Instrument zur Steigerung der Effektivität und Effizienz von Dienstleistungsprozessen, *Technischer Vertrieb*, Vol. 1, No. 2, pp. 33–39.

Kleinaltenkamp, M. (2000): Einführung in das Business-to-Business Marketing, in Kleinaltenkamp, M. and Plinke, W. (Eds.): *Technischer Vertrieb: Grundlagen des Business-to-Business Marketing*, Berlin: Springer, pp. 171–249.

Kleinaltenkamp, M. (2001): Begriffsabgrenzungen und Erscheinungsformen von Dienstleistungen, in Bruhn, M. and Meffert, H. (Eds.): *Handbuch Dienstleistungsmanagement*, Wiesbaden: Gabler, pp. 29–52.

Kleinaltenkamp, M., Fließ, S. and Jacob, F. (1996): *Customer Integration: Von der Kundenorientierung zur Kundenintegration*, Wiesbaden: Gabler.

Kleinaltenkamp, M., Macdonald, E. and Wilson, H. (2011): How co-creation processes create value: An exploration in an industrial maintenance context using repertory grid technique, *Proceedings of the 14th Australian and New Zealand Marketing Academy Conference*, 28.- 30. November, Perth.

Kleinaltenkamp, M., Macdonald, E. and Wilson, H. (2012a): Value Co-creation in a Usage Center, *Proceedings of the 20th Academic Conference of the Institute of the Study of Buiness Markets*, 15.-16. August, Chicago.

Kleinaltenkamp, M., Macdonald, E. and Wilson, H. (2012b): 'You'll Never Walk Alone' - Value Co-creation in a Usage Center, *Proceedings of the 3rd Global Marketing Conference*, 19.-22. July, Seoul.

Kleinaltenkamp, M. and Macdonald, E.K. (2011): Usage Processes and Value-in-Use: Important Areas of Focus for Marketing in the "The Day After", *Proceedings of the 40th Annual Conference of the European Marketing Academy (EMAC)*, 24.-27. May, Ljubljana.

Kleinaltenkamp, M., van Stiphout, J. and Eichentopf, T. (2010): The customer script as a model of customer process activities in interactive value creation, *Proceedings of the 11th International Research Seminar in Service Management*, 25.-28. May, La Londes les Maures, pp. 457–475.

Klose, K., Knackstedt, R. and Becker, J. (2005): Process Modelling for Service Processes - Modelling Methods Extensions for Specifying and Analysing Customer Integration, *Proceedings of the 7th International Conference on Enterprise Information Systems (ICEIS)*, 25.-28. May, Miami, pp. 260–265.

Knackstedt, R. and Dahlke, B. (2004): Customer Process Management, *Das Wirtschaftsstudium*, Vol. 33, No. 1, pp. 47–54.

Knackstedt, R. and Pellengahr, M. (2007): Plädoyer für die Entwicklung perspektivenspezifischer Problemlösungskomponenten zur Unterstützung der Prozessverbesserung, *Proceedings of the 8th Conference on Wirtschaftsinformatik*, 28. February-02. March, Karlsruhe.

Kohli, A.K. and Jaworski, B.J. (1990): Market Orientation: The Consturct, Research Propositions, and Managerial Implications, *Journal of Marketing*, Vol. 54, No. April, pp. 1–18.

Kotler, P. and Armstrong, G. (2011): *Principles of Marketing*, Upper Saddle River: Prentice Hall.

Kotler, P., Keller, D.K.L., Brady, D.M., Goodman, M. and Hansen, M.T. (2012): *Marketing Management*, Harlow: Prentice Hall.

Kuhn, T.S. (2012): *The Structure of Scientific Revolutions*, Chicago: University of Chicago Press.

Langeard, E., Bateson, J., Lovelock, C.H. and Eiglier, P. (1981): *Marketing of Services: New Insight from Consumers and Managers*, Report No. 81-104, Cambridge: Marketing Science Institute.

Laß, D. (2002): *Kundenwünsche analysieren und verstehen. Theorien, Methoden und Anwendungsbeispiele für Wissenschaft, Marktforschungs- und Managementpraxis*, Berlin: Weißensee Verlag.

Lasshof, B. (2006): *Produktivität von Dienstleistungen: Mitwirkung und Einfluss des Kunden*, Wiesbaden: Gabler.

Laudon, K.C. and Laudon, J.P. (2012): *Management Information Systems: Managing the Digital Firm*, Boston: Pearson.

Lebas, M.J. (1995): Performance measurement and performance management, *International Journal of Production Economics*, Vol. 41, No. 1–3, pp. 23–35.

Lehr, C. (2012): *Web 2.0 in higher education - A framework for designing technology-based learning scenarios*, Glückstadt: vwh Verlag.

Leist, S. (2002): Bankenarchitektur des Informationszeitalters - Zielsetzung und Gestaltungsebenen, in Leist, S. and Winter, R. (Eds.): *Retail Banking im Informationszeitalter*, Berlin: Springer, pp. 4–28.

Leister, J.E. (2011): *Die Dienstleistungsumgebung als Indikator in der Vertrauensbildung bei Auswahlentscheidungen Eine empirische Analyse am Beispiel des Krankenhauses*, Berlin: Pro Business.

Lemke, F., Clark, M. and Wilson, H. (2011): Customer experience quality: an exploration in business and consumer contexts using repertory grid technique, *Journal of the Academy of Marketing Science*, Vol. 39, No. 6, pp. 846–869.

Levitt, T. (1960): Marketing Myopia, *Harvard Business Review*, Vol. 82, No. 7-8, pp. 138–49.

Levy, Y. and Ellis, T.J. (2006): A Systems Approach to Conduct an Effective Literature Review in Support of Information Systems Research, *Science Journal*, Vol. 9, No. 1, pp. 181–212.

Li, C., Reichert, M. and Wombacher, A. (2011): Mining business process variants: Challenges, scenarios, algorithms, *Data and Knowledge Engineering*, Vol. 70, No. 5, pp. 409–434.

Lovelock, C. and Wirtz, J. (2006): *Services Marketing: People, Technology, Strategy*, Upper Saddle River: Prentice Hall.

Ludolph, F. (1997): Model-based user interface design: successive transformations of a task/object model, in Wood, L.E. (Ed.): *User Interface Design: Bridging the Gap from User Requirements to Design*, Boca Raton: CRC Press, pp. 81–108.

Lusch, R.F. and Vargo, S.L. (2006): Service-dominant logic: reactions, reflections and refinements, *Marketing Theory* , Vol. 6 , No. 3 , pp. 281–288.

Lusch, R.F., Vargo, S.L. and O'Brien, M. (2007): Competing through service: Insights from service-dominant logic, *Journal of Retailing*, Vol. 83, No. 1, pp. 5–18.

Lutherer, E., Ghroud, S., Martinez, M. and Favrel, J. (1994): Modelling with CIMOSA: A case study, *Proceedings of the IFIP WG5.7 Working Conference on Evaluation of Production Management Methods*, 21.-24. March, Gramado, pp. 195–203.

Mabo, P., Victor, F., Bazin, P., Ahres, S., Babuty, D., Da Costa, A., Binet, D. and Daubert, J.-C. (2012): A randomized trial of long-term remote monitoring of pacemaker recipients (The COMPAS trial), *European Heart Journal*, Vol. 33, No. 9, pp. 1105–1111.

Macdonald, E.K., Wilson, H. and Konus, U. (2012): Better customer insight - in real time, *Harvard Business Review*, Vol. 90, No. 9, pp. 102–108.

Macdonald, E.K., Wilson, H., Martinez, V. and A., T. (2011): Assessing value-in-use: A conceptual framework and exploratory study, *Industrial Marketing Management*, Vol. 40, No. 5, p. 12.

Maddern, H., Maull, R., Smart, A. and Baker, P. (2007): Customer satisfaction and service quality in UK financial services, *International Journal of Operations and Production Management*, Vol. 27, No. 9, pp. 999–1019.

Maklan, S. and Klaus, P.P. (2011): Customer Experience: Are We Measuring the Right Things?, *International Journal of Market Research*, Vol. 53, No. 6, p. 771.

Malone, T.W., Crowston, K., Lee, J., Pentland, B., Dellarocas, C., Wyner, G., Quimby, J., Osborn, C.S., Bernstein, A., Herman, G., Klein, M. and O'Donnell, E. (1999): Tools for Inventing Organizations: Toward a Handbook of Organizational Processes, *Management Science*, Vol. 45, No. 3, pp. 425–443.

Malthus, T.R. (1820): *Principles of Political Economy, 1820*, London: John Murray.

Markus, M.L., Majchrzak, A. and Gasser, L. (2002): A design theory for systems that support emergent knowledge processes, *MIS Quarterly*, Vol. 26, No. 3, pp. 179–212.

Martini, A. (2008): *Search, Experience and Trust in the "Moments of Truth" - An analysis of dynamic quality assessment for professional services at the example of educational services*, Dissertation, Berlin: Freie Universität Berlin.

Marzegalli, M., Lunati, M., Landolina, M., Perego, G.B., Ricci, R.P., Guenzati, G., Schirru, M., Belvito, C., Brambilla, R., Masella, C., Di Stasi, F., Valsecchi, S. et al. (2008): Remote Monitoring of CRT-ICD: The Multicenter Italian CareLink Evaluation - Ease of Use, Acceptance, and Organizational Implications, *Pacing and Clinical Electrophysiology*, Vol. 31, No. 10, pp. 1259–1264.

Marzilli, T. (2011): iPhone user tracking. Retrieved January 9, 2013, from http://www.brandindex.com/article/iphone-user-tracking

Maslow, A.H. (1943): A Theory of Human Motivation, *Psychological Review*, Vol. 50, No. 4, pp. 370–396.

Maslow, A.H. (1998): *Maslow on Management*, New York: Wiley.

McCarthy, J.E. (1960): *Basic Marketing - A Managerial Approach*, Homewood: Irwin.

McColl-Kennedy, J.R., Vargo, S.L., Dagger, T.S., Sweeney, J.C. and van Kasteren, Y. (2012): Health Care Customer Value Cocreation Practice Styles, *Journal of Service Research*, Vol. 15, No. 4, pp. 370–389.

Meis, J., Menschner, P. and Leimeister, J.M. (2010): Modellierung von Dienstleistungen mittels Business Service Blueprinting Modeling, in Thomas, O. and Nüttgens, M. (Eds.): *Dienstleistungsmodellierung 2010: interdisziplinäre Konzepte und Anwendungsszenarien*, Berlin: Physica, pp. 39–64.

Milton, S.K. and Johnson, L.W. (2012): Service blueprinting and BPMN: a comparison, *Managing Service Quality*, Vol. 22, No. 6, pp. 606–621.

Mitreva, V. (2012): *Conjoint-Analyse zur Bewertung integrativer (Teil-)Prozessdesigns auf Basis des Business Process Blueprintings*, Diploma thesis, Berlin: Freie Universität Berlin.

Möller, S. (2004): *Interaktion bei der Erstellung von Dienstleistungen: Die Koordination der Aktivitäten von Anbieter und Nachfrager*, Wiesbaden: DUV.

Montreuil, B. and Poulin, M. (2005): Demand and supply network design scope for personalized manufacturing, *Production Planning and Control*, Vol. 16, No. 5, pp. 454–469.

Narver, J.C. and Slater, S.F. (1990): The Effect of a Market Orientation on Business Profitability, *Journal of Marketing*, Vol. 54, No. 4, p. 20.

Narver, J.C., Slater, S.F. and MacLachlan, D.L. (2004): Responsive and Proactive Market Orientation and New-Product Success, *Journal of Product Innovation Management*, Vol. 21, No. 5, pp. 334–347.

Nelson, P. (1970): Information and Consumer Behavior, *Journal of Political Economy*, Vol. 78, No. 2, pp. 311–329.

Nunamaker, J.F., Chen, M. and Purdin, T.D.M. (1990): Systems development in information systems research, *Journal of Management Information Systems*, Vol. 7, No. 3, pp. 89–106.

Oliver, R.L. (1980): A Cognitive Model of the Antecedents and Consequences of Satisfaction Decisions, *Journal of Marketing Research*, Vol. 17, No. 4, pp. 460–469.

Oliver, R.L. (1993): Cognitive, affective, and attribute bases of the satisfaction response, *Journal of consumer research*, Vol. 20, No. 3, pp. 418–430.

OMG (2011): Business Process Model and Notation (BPMN) 2.0, *Object Management Group, Inc. (OMG)*. Retrieved from http://www.omg.org/spec/BPMN/2.0/PDF

Orme, B.K. (2009): *Getting Started with Conjoint Analysis: Strategies for Product Design and Pricing Research*, Chicago: Research Publishers.

Österle, H., Winter, R. and Brenner, W. (2010): *Gestaltungsorientierte Wirtschaftsinformatik: Ein Plädoyer für Rigor und Relevanz*, Nuremberg: Infowerk.

Oxford English Dictionaries Online. (2012a): Oxford English Dictionary Online, *Oxford English Dictionary*. Retrieved from http://oxforddictionaries.com/definition/english/need

Oxford English Dictionaries Online. (2012b): Oxford English Dictionary Online, *Oxford English Dictionary*. Retrieved from http://oxforddictionaries.com/definition/english/need

Parasuraman, A., Berry, L.L. and Zeithaml, V.A. (1991): Refinement and reassessment of the SERVQUAL scale, *Journal of Retailing*, Vol. 67, No. 4, pp. 420–450.

Parasuraman, A., Zeithaml, V.A. and Berry, L.L. (1985): A Conceptual Model of Service Quality and Its Implications for Future Research, *Journal of Marketing*, Vol. 49, No. 4, pp. 41–50.

Parasuraman, A., Zeithaml, V.A. and Berry, L.L. (1988): SERVQUAL: A Multiple-Item Scale for Measuring Consumer Perceptions of Service Quality, *Journal of Retailing*, Vol. 64, No. 1, pp. 12–40.

Park, C.W., Jaworski, B.J. and MacInnis, D.J. (1986): Strategic brand concept-image management, *The Journal of Marketing*, Vol. 50, No. 4, pp. 135–145.

Patrício, L., Fisk, R.P., Cunha, J. and Constantine, L. (2011): Multilevel Service Design: From Customer Value Constellation to Service Experience Blueprinting, *Journal of Service Research*, Vol. 14, No. 2, pp. 180–200.

Paulssen, M. and Bagozzi, R.P. (2006): Goal hierarchies as antecedents of market structure, *Psychology and Marketing*, Vol. 23, No. 8, pp. 689–709.

Payne, A.F., Storbacka, K. and Frow, P. (2008): Managing the co-creation of value, *Journal of the Academy of Marketing Science*, Vol. 36, No. 1, pp. 83–96.

Peffers, K., Tuunanen, T., Rothenberger, M.A. and Chatterjee, S. (2007): A Design Science Research Methodology for Information Systems Research, *Journal of Management Information Systems*, Vol. 24, No. 3, pp. 45–77.

Peyret, H. (2009): *The Forrester wave: business process analysis*, Cambridge: Forrester Research.

Plinke, W. (1991): Investitionsgütermarketing, *Marketing - ZFP*, Vol. 13, No. 3, pp. 172–177.

Polyvyanyy, A., Smirnov, S. and Weske, M. (2010): Business Process Model Abstraction, in vom Brocke, J. and Rosemann, M. (Eds.): *Handbook on Business Process Management 1*, Heidelberg: Springer, pp. 149–166.

Porter, M.E. (1980): *Competitive Strategy: Techniques for Analyzing Industries and Competitors, Competitive Strategy*, New York: Free Press.

Porter, M.E. (1985): *Competitive Advantage: Creating and Sustaining Superior Performance*, New York: Free Press.

Porter, M.E. (1996): What is strategy?, *Harvard Business Review*, Vol. 74, No. 6, pp. 61–78.

Potts, C. (2010): *recrEAtion: Realizing the Extraordinary Contribution of Your Enterprise Architects*, Bradley Beach: Technics Publications.

Pries-Heje, J., Baskerville, R. and Venable, J.R. (2008): Strategies for Design Science Research Evaluation, *Proceedings of the 16th European Conference on Information Systems (ECIS)*, 9.-11. June, Galway.

Quantified Self. (2013): Quantified self press. Retrieved January 9, 2012, from http://quantifiedself.com/quantified-self-press/

Raatikainen, P.M.J., Uusimaa, P., van Ginneken, Mireille M.E. Janssen, J.P.G. and Linnaluoto, M. (2008): Remote monitoring of implantable cardioverter defibrillator patients: A safe, time-saving, and cost-effective means for follow-up, *Europace*, Vol. 10, No. 10, pp. 1145–1151.

Rachmann, A., Maucher, I., Schöler, B. and Hewing, M. (2011): Benutzerzentriertes Service Engineering am Beispiel einer Telemonitoring-Dienstleistung, in Bieber, D. and Schwarz, K. (Eds.): *Mit AAL-Dienstleistungen altern. Nutzerbedarfsanalysen im Kontext des Ambient Assisted Living*, Saarbrücken: ISO-Institut, pp. 197–218.

Rajala, M. and Savolainen, T. (1996): A framework for customer oriented business process modelling, *Computer Integrated Manufacturing Systems*, Vol. 9, No. 3, pp. 127–135.

Ramaswamy, R. (1996): *Design and Management Service Processes: Keeping Customers for Life*, Upper Saddle River: Prentice Hall.

Randall, L. (1993): Perceptual blueprinting, *Managing Service Quality*, Vol. 3, No. 4, pp. 7–12.

Randolph, J.J. (2009): A Guide to Writing the Dissertation Literature Review, *Practical Assessment Research Evaluation*, Vol. 14, No. 13, pp. 1–13.

Rappa, M. (2010): Business models on the web, *Managing the digital enterprise*. Retrieved January 7, 2013, from http://digitalenterprise.org/models/models.html#Infomediary

Reichert, M. and Weber, B. (2012): *Enabling Flexibility in Process-Aware Information Systems: Challenges, Methods, Technologies*, Berlin: Springer.

Richardson, A. (2010): Using Customer Journey Maps to Improve Customer Experience, *Harvard Business Review Blog*. Retrieved December 10, 2012, from http://blogs.hbr.org/cs/2010/11/using_customer_journey_maps_to.html

Roos, D. and Anemo, M. (2011): Ground-breaking Innovation Management Concepts from the Past 25 Years, *Prism*, Vol. 11, No. 1, pp. 13–17.

Rosemann, M. (2011a): Challenges in business process management: new frontiers and new paradigms, *Keynote of the 9th International Conference on Business Process Management (BPM)*, 28. August-02. September, Clermont-Ferrand.

Rosemann, M. (2011b): Birth-to-Death Value Chain. Retrieved April 18, 2013, from http://www.michaelrosemann.com/uncategorized/113/

Rosemann, M. (2013a): Life Systems - How to best support the birth-to-death-value chain, *Invited keynote at the School of Business and Economics (Freie Universität Berlin)*, 11. March, Berlin.

Rosemann, M. (2013b): Ambidextrous BPM, *Keynote at the Gartner Business Process Management Summit*, 13. March 2013, London.

Rosemann, M. and vom Brocke, J. (2010): The Six Core Elements of Business Process Management, in vom Brocke, J. and Rosemann, M. (Eds.): *Handbook on Business Process Management 1*, Heidelberg: Springer, pp. 107–122.

Rust, R.T. and Oliver, R.L. (1994): *Service Quality: New Directions in Theory and Practice*, Thousand Oaks: Sage.

Salman, R. (2004): *Kostenerfassung und Kostenmanagement von Kundenintegrationsprozessen*, Wiesbaden: DUV.

Salo, O. and Abrahamsson, P. (2004): Empirical Evaluation of Agile Software Development: The Controlled Case Study Approach, in Bomarius, F. and Iida, H. (Eds.): *Product Focused Software Process Improvement Lecture Notes in Computer Science Volume 3009*, Berlin: Springer, pp. 408–423.

Santerre, R.E. and Neun, S.P. (2012): *Health Economics*, Cincinnati: South-Western College Pub.

Sawhney, M., Balasubramanian, S. and Krishnan, V. V. (2003): Creating growth with services, *MIT Sloan Management Review*, Vol. 45, No. 2, pp. 34–44.

Saxon, L.A., Hayes, D.L., Gilliam, F.R., Heidenreich, P.A., Day, J., Seth, M., Meyer, T.E., Jones, P.W. and Boehmer, J.P. (2010): Long-term outcome after ICD and CRT implantation and influence of remote device follow-up: the ALTITUDE survival study, *Circulation*, Vol. 122, No. 23, pp. 2359–2367.

Say, J.-B. (1855): *A Treatise on Political Economy*, Lippincott: Grambo.

Schank, R. C. (1975): The Structure of Episodes in Memory, in Bobrow, D.G. and Collins, A. (Eds.): *Representation and Understanding: Studies in Cognitive Science* New York: Academic Press, pp. 237–272.

Scheer, A.-W. (2000a): *ARIS - Business Process Frameworks*, Heidelberg: Springer.

Scheer, A.-W. (2000b): *ARIS - Business Process Modeling*, Berlin: Springer.

Scheer, A.-W. and Bräbander, E. (2010): The Process of Business Process Management, in vom Brocke, J. and Rosemann, M. (Eds.): *Handbook on Business Process Management 2*, Heidelberg: Springer, pp. 293–265.

Scheuing, E.E. and Johnson, E.M. (1989): A proposed model for new service development, *Journal of Services marketing*, Vol. 3, No. 2, pp. 25–34.

Schneider, K., Daun, C., Behrens, H. and Wagner, D. (2006): Vorgehensmodelle und Standards zur systematischen Entwicklung von Dienstleistungen, in Bullinger, H.-J. and Scheer, A.-W. (Eds.): *Service Engineering*, Berlin: Springer, pp. 113–138.

Schoenfeld, M.H., Compton, S.J., Mead, R.H., Weiss, D.N., Sherfesee, L., Englund, J. and Mongeon, L.R. (2004): Remote monitoring of implantable cardioverter defibrillators: a prospective analysis., *Pacing and clinical electrophysiology*, Vol. 27, No. 6 Pt 1, pp. 757–763.

Schwab, J.O., Müller, A., Oeff, M., Neuzner, J., Sack, S., Pfeifer, D. and Zugck, C. (2008): Telemedizin in der Kardiologie – Relevanz für die Praxis?, *Herz*, Vol. 33, No. 6, pp. 420–430.

Schweikart, J. (1997): *Integrative Prozeßkostenrechnung: Kundenorientierte Analyse von Leistungen im industriellen Business-to-Business-Bereich*, Wiesbaden: DUV.

Shahin, A. (2010): Service Blueprinting: An Effective Approach for Targeting Critical Service Processes - With a Case Study in a Four-Star International Hotel, *Journal of Management Research*, Vol. 2, No. 2, pp. 1–16.

Shapiro, B.P. (1988): What the Hell Is 'Market Oriented'?, *Harvard Business Review*, Vol. 66, No. 6, pp. 119–125.

Shaw, C. and Ivens, J. (2004): *Building Great Customer Experiences*, Basingstoke: Palgrave Macmillan.

Shostack, G.L. (1977): Breaking Free from Product Marketing, *Journal of Marketing*, Vol. 41, No. 2, pp. 73–80.

Shostack, G.L. (1982): How to Design a Service, *European Journal of Marketing*, Vol. 16, No. 1, pp. 49–63.

Shostack, G.L. (1984): Designing services that deliver, *Harvard Business Review*, Vol. 62, No. 1, pp. 133–139.

Siau, K. and Rossi, M. (2011): Evaluation techniques for systems analysis and design modelling methods - a review and comparative analysis, *Information Systems Journal*, Vol. 21, No. 3, pp. 249–268.

Siemens, G. and Long, P. (2011): Penetrating the fog: Analytics in learning and education, *Educause Review*, Vol. 46, No. 5, pp. 30–40.

Slater, S.F. and Narver, J.C. (1994): Market orientation, customer value, and superior performance, *Business Horizons*, Vol. 37, No. 2, pp. 22–28.

Smith, A. (2010): *The Wealth of Nations - An Inquiry into the Nature and Causes of the Wealth of Nations*, Chichester: Capstone.

Smith, A.M. (1995): Measuring Service Quality: is SERVQUAL now Redundant?, *Journal of Marketing Management*, Vol. 11, No. 1-3, pp. 257–276.

Sonnenberg, C. and vom Brocke, J. (2012a): Evaluation Patterns for Design Science Research Artefacts, in Helfert, M. and Donnellan, B. (Eds.): *Practical Aspects of Design Science: Communications in Computer and Information Science Volume 286*, Berlin: Springer, pp. 71–83.

Sonnenberg, C. and vom Brocke, J. (2012b): Evaluations in the Science of the Artificial - Reconsidering the Build-Evaluate Pattern in Design Science Research, in Peffers, K., Rothenberger, M. and Kuechler, B. (Eds.): *Design Science Research in Information Systems. Advances in Theory and Practice Lecture Notes in Computer Science Volume 7286*, Berlin: Springer, pp. 381–397.

Spohrer, J.C. and Maglio, P.P. (2011): Towards a Science of Service Systems, in Demirkan, H., Spohrer, J.C. and Krishna, V. (Eds.): *The Science of Service Systems*, New York: Springer, pp. 157–194.

Stachowiak, H. (1973): *Allgemeine Modelltheorie*, Vienna: Springer.

Stake, R.E. (1994): Case studies, in Denzin, N.K. and Lincoln, Y.S. (Eds.): *Handbook of Qualitative Research*, Sage, pp. 236–247.

Stamatis, D.H. (2003): *Failure Mode and Effect Analysis: FMEA from Theory to Execution*, Milwaukee: Quality Press.

Stauss, B. and Weinlich, B. (1997): Process-oriented measurement of service quality: Applying the sequential incident technique, *European Journal of Marketing*, Vol. 31, No. 1, pp. 33–55.

Strametz, R., Fließ, S., L'Allemand, N., Roßkopf, W. and Iber, T. (2012): Process optimization by means of the service blueprint technique - Restructuring the preoperative clinic at Frankfurt University Hospital from the patient's point of view, *Anästhesiologie und Intensivmedizin*, Vol. 53, No. 4, pp. 228–235.

Strong, C.A. and Harris, L.C. (2004): The drivers of customer orientation: an exploration of relational, human resource and procedural tactics, *Journal of Strategic Marketing*, Vol. 12, No. 3, pp. 183–204.

Swenson, K.D. (2010): The Nature of Knowledge Work, in Swenson, K.D. (Ed.): *Mastering the Unpredictable: How Adaptive Case Management Will Revolutionize the Way That Knowledge Workers Get Things Done*, Tampa: Meghan-Kiffer Press, pp. 5–27.

Swenson, K.D., Palmer, N., Pucher, M.J., MD, C.W. and Manuel, A. (2012): *How Knowledge Workers Get Things Done*, Lighthouse Point: Future Strategies.

Taylor, F.W. (2001): *The Principles of Scientific Management*, Mineola: Dover Publications.

Teixeira, J., Patrício, L., Nunes, N.J., Nóbrega, L., Fisk, R.P. and Constantine, L. (2012): Customer experience modeling: from customer experience to service design, *Journal of Service Management*, Vol. 23, No. 3, pp. 362–376.

Telefónica. (2013): Dynamic Insights. Retrieved January 7, 2013, from http://dynamicinsights.telefonica.com/

Timmers, P. (1998): Business Models for Electronic Markets, *Electronic Markets*, Vol. 8, No. 2, pp. 3–8.

Tse, D.K. and Wilton, P.C. (1988): Models of consumer satisfaction formation: an extension, *Journal of marketing research*, Vol. 25, No. 2, pp. 204–212.

Tseng, M.M., Qinhai, M. and Su, C.-J. (1999): Mapping customers' service experience for operations improvement, *Business Process Management Journal*, Vol. 5, No. 1, pp. 50–64.

Tuli, K.R., Kohli, A.K. and Bharadwaj, S.G. (2007): Rethinking Customer Solutions: From Product Bundles to Relational Processes, *Journal of Marketing*, Vol. 71, No. 3, pp. 1–17.

Turnbull, J. (2009): Customer value-in-experience: theoretical foundation and research agenda, *Proceedings of the 12th Australian and New Zealand Marketing Academy Conference (ANZMAC)*, 30.November-2. December, Melbourne.

Ulaga, W. and Chacour, S. (2001): Measuring Customer-Perceived Value in Business Markets: A Prerequisite for Marketing Strategy Development and Implementation, *Industrial Marketing Management*, Vol. 30, No. 6, pp. 525–540.

Vaishnavi, V.K.. and William, K.J. (2007): *Design Science Research Methods and Patterns: Innovating Information and Communication Technology*, Boca Raton: Auerbach Publications.

Vanwersch, R.J.B., Shahzad, K., Vanhaecht, K., Grefen, P., Pintelon, L.M., Mendling, J., van Merode, G.G. and Reijers, H.A. (2011): Methodological support for business process redesign in health care: a literature review protocol, *International Journal of Care Pathways*, Vol. 15, No. 4, pp. 119–126.

Vargo, S.L. (2011): On marketing theory and service-dominant logic: Connecting some dots, *Marketing Theory*, Vol. 11, No. 1, pp. 3–8.

Vargo, S.L. and Lusch, R.F. (2004a): Evolving to a New Dominant Logic for Marketing, *Journal of Marketing*, Vol. 68, No. 1, pp. 1–17.

Vargo, S.L. and Lusch, R.F. (2004b): The Four Service Marketing Myths: Remnants of a Goods-Based, Manufacturing Model, *Journal of Service Research*, Vol. 6, No. 4, pp. 324–335.

Vargo, S.L. and Lusch, R.F. (2008a): From goods to service(s): Divergences and convergences of logics, *Industrial Marketing Management*, Vol. 37, No. 3, pp. 254–259.

Vargo, S.L. and Lusch, R.F. (2008b): Service-dominant logic: continuing the evolution, *Journal of the Academy of Marketing Science*, Vol. 36, No. 1, pp. 1–10.

Varma, N., Pavri, B., Michalski, J. and Stambler, B. (2011): Do heart failure patients with ICDs managed remotely suffer increased adverse event rates? automatic remote monitoring compared to conventional follow up in the TRUST trial, *Europace Journal*, Vol. 13, No. 3 (supplement 3).

Verhoef, P.C., Lemon, K.N., Parasuraman, A., Roggeveen, A., Tsiros, M. and Schlesinger, L.A. (2009): Customer Experience Creation: Determinants, Dynamics and Management Strategies, *Journal of Retailing*, Vol. 85, No. 1, pp. 31–41.

Voss, C., Roth, A. V and Chase, R.B. (2008): Experience, Service Operations Strategy, and Services as Destinations: Foundations and Exploratory Investigation, *Production and Operations Management*, Vol. 17, No. 3, pp. 247–266.

Webster, J. and Watson, R.T. (2002): Analyzing the past to prepare the future: writing a literature review, *MIS Quarterly*, Vol. 26, No. 2, pp. xiii–xxiii.

Weiber, R. and Hörstrup, R. (2009): Von der Kundenintegration zur Anbieterintegration: Die Erweiterung anbieterseitiger Wertschöpfungsprozesse auf kundenseitige Nutzungsprozesse, in Bruhn, M. and Stauss, B. (Eds.): *Kundenintegration*, Wiesbaden: Gabler, pp. 281–312.

Weske, M. (2009): *Business Process Management: Concepts, Languages, Architectures*, Berlin: Springer.

Westbrook, R.A. (1987): Product/consumption-based affective responses and postpurchase processes, *Journal of marketing research*, Vol. 24, No. 3, pp. 258–270.

WHO (2003): *Adherence to long-term therapies - Evidence for action*, Geneva: World Health Organization (WHO).

WHO (2004): *Annex table 2: Deaths by cause, sex and mortality stratum in WHO regions, estimates for 2002, The world health report 2004 - changing history*, Geneva: World Health Organization (WHO).

Wieners, W.W. (2000): *Global Health Care Markets: A Comprehensive Guide to Regions, Trends, and Opportunities Shaping the International Health Arena*, San Francisco: Jossey-Bass.

Williamson, O.E. (1979): Transaction-Cost Economics: The Goverance of contractual Relations, *Governance And International Journal Of Policy And Administration*, Vol. 22, No. 2, pp. 233–261.

Winn, J.K. and Wrathall, J.R. (2000): Who Owns the Customer - The Emerging Law of Commercial Transactions in Electronic Customer Data, *Business Lawyer*, Vol. 56, No. 1, p. 213.

Winter, A., Alt, R., Ehmke, J., Haux, R., Ludwig, W., Mattfeld, D., Oberweis, A. and Paech, B. (2012): Manifest - Kundeninduzierte Orchestrierung komplexer Dienstleistungen, *Informatik-Spektrum*, Vol. 35, No. 6, pp. 399–408.

Winter, R. (2003): Modelle, Techniken und Werkzeuge im Business Engineering, in Österle, H. and Winter, R. (Eds.): *Business Engineering - Auf dem Weg zum Unternehmen des Informationszeitalters.*, Berlin: Springer, pp. 87–118.

Wood, A. (1993): Efficient consumer response, *Logistics Information Management*, Vol. 6, No. 4, pp. 38–40.

Xie, C., Bagozzi, R.P. and Troye, S. V. (2007): Trying to prosume: toward a theory of consumers as co-creators of value, *Journal of the Academy of Marketing Science*, Vol. 36, No. 1, pp. 109–122.

Yin, R.K. (2009): *Case Study Research: Design and Methods, Case study research design and methods*, Los Angeles: Sage.

Zablah, A.R., Franke, G.R., Brown, T.J. and Bartholomew, D.E. (2012): How and When Does Customer Orientation Influence Frontline Employee Job Outcomes? A Meta-Analytic Evaluation, *Journal of Marketing*, Vol. 76, No. 3, pp. 21–40.

Zeithaml, V.A., Parasuraman, A. and Berry, L.L. (1985): Problems and Strategies in Services Marketing, *Journal of Marketing*, Vol. 49, No. 2, pp. 33–46.

Zeitfracht Medien GmbH
Ferdinand-Jühlke-Straße 7
99095 Erfurt, Deutschland
produktsicherheit@kolibri360.de